MALLORY, IRVINE AND EVEREST

To Radhanath Sikdar, who computed the mountain

To Noel Odell, the last man who saw Mallory and Irvine alive

To my wife Nadia for putting up with the building of this book

MALLORY, IRVINE AND EVEREST

THE LAST STEP BUT ONE

ROBERT H. EDWARDS

PEN & SWORD
HISTORY
AN IMPRINT OF PEN & SWORD BOOKS LTD.
YORKSHIRE – PHILADELPHIA

First published in Great Britain in 2024 by
PEN AND SWORD HISTORY
An imprint of
Pen & Sword Books Ltd
Yorkshire – Philadelphia

ISBN 978 1 39903 434 0

A CIP catalogue record for this book is available from the British Library.

Typeset in Times New Roman 9.5/11.5 by SJmagic DESIGN SERVICES, India.
Printed and bound in the UK on paper from a sustainable source by CPI Group (UK) Ltd., Croydon. CR0 4YY.

Pen & Sword Books Ltd. incorporates the imprints of Pen & Sword Books: After the Battle, Archaeology, Atlas, Aviation, Battleground, Discovery, Family History, History, Maritime, Military, Politics, Select, Transport, True Crime, Fiction, Frontline Books, Leo Cooper, Praetorian Press, Seaforth Publishing, Wharncliffe and White Owl.

For a complete list of Pen & Sword titles please contact
PEN & SWORD BOOKS LIMITED
George House, Units 12 & 13, Beevor Street, Off Pontefract Road,
Barnsley, South Yorkshire, S71 1HN, England
E-mail: enquiries@pen-and-sword.co.uk
Website: www.pen-and-sword.co.uk

or

PEN AND SWORD BOOKS
1950 Lawrence Rd, Havertown, PA 19083, USA
E-mail: uspen-and-sword@casematepublishers.com
Website: www.penandswordbooks.com

MIX
Paper | Supporting responsible forestry
FSC® C013604

'My dear Watson, whenever you have eliminated the impossible, then whatever remains, however improbable, must be the truth.'
– Sherlock Holmes

'It is futile to do with more things, that which can be done with less.'
– William of Ockham

'Well, blind man, have you seen the elephant?'
– attributed to the Buddha

'Perfect weather for the job'
– George Mallory

Note on altitudes and times

Altitudes

The British expeditions of the 1920s and 1930s to Mount Everest estimated the altitude of the summit at 29,002 feet above mean sea level. The modern calibration, agreed by the governments of China and Nepal, is 8,849m (29,032 feet).

To altitudes reported by the expeditions of the 1920s and 1930s, 30 feet should be added to correspond to the modern calibration.

To altitudes reported by modern climbers, 30 feet should be subtracted to correspond to the calibration of the 1920s and 1930s.

Times

The British expeditions of the 1920s and 1930s to Mount Everest did not specify, in their published accounts, what time zone they used. This author has assumed that all times of day given in contemporary accounts were based on Darjeeling time.

Contents

Prologue

Early on the morning of 8 June 1924, the English mountaineers George Leigh Mallory and Andrew Comyn Irvine left their tent on the high slopes of the north face of Mount Everest. They had had no companions in their camp. No-one saw them leave; no-one knows at what time they left; no-one knows what they were carrying. Their team-mates on the British expedition, camped far below them on the mountain, knew only that they planned to reach the summit. Calibrated, at that time, at 29,002 feet above sea level[1], it was the highest point in the world.

Mallory was thirty-seven years old, an immensely gifted climber on his third expedition to Everest. He surely knew that if he did not succeed this time, he would yield his place to younger men. This was his last chance.

Irvine was a student from Oxford University, twenty-two years old. He was fit and strong, but he had little mountaineering experience. Mallory had chosen him unexpectedly as partner for the final assault on Everest.

That morning, their colleague Noel Odell set out to prospect for rocks and fossils, two thousand feet below. Shortly after mid-day, he thought that he glimpsed Mallory and Irvine through a brief parting of the clouds. Throughout his long life, often in the face of disbelief, he would insist that they had been a few hundred feet below the summit, and 'going strong for the top'.

Whatever Odell saw, it is a matter of record that Mallory and Irvine were never seen alive again.

Colonel Edward Norton, the leader of the expedition, sent Odell on a desperate mission to look for the missing climbers. Odell located their tent; he made brief observations of what remained in and around it; and on Norton's orders, quickly abandoned the search. In his dispatches to *The Times* of London and to the Royal Geographical Society, Norton expressed his grief and bewilderment at the undoubted loss of the two men. He and other members of the expedition, then and later, advanced various theories as to what had befallen them; but no-one knew what had happened.

In 1933 another British expedition returned to the north face of Everest. Two different parties, in separate attempts, approached but did not reach the summit. On the first attempt, Percy Wyn Harris found an ice axe[2] in perfect condition, just below the northeast ridge. Its location, and the manufacturer's stamp, affirmed that it could only have belonged to Mallory or Irvine. This discovery engendered speculation that Mallory or Irvine, or both, had suffered a fatal fall; but the expedition made no attempt to search for their remains. There the matter would rest. For over sixty years, the ice axe would be the only physical evidence of Mallory's and Irvine's last climb.

History records that on 29 May 1953, Edmund Hillary and Tenzing Norgay reached the summit of Everest. Their approach was from the south side, in Nepal; the Chinese government had closed the north face to foreigners. No part of their ascent could have intersected with any possible route of Mallory and Irvine. They later reported that at the summit, they had looked for traces of Mallory and Irvine, and had found none.

In 1960, the People's Republic of China sent a vast and highly organized expedition to the north face of Everest. They retraced some portions of the known routes of the pre-war British expeditions; but in their final approach, they followed the crest of the northeast ridge. Only Mallory and Irvine could possibly have taken this route; but the Chinese had no way to know. In the pre-dawn darkness of 25 May 1960, three climbers – Wang Fu-zhou, Qu Yin-hua[3] and Gombu[4] - reached the summit.

No official account of the 1960 Chinese expedition has ever made reference to Mallory and Irvine. Modern Chinese media assert that the 1960 climb was the first ascent of Everest from the north; their implication is that Mallory and Irvine did not reach the summit. Yet in 1965, Wang Fu-zhou spoke in what was then Leningrad[5] to what was then the Geographical Society of the Soviet Union[6]. He made the remark that at an altitude of 28,215 feet[7], or some 800 feet below the summit, they had seen the body of a European, wearing braces[8]. Before or since, there is nothing in the public domain (at least outside China or Russia) that would shed light on this extraordinary statement.

The Chinese made a second successful ascent of Everest in 1975. From this climb, one final clue would come to light. Wang Hong-bao[9] was a member of that team. Four years later, he participated in another Everest expedition with Chinese and Japanese participants; during that journey, he lost his life in an accident. The day before his death, he told a Japanese colleague (in sign language and with one word of English) that in 1975, he had seen 'old English dead'.

In 1999, an American expedition set out for Everest with the express purpose of finding Mallory or Irvine. They had the benefit of the remarkable research of the German geologist Jochen Hemmleb, who had identified the approximate location of the 1975 Chinese camp, and who accompanied the expedition. They succeeded beyond their highest expectations. On 1 May 1999, five climbers – Conrad Anker[10], Dave Hahn, Jake Norton, Andy Politz, and Tap Richards – found the body of George Mallory.

Mallory was partly buried in ice and scree. He was three-quarters of a mile horizontally from the summit and over two thousand feet below. He was close to the altitude of the last known camp of 1924. He had fallen; but to all appearances, he had not fallen far. His right leg was broken. The American climbers excavated his remains, collected artifacts from his body and attempted a makeshift burial. On 16 May, Politz and Pollard returned for a further search, found Mallory's watch, and discovered a head injury which might have caused his death.

Irvine's body has not been found, to this day.

The location and position of Mallory's body, and the condition of the artifacts, predictably gave rise to narratives about his final hours and those of Irvine. Yet the climbers themselves have acknowledged that nothing that they found shed substantive light on the central mystery – whether Mallory or Irvine, or both, had reached the summit.

As early as the 1930s, there had been a school of thought among climbers that Mallory and Irvine had stood at the summit; and an opposing view that they had not. The differences largely stemmed from whether the protagonist accepted Odell's sighting, or not. For if Mallory and Irvine had been where Odell believed he had seen them, there was no obstacle between them and the summit.

The 1999 discovery shifted the debate towards the narrative of failure. Among climbers and authors, the predominant narrative has been based on the assumptions (and they are assumptions) that Mallory and Irvine took a route along the northeast ridge; that this led them to the daunting Second Step; and that this obstacle was beyond even Mallory's climbing abilities and far beyond those of Irvine. In this narrative, Mallory and Irvine turned around at the Second Step, and through some misfortune, died on the descent.

This book is about the facts of Mallory's and Irvine's last climb. We shall set aside all speculation, opinion, assumptions and preconceived narrative. We shall bring a mathematical and analytical approach to the mystery. We shall return to the contemporary source documents, including the writings and speeches of Mallory himself. We shall examine the topography of Mount Everest; what ascent rates were physically possible or probable; where Odell was and what he could have seen; and what, for the climb, would have been a realistic mission plan. We shall construct a hypothesis of Mallory's and Irvine's last climb.

With that, our story begins.

Part I

PRELUDES TO EVEREST

Chapter 1

Sikdar

In December 1831, Radhanath Sikdar started work at the Survey of India in Dehradun, capital of the Indian state of Uttarakhand. He was a Brahmin from Bengal, nineteen years old. His job title was Computor; he was the first Indian to hold this position. In those days the term 'computor' (later, 'computer') referred to a human occupation, not to a machine. Sikdar's salary was thirty rupees (two British pounds) per month.[1]

India was then part of the British Empire. An Englishman was the Superintendent of the Survey of India and Surveyor-General. His name was Colonel George (later Sir George) Everest.

One of the responsibilities of the Survey of India was the Great Trigonometric Survey, a task which had been underway since 1802. Its original objective had been to map the Great Arc: the meridian of 78 degrees east longitude, from the far south of India to the Himalayas. Over time, its objective had expanded to encompass a complete mapping of the Indian subcontinent by geodetic survey and the application of trigonometry. It was a cartographic exercise on an unprecedented scale. A president of the Royal Geographical Society described it as 'one of the most stupendous works in the whole history of science'.[2]

Within the obscure world of the Survey of India, Sikdar was acknowledged as a talented mathematician. His creative and meticulous work came to the attention of Colonel Everest, a man not known for accolades, who said of him in 1838:

> *'... there are few in India whether European or native [Indian] that can at all compete with him. Even in Europe these mathematical attainments would rank very high'.*[3]

In 1842, Colonel Everest retired. His job as Surveyor-General passed to his protege Colonel Andrew (later Sir Andrew) Scott Waugh.

On 20 October 1850, by order of the British Parliament, Colonel Waugh submitted his report on the progress, and not incidentally, the expenses, of the Great Trigonometric Survey up to the fiscal year 1849/50. Therein, he devoted a paragraph to the civil servants working under his command. He wrote:

> *'A more loyal, zealous, and energetic body of men ... is nowhere to be found ... Among these may be mentioned, as most conspicuous for ability, Babu Radanath Sikhdar, a native of India, of Brahminical extraction, whose mathematical acquirements are of a high order ...'*[4]

It was a logical consequence of Waugh's high regard for him that sometime in 1852, Sikdar was appointed Chief Computor of the Great Trigonometric Survey. He was

Figure 1.1. (left) Radhanath Sikdar, date unknown. (right) Col. Andrew Scott Waugh, 1861. (Unknown, public domain)

thirty-eight years old. For this new position, he was transferred to Kolkata[5]. He was now reporting directly to Waugh.

In Kolkata, he received the raw data from geodetic field stations throughout India. Not all stations were close to the objects of their measurement. Waugh gave Sikdar the task of computing the latitudes, longitudes and altitudes of mountain peaks which had been observed from 'distances of over 100 miles'.[6]

One such mountain bore the name Peak XV. It was apparently in Nepal, but it was within India's (and therefore Britain's) sphere of interest. The border between India and Nepal was imprecise, that between Nepal and Tibet even more so, and the government of Nepal would not permit the entry of foreigners other than diplomats. The first European observation of Peak XV had been made by J. O. Nicholson in 1847, by theodolite from near Darjeeling, a distance of 105 miles. The field data had been assembled by John Hennessy. At that time, Peak XV was considered 'a possible contender for the world's highest peak'[7]; however, its altitude had not been calculated, and officially the highest mountain in the world was Kanchenjunga, also in the Himalayas but in Sikkim, at that time an independent country.

Sikdar executed his calculations, using data from six field stations. Applying the average of the six measurements, he arrived at an altitude of 29,000 feet above mean sea level. If correct, that would establish Peak XV as the highest in the world. Legend has it that Waugh was concerned that this estimate might seem like a rounded number, and that he arbitrarily added two feet. In any event, history records that from 1852 until the late twentieth century, the peak of this mountain was calibrated at 29,002 feet. What history did not record, for over fifty years, was that this estimate was essentially Sikdar's work.

For some years, Colonel Waugh retained the name Peak XV for the highest mountain in his database. It was something of an irony that Waugh, who had followed the example of Colonel Everest as a champion of Sikdar, should subsequently attempt to impose an English name on the mountain that his Indian collaborator had identified.

On 1 March 1856, he wrote to his friend Henry Edward Landor Thuillier, the deputy Surveyor-General, in the following terms:

> *'I was taught by my respected chief and predecessor, Colonel George Everest, to assign to every geographical object its true local or native appellation, and I have always scrupulously adhered to this rule, as I have in fact to all other principles laid down by that eminent geodist.*
>
> *'But here is a mountain, most probably the highest in the world, without any local name that we can discover, whose native appellation, if it has any, will not very likely be ascertained until we are allowed to penetrate into Nepal.'*[8]

Waugh then explained that he had decided to give the mountain the name Mount Everest, in honour of his predecessor.

Until then, the British administration had preserved a tradition of using indigenous names. To this tradition, there arose a defender in the person of Brian Houghton Hodgson, who had been the British political resident in Nepal. On 27 October 1856 he wrote to the Royal Asiatic Society of Great Britain and Ireland, asserting that the mountain already had an indigenous name; and that name was Deodanga. This Nepali expression could be rendered approximately as 'sacred mountain'.

Edward Norris, secretary of the Society, wrote in reply:

> *'Your letter of the 27th October [1856], together with your observation on the incongruity of assigning a European name to Indian localities already provided with native appellations, was received and read at our last meeting of the 17th inst. [November 1856?] and I have the pleasure to inform you that the members present unanimously expressed their concurrence with your view of the case. A notice of the paper was communicated to the Athenaeum and Literary Gazette, and has appeared already in full in the latter journal.'*[9]

What followed was a battle of cultures: more precisely, a battle between two Englishmen for the ascendancy of British or Asian culture. The mountain in Nepal with an altitude of 29,002 feet was, for Waugh and his friends and supporters, Mount Everest; and for Hodgson and the Royal Asiatic Society (and possibly the influential *Literary Gazette*), it was Deodanga.

On 15 August 1857, the *Illustrated London News* published a drawing, of which we reproduce an extract below, with the caption: 'View from Darjeeling of Deodhunga, the highest mountain in the world, lately measured by Colonel A. S. Waugh. Height above sea level, 29,002 feet.'

In an accompanying article, the newspaper went on to say:

> *'On the 12th of May last [1857] two very interesting communications were read to the Royal Geographical Society upon Deodhunga, which mountain Colonel Waugh, in the first paper, refers to as 'higher than any other hitherto measured mountain in India, and most probably the highest in the whole world.' ... The Colonel then proposed to name this*

Figure 1.2. An extract from an artist's impression of the Himalayas as seen from the Darjeeling Sanitarium in August 1857. The image and caption gave no clue as to which mountain was identified as Deodhunga. (Samuel Read, after a sketch by Capt. Walter Stanhope Sherwill / *Illustrated London News*)

> *noble peak of the Himalayas after his respected chief and predecessor in office (Col. George Everest) 'Mount Everest.'*[10]

The *Illustrated London News* then quoted the second paper read to the Society, as submitted by Hodgson from Darjeeling and dated 26 October 1856. The critical extract of Hodgson's paper was as follows:

> *'... he must add, in justice to the Nepaulese [Nepalis] ... that the mountain in question does not lack a native and ascertained name; that that name is Deodhunga, Holy Hill, or Mons Sacer.'*[11]

The Society proceeded to a swift and very British wrapping-up. Colonel Everest (who was present) acknowledged the compliment, while allowing that Indians might not be able to write or pronounce his name (phonetically, Eve-rest, unlike the modern pronunciation). After a brief reference to 'whatever might be its name in India', the appellation of Mount Everest was duly adopted. Colonel Walsh received the Gold Medal of the Royal Geographical Society. The rest is history.

Almost fifty years later it became known (outside the Great Trigonometric Survey) that Radhanath Sikdar had identified the highest point in the world. In 1904, the then Surveyor-General, Sidney Gerald Burrard, wrote:

> *'About 1852 the chief computer of the office at Calcutta informed Sir Andrew Waugh that a peak designated XV had been found to be higher*

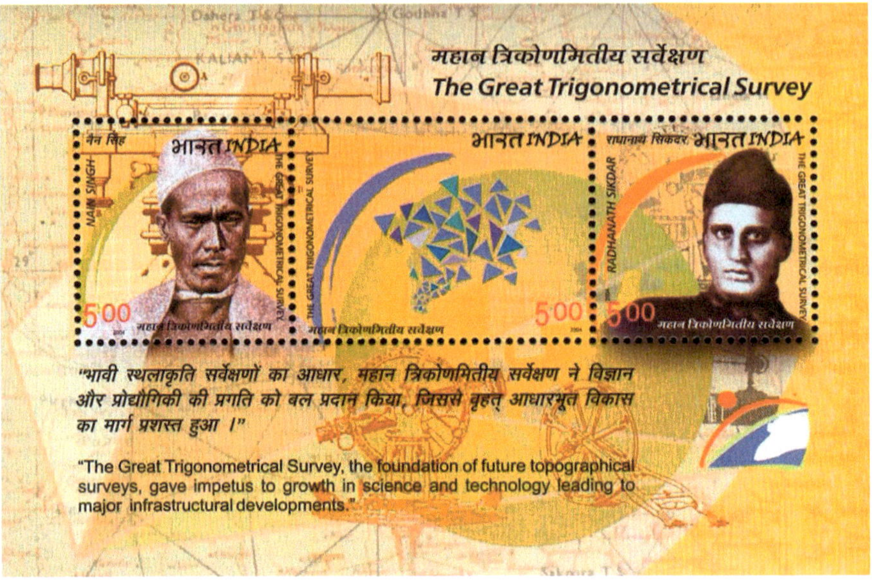

Figure 1.3. Radhanath Sikdar and the Great Trigonometric Survey, portrayed on a Rs.5 postage stamp in 2004. (India Post Office)

> *than any other hitherto measured in the world. The peak was discovered by the computers to have been observed from six different stations; on no occasion had the observer suspected that he was viewing through the telescope the highest point of the earth.'*[12]

Burrard did not see fit to name the 'chief computer'.

In 1870, Radhanath Sikdar passed away. In 1921, over fifty years after his death, the British would return in the hope of climbing the mountain that he had computed.

Postscript: the Schlagintweit mission

In his arguments before the Royal Geographical Society, with a view to demolishing Brian Hodgson's position, Colonel Waugh was disparaging of the opposition's references to German explorers. He wrote:

> *'Great stress has been laid in some quarters on the fact that the position of Deodanga is given in German Maps; now this proves no more than that German geographers are rash enough to lay down anything upon hearsay; for we know beyond all question that no competent European with adequate means has ever been in the vicinity of Deodanga so as to be able to fix it. Deodanga does not appear in English maps, because it would be inconsistent with the rigorous notions which prevail among*

> *English scientific men in general to pretend to give the position of a point on the earth's surface on hearsay evidence.'*[13]

Nevertheless, in an intriguing postscript, a party of German scientists would support Waugh's identification and naming of the highest peak in the world. The three Schlagintweit brothers (Adolphe, Hermann and Robert) were Alpine glaciologists. There was no question of their competence or the adequacy of their means. The British East India Company, acting on the highest recommendations, had commissioned them in 1854, to complete the Magnetic Survey of India[14] – a project unrelated to the Great Trigonometric Survey. They were personally well known to the officials of the Survey of India, including Waugh and Everest himself.

Hermann Schlagintweit obtained permission in 1855 to enter Nepal, where no British scientist or surveyor had been allowed to set foot. His brother Robert, writing in *The Athenaeum*, claimed that Hermann had visited both Mount Everest and Deodhunga; he affirmed that these two mountains were not the same:

> *'Hermann Schlagintweit ... came to the high mountain of Nepaul {Nepal], which was lately called Mount Everest by Col. Waugh, after his distinguished predecessor. This is the highest Mountain in the world at present known, being considerably over 29,000 feet above the level of the sea. The natives have two names for it — one of them, Gorishanta, which is mythological, is to be found only in the Nepaulese [Nepali], and the second name, Chingofanmara, is that by which it is known among the people of Thibet [Tibet]. The name Deudunga which was mentioned by Mr. Hodgson in connexion with this peak, was not the name of it at all, but of a small mountain some 8,000 feet high, which lies in the same direction ... '*[15]

In one important respect, Hermann Schlagintweit was wrong.

The brothers' map of their routes makes it clear that none of them was ever in the vicinity of Mount Everest. Nevertheless, Hermann took two bearings by theodolite on the mountain that he would later call Everest: once from Falut (Phalut), on the border between Nepal and Sikkim[16], and once from Kaulia Hill[17] near Kathmandu. He would later estimate the distance (presumably from Falut) as 'over 84 miles'[18] (135 km). The diagram of his observations places this mountain on a bearing of 308 degrees from true north. By the modern calibration, Everest as viewed from Falut is on a bearing of 310 degrees from true north. Hermann was certainly looking in the right direction.

Figure 1.4. Hermann von Schlagintweit in 1858. (Unknown, public domain)

Figure 1.5. Hermann Schlagintweit's observations of what he reported as Mount Everest, superimposed on a modern map. Base map ©2022 Google Maps; additional graphics by author, based on the Schlagintweit Atlas, page 'm', by courtesy of the University of Heidelberg.

The second observation, from Kaulia, placed 'Everest' on a bearing of 85 degrees from true north. However, from Kaulia this radial passes through the mountain known today as Gaurishankar. It is readily identifiable by its twin peaks; its main peak has an altitude of 23,406 feet. It is thirty-six miles from Everest.

Only by combining these two bearings, taken from known locations, could Hermann draw a triangle whose third apex would establish the location of his 'Everest'. He did so (as shown in Figure 1.5), and thereby located Everest at latitude 27° 59' 17' N, 86° 54' 40' E, which is less than a mile from the modern co-ordinates (for the summit) of latitude 27° 59' 10" N, longitude 86° 55' 21" E.

Hermann executed and published a painting titled 'Gaurisankar (Mount Everest)', based on his view from near Falut. In his painting, Everest is a prominent peak, dominating the skyline. In reality, as viewed from Falut, it is partly hidden behind Makalu and appears lower than Makalu, as shown in Figure 1.6. It seems probable that the main peak in Hermann's painting is Makalu, with Everest depicted inaccurately as a subsidiary peak rather than a distinct mountain.

It is easy to see what went wrong. From Falut, Hermann saw a group of mountains with Everest probably among them. From Kaulia, he saw Gaurishankar (at an unknown distance, but much closer to him than Everest) and assumed that he was seeing Everest. The Schlagintweit brothers in due course identified Gaurishankar (or Gorishanta as they had first called it) with Everest.

The Schlagintweit brothers published the results of their scientific mission in four volumes from 1861 onwards[19], in flawless English, with a dedication to Queen Victoria. However, rivalries and animosities towards the Germans were such that their mission would be erased from the British version of Himalayan history.

The observations of the Schlagintweit brothers caused a sensation in Germany and confusion for many years in Britain. But that is another story.

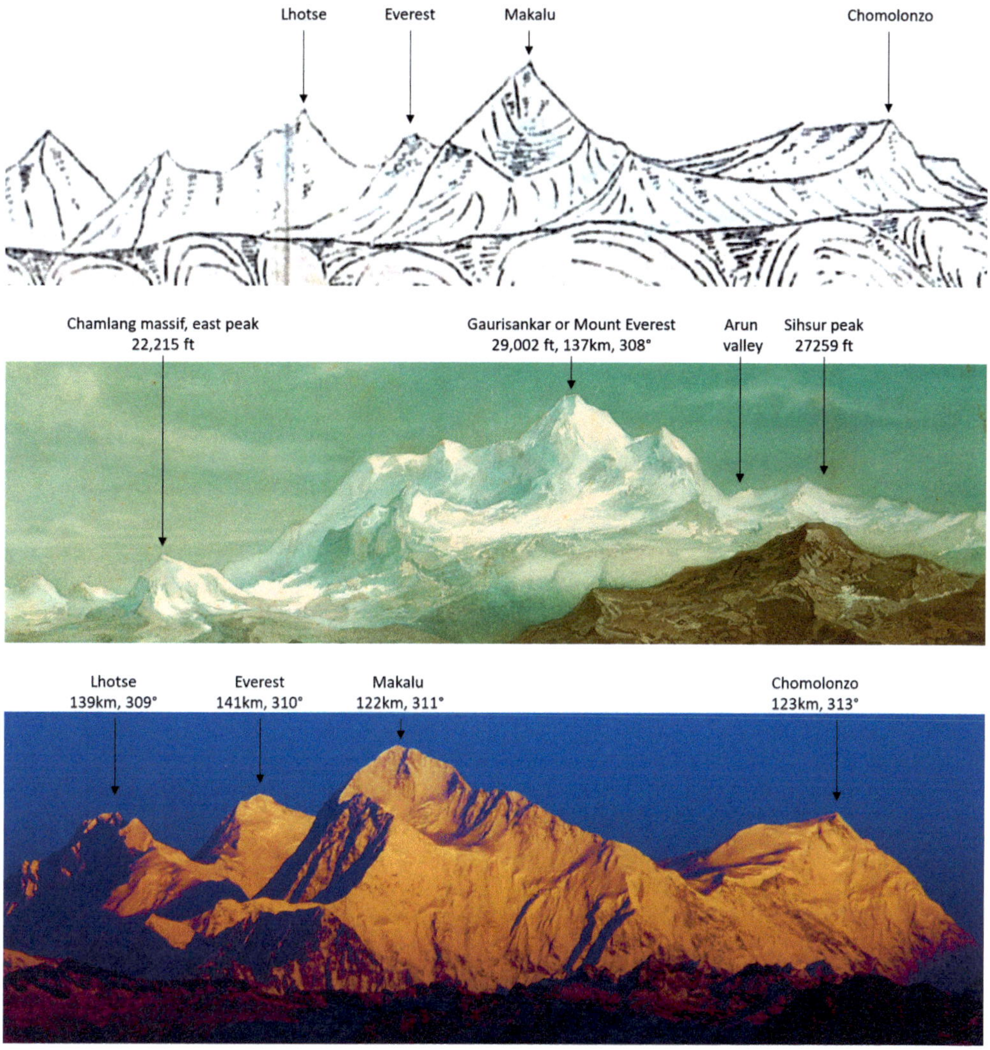

Figure 1.6. Three views of Mount Everest and neighboring peaks, from the Singalila ridge, Nepal/Sikkim border.

(above) detail from Walter Sherwill's sketch No.5, made in 1852, captioned 'Great peak in the snowy Nepal range, about 27,000 feet, N.W. from near Tombuk Pass'. By courtesy of June Harvey. (Walter Sherwill; annotations by author)

(middle) A detail from Hermann Schlagintweit's painting 'Gaurísánkar (Mount Everest)', made in 1857. (Hermann Schlagintweit, public domain; annotations added by author from Schlagintweit brothers, *Atlas, Part 1*, p.29)

(below) Everest and nearby peaks, viewed from Falut in 2011. (Shilbhadra, public domain; additional graphics by author, showing distances and bearings from true north)

Chapter 2

The Third Pole

As late as 1920, neither the British nor any other Western power had a hope of exploring Everest, nor even of venturing anywhere near the mountain that now bore a very British name. By now it was acknowledged that Mount Everest straddled the border between Nepal and Tibet. Nepal was nominally independent, but under the Sugauli Treaty of 1923, was subject to unwelcome British arbitration of its foreign relations. Tibet was also independent but had been invaded by the British as recently as 1904.

The British exploration establishment needed a new geographical triumph. They believed that American-led expeditions had beaten them to the North Pole – either Cook's party in 1908 or Peary's in 1909 – although modern scholars dispute Cook's claim and are divided about Peary's. There was (and remains) no doubt that in 1911, the Norwegian expedition led by Roald Amundsen had been the first to reach the South Pole. The British needed a third Pole, and Everest fitted the bill.

In the summer of 1920, Lieutenant-Colonel Charles Kenneth Howard-Bury[1] travelled to India on behalf of the Royal Geographical Society. His mission was to propose an expedition to Everest, which would need the backing of the Government of India. He met Sir Charles Bell, the Political Officer for India, and Lord Chelmsford, the Viceroy (Governor) of India. At first, the prospects were dim. At a meeting of the Society in London on 8 November 1920, its president, Sir Francis Younghusband, admitted that there were 'political obstacles in the way of our proceeding with preparations for the expedition to Mount Everest'[2]. In plain English, he meant that neither the Nepali government nor the Dalai Lama of Tibet was prepared to grant entry to British mountaineers.

Within the next five weeks, the obstacles somehow disappeared. On 15 December 1920, Lord Chelmsford sent the following message to the India Office in London:

> *'Bell telegraphs that he has explained to Dalai Lama object of desired exploration (i.e. Mount Everest) and necessity of travelling through Tibetan territory, and obtained Tibetan Government's consent.'*[3]

Younghusband told the Society at its meeting on 10 January 1921:

> *'... the Alpine Club and our Society will now organize an expedition which will have as its object the ascent of the highest mountain in the world, a mountain to which even the approaches are as yet unknown to Europeans.*
>
> *... the summit of Mount Everest will never be reached unless we have first explored with the greatest care all the approaches to it through*

country at present entirely unknown; and then examined, mapped, and photographed the mountain itself in fullest detail.

'In the present year the Alpine Club and our Society propose to organize a reconnaissance party to acquire this geographical knowledge.'[4]

On 24 January 1921, Younghusband announced that Colonel Howard-Bury would be chief of the Expedition, and that the illustrious Scottish mountaineer Harold Raeburn would lead the reconnaissance, now scheduled for the later part of the same year.

Enter Mallory

The definitive story of the 1921 expedition has been told in the book *Mount Everest, the Reconnaissance, 1921*, of which Colonel Howard-Bury was the principal author. At this juncture, George Herbert Leigh Mallory[5] enters our story. Of the prospective members of the reconnaissance, Howard-Bury wrote:

'The mountain party was to consist of four members, two of whom were to be men of considerable experience and two younger men who it was hoped would form the nucleus of the climbing party the next year [1922].

... Mr. Harold Raeburn, a member of the Alpine Club who had had great experience of snow and rock work in the Alps, and who had in 1920 been climbing on the spurs of Kanchenjunga, was invited to lead the mountain party.

Dr [Alexander Mitchell] Kellas, who had made several climbing expeditions in the Himalaya and had in 1920 ascended to a height of 23,400 feet on Mount Kamet, was also invited to join the climbing party.

The two younger members selected for the climbing party were Mr. George Leigh Mallory and Captain George Finch, both with a very high reputation for climbing in the Alps. Unfortunately Captain Finch was for the time indisposed and his place at the last moment had to be taken by Mr. [Guy Henry] Bullock of the Consular Service ...'[6]

In the spring of 1921, when the expedition set sail for India, Raeburn was fifty-five years old; Dr Kellas was fifty-two; Bullock was thirty-three, though he looked much older; Mallory was thirty-four.

Dr Kellas would never see Mount Everest. On the journey through Tibet, his health progressively declined. Inexplicably, his companions did not send him back to safety; at times, they carried him onwards, first on a chair and then on a stretcher. On 5 June 1921, he died suddenly of a heart attack. His colleagues buried him near the village of Kampa Dzong in Tibet.

Four other British citizens would join the party as specialists: Major Henry Treise Morshead (whom Mallory would meet again in 1922), and Major Edward Oliver Wheeler, both as surveyors, seconded from the Survey of India; Dr Alexander Macmillan Heron as geologist; and Alexander Frederick Richmond Wollaston as medical doctor, naturalist and botanist.

Figure 2.1. George Mallory on the 1921 British Everest Expedition. (Author, after photographs by Alexander Wollaston)

We need here, for our present purposes and no more, to define Mallory. He came from a family that nowadays would be called wealthy. He had been educated at Winchester College and Cambridge University; he had served from 1915 to 1918 in combat in the Great War and had risen to the rank of lieutenant; in 1921, he was employed as a teacher at Charterhouse, a renowned English public (meaning private) school. Volumes have been written on Mallory the man, and Mallory the soldier; they are not part of our story. Here, we are interested in Mallory the mountaineer: how he climbed, how he planned, and (to the extent that anyone can know another) how he thought about Mount Everest.

The reconnaissance

We are fortunate that in *Mount Everest, the Reconnaissance, 1921*, Mallory was the author of the centrepiece of the book, consisting of six chapters under the rubric 'The Reconnaissance of the Mountain'. The first two chapters were titled 'The Northern Approach', set mainly in the Rongbuk glacier, and included the story of a side trip that could have been called 'The Western Approach'. A third chapter was titled 'The Eastern Approach', in which Mallory searched unnecessarily for a way to Everest via the Kharta glacier. A fourth chapter was misleadingly titled 'The Assault', in which Mallory wrote of reaching the North Col and contemplating (but wisely not attempting) the North Ridge. He devoted an entire chapter to an analysis of snow and its properties. He concluded with his identification of the route to the summit, which in its essence was the route that would be followed in 1922 and 1924, and by all subsequent pre-war expeditions.

There was no southern approach, and there could not be, for Nepal remained out of bounds. If the British had been allowed into Nepal, Mallory might well have found the route on which the Swiss almost succeeded in 1952, and by which Hillary and Tenzing reached the summit in 1953. Then history might have been different.

Mallory's writing was at times tender and lyrical, and at others ponderous, stupefyingly detailed, and often confusing. In our reading of 'The Reconnaissance of the Mountain', we are seeking insights into his perception of the mountain: how he assessed it, how he calibrated it, how he loved and feared it; how he framed his eventual challenge to it. For the moments when Mallory articulated and recorded those perceptions, the reader's patience is rewarded.

The chronology of Mallory's reconnaissance is important. His first sighting of Everest prepared him for a mystery; the second sighting made an indelible impression on him; later sightings modified and built on that impression. As he came closer to the mountain, he became increasingly convinced that, stupendous as it was, he could climb it. We shall see that in the autumn of 1921, tasked only with a reconnaissance and not with an ascent, the thought crossed his mind that he could even then climb the North Ridge and reach the Northeast Shoulder. And obliquely he implied: if the shoulder, why not the top?

With that, we can set out in Mallory's footsteps, and metaphorically, we may approach the mountain as he did.

The vision

We join Mallory on 6 June 1921, at the village of Kampa Dzong, about 100 miles east of Everest. On a hilltop above the village there was an ancient stone fort and monastery. It was the day after the death of Dr Kellas. Raeburn was ill and would soon be sent back to Sikkim. Mallory wrote:

> *'Mr. G. H. Bullock and myself [were] the only representatives of the Alpine Club now remaining in the Expedition.'*[7]

Behind this offhand remark, there were profound implications. The two older men who had been supposed to mentor Mallory and Bullock were gone. Colonel Howard-Bury had no functional authority over the two young mountaineers; he was in any case in a separate party and made no great demands on Mallory for synchronized movements or for reporting. As far as climbing was concerned, Mallory was now, in effect, the head of the expedition.

In principle, the young diplomat Guy Bullock was co-equal with Mallory, but from Mallory's writing, we would not know it. However, unlike Mallory and the other members of the expedition, Bullock kept a detailed diary. His notes were eventually published in *The Alpine Journal* in 1962. His terse entries serve as a counterpoint to Mallory's lyricism.

Early that morning, Mallory and Bullock climbed past the fort at Kampa Dzong and continued upwards for about a thousand feet. Of the panorama that then unfolded before them, Mallory wrote:

> *'... we experienced the strange elation of seeing Everest for the first time. ... There was no mistaking the two great peaks in the West: that to the left must be Makalu, grey, severe and yet distinctly graceful, and the other away to the right—who could doubt its identity? It was a prodigious*

> *white fang excrescent from the jaw of the world. We saw Mount Everest not quite sharply defined on account of a slight haze in that direction; this circumstance added a touch of mystery and grandeur ...* '[8]

Mallory here was creating an Everest of the mind: a mountain outside the realms of normal human experience; a mountain with properties bordering on the supernatural. His description was not entirely accurate. Mount Everest does not resemble a white fang; it is a bulky object, pyramidal and massive. Its great height is tempered by its comparably vast breadth. As Mallory came closer, his descriptions, and we imagine his perceptions, would evolve.

Of this same sighting, Bullock wrote, with no evident emotion:

> '*... had excellent view of Everest range, as well as Kanchen[junga], etc. Makalu appears rather solitary well to the left (4°) [four degrees of arc].*'[9]

Proceeding west from Kampa Dzong, Mallory and Bullock skirted a mountain range that Mallory recorded as the Gyanka (but which is not to be found under this name in modern maps). Among these mountains, Everest could no longer be seen. They planned to follow the gorge of the river Yaru, which winds in a generally westward direction. Early on the morning of 11 June, they set out from Gyanka Nangpa. Again, this place is unknown to modern cartographers, but it is shown on the expedition map, where it appears to be about sixty miles northeast of Everest. Mallory wrote that they had almost halved the distance to be travelled.

On 13 June, at a place called Shiling, Bullock's diary records a sighting of Everest. At some moment during that day, Mallory would recall:

> '*... we were out on the edge of a wide sandy basin ... we saw the long Arun Valley proceeding Southwards to cut through the Himalayas and its western arm which we should have to follow to Tingri ...* '[10]

Here, Mallory was using the Nepali name for the river. In modern maps, it is shown as the Bum-Chu in Tibetan (or Pum Qu in Chinese); as Mallory knew, it eventually crosses into Nepal, where it becomes the Arun. At this junction of the two rivers, they were fifty-seven miles from Everest. They expected that looking towards the southwest, they would again see their objective.

> '*... we made our way up a steep hill to a rocky crest overlooking the gorge ... We were now able to make out almost exactly where Everest should be; but the clouds were dark in that direction. ... We caught the gleam of snow behind the grey mists. A whole group of mountains began to appear in gigantic fragments. Mountain shapes are often fantastic seen through a mist; these were like the wildest creation of a dream.* '[11]

Here, Mallory would have his second transcendent vision of the mountain:

> '*A preposterous triangular lump rose out of the depths; its edge came leaping up at an angle of about 70° and ended nowhere. To the left a*

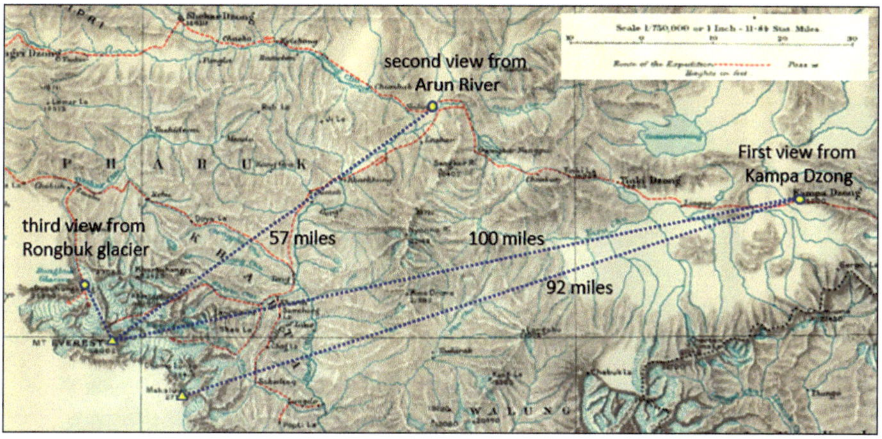

Figure 2.2. Mallory's first, second and third significant sightings of Mount Everest. (Base map from Howard-Bury: *Mount Everest, The Reconnaissance, 1921,* Map 1; additional graphics by author)

> *black serrated crest was hanging in the sky incredibly. Gradually, very gradually, we saw the great mountain sides and glaciers and aretes, now one fragment and now another through the floating rifts, until 'far higher in the sky than imagination had dared to suggest' the white summit of Everest appeared. And in this series of partial glimpses we had seen a whole; we were able to piece together the fragments, to interpret the dream. However much might remain to be understood, the centre had a clear meaning as one mountain shape, the shape of Everest.'*[12]

We see in this, as in other passages, Mallory's emotional bond with Everest: a bond that he would hardly speak or write of in 1922, and not at all in 1924. His description was again exaggerated; neither the eastern nor the western ridge of the mountain has a slope approaching seventy degrees. On the reconnaissance, Mallory was free to articulate his poetic impulses; and yet, he was able to leap in a moment from a mystical contemplation to a pragmatic climber's assessment of the mountain:

> *'We were looking at Everest from about northeast and evidently a long arete [ridge] was thrust out towards us. Some little distance below the summit the arete came down to a black shoulder, which we conjectured would be an insuperable obstacle. To the right of this we saw the sky line in profile and judged it not impossibly steep.'*[13]

Mallory had made three actionable observations. He had correctly identified the Northeast Ridge (or *arete* in the terminology of an Alpine climber). He had seen the junction of two ridges which would later be called the Northeast Shoulder; it looked impossible, but later he would change his mind. What he called the 'sky line' seems to be the section of the Northeast Ridge between the shoulder and the summit; and he was right, it is a comparatively gentle slope. Here we should remember his use of the term "sky line"; he would use it again on 7 June 1924, and would be completely misunderstood.

Finally, Mallory acknowledged the profound effect that this specific sight had had upon him, above all those before and after:

> *'... it is for me beyond other adventures unforgettable; ... the vision of Everest inhabiting our minds after this day had no small influence upon our deductions when we came to close quarters with the mountain.'*[14]

Of the same vision, Bullock wrote prosaically:

> *'... as Evt. [Everest] gradually cleared, we took its bearings ... NE ridge of Ev. [Everest] straight towards us. On E face seems to be very steep slope not far from top. N face seems rock with some snow on it. Lower part perhaps moderate angle ... W ridge possibly easy angle.'*[15]

Pushing the envelope

From 11 June 1921 onwards, Mallory and Bullock were travelling westwards, making a long detour to the north of Everest that was probably dictated by topography. They would have a few more sightings of Everest, notably one from near the village of Shekar Dzong, without adding appreciably to their knowledge of the mountain. On 23 June, they departed the village of Tingri Dzong, about forty-two miles north-north-west of Everest. Mallory would later write that even at this early stage, he envisaged a reconnaissance of several approaches, probably along valleys separated by high ridges. In other words, there would be a need for strategic decisions; once an expedition was committed to a valley, it would not lightly side-step to a neighbouring one.

The reconnaissance of the approaches would necessarily be followed by an assessment of all the accessible faces and ridges of Mount Everest itself. Like a good soldier going into battle (which in a sense he was), Mallory wrote:

> *'Our reconnaissance must aim at a complete knowledge of the various faces and aretes, a correct understanding of the whole form and structure of the mountain and the distribution of its various parts; we must distinguish the vulnerable places in its armour and finally pit our skill against the obstacles wherever an opportunity of ascent should appear until all such opportunities were exhausted.'*[16]

There was a third objective in the back of Mallory's mind, which was not self-evidently part of the mission as it had been conceived in London. We perhaps will never know what parameters the Royal Geographical Society had placed on the expedition. But Mallory's narrative makes it clear that his first objective was an identification of the best approach; his second was a determination of the shape of the mountain; and his third was something along the lines of an ascent. Mallory wrote:

> *'... anything in the nature of an assault should be left to the last as a separate stage of organisation and effort. ... So long as a doubt remained as to the way we should choose[,] we made no attempt to climb the peak ...'*[17]

Shortly, we shall see that at a certain point in this reconnaissance, Mallory was able to convince himself that no doubt remained; and he was then able in good conscience to attempt a climb. As to how far his ambition stretched at this moment, his writing gives little clue. He was acting the good test pilot, with the right stuff, who was just *pushing the envelope*.

Twenty-six years later, Chuck Yeager would be just pushing the envelope a little bit in the Bell X-1, and maybe by accident he just broke the sound barrier:

> *'We didn't know it (the flight) was going to be above Mach 1. ... All I was going to do was to go on up and probably run it out to about .98.'*[18]

We may wonder whether in 1921, Mallory was not planning accidentally to climb Mount Everest.

The northern approach

At Tingri Dzong, Mallory made his first strategic decision, which was to focus on a northern approach. This was dictated largely by the need to stay clear of Nepali territory. This approach necessarily would pass through the village of Chobuk. Thence the itinerary would follow the Rongbuk stream, which would lead to the Rongbuk glacier, and in turn to Everest. Mallory's party crossed the stream at Chobuk on 25 June 1921. As Mallory would write later, the Rongbuk valley is over twenty miles long, predominantly straight, broad and gently sloping throughout its length; and at its southern extremity is Mount Everest.

An hour out of Chobuk, they would see the sight that has become synonymous with the northern approach to Everest:

> *'We paused here in sheer astonishment. Perhaps we had half expected to see Mount Everest at this moment. ... But the sight of it now banished every thought. ... At the end of the valley and above the glacier Everest rises not so much a peak as a prodigious mountain-mass. There is no complication for the eye. The highest of the world's great mountains, it seems, has to make but a single gesture of magnificence to be lord of all, vast in unchallenged and isolated supremacy.'*[19]

From where he stood, Mallory could see the North Face, rising over 10,000 feet from the valley floor, and the two great ridges enclosing the Face. On the right in Mallory's view, the Northwest Ridge falls steeply below the summit (in photographs taken from the north, it looks like around 45 degrees). The Northeast Ridge, on the left in Mallory's view, was now confirmed to descend gently from the summit. Where the ridge reached the Northeast Shoulder, the slope became much steeper; Mallory must have surmised immediately that if he could reach the Shoulder, the climb to the summit would be relatively easy.

Figure 2.3. Mallory's view of Mount Everest from the Rongbuk glacier, at a distance of nine miles. (George Mallory, public domain; additional graphics by author)

What Mallory did not yet see, and was glad not to see, was any sign of pinnacles, jagged edges, crenelations and suchlike obstacles to the climber's path. He saw a smooth and bulky mass of rock, with here and there a dusting of snow. In this first view from nearby, the mountain must have seemed almost benign.

Bullock, stoic as always, had only this to say about Mallory's transcendent experience:

> *'Saturday June 25. To Choyling. ... At Chobuk cross the river by cantilever bridge. ... This river runs straight to NW coombe [roughly, hollow] of Everest. ... Finally valley turns a little east and Everest appears full in view at the end ...'*[20]

On 26 June, the party established a base camp in the Rongbuk valley, at an altitude of 17,500 feet by their barometer, sixteen miles from Everest and with the mountain in plain sight. Mallory recorded that their camp was not far from a major monastery which he referred to as Choyling (but which today is known as the Rongbuk Monastery).

In Mallory's diary for 28 June, he confirmed his thoughts about the Northeast Ridge:

> *'[Everest] is, generally speaking, convex, steep in lower parts and slanting back to summit. Last section of East arete [the Northeast Ridge] should go; but rocks up to the shoulder are uninviting. An arete must join up here, coming down towards us and connecting up with first peak to N.'*[21]

It was clear that the Northeast Shoulder was one of the keys to the climb. It was also evident that this shoulder must be the culmination of a ridge or saddle, which Mallory could not then see, but which he rightly deduced would link Everest with the unnamed peak to the north (later known as Chang Tse). Later he would find that saddle, to which he would often refer as Chang La (Tibetan for 'North Pass'). He and others would adopt an alternative name for the saddle: the North Col, as it is known today. After the Northeast Shoulder, it is the second key to the northern ascent of Everest.

Here also is Mallory's first written use of the phrase 'should go': meaning simply, 'can be climbed'. From the Northeast Shoulder to the summit, he saw no impassable obstacle. Here we may reflect that at least through binoculars, he must have seen some of the discontinuities on the Northeast Ridge: for example, those that would later be known as the First Step and the Second Step. Subsequent expeditions would learn that the Second Step was a cliff about 120 feet high from base to crest. From nine miles away, it would subtend a visual angle of about eight minutes of arc[22]: about a quarter the diameter of the full moon, as viewed with the naked eye. Mallory certainly carried binoculars on this journey; they probably had a magnification of five times. If so, they would have displayed the Second Step with a visual height of forty arc-minutes, more than the diameter of the moon.

Much later, the Second Step would become central to the debate about whether Mallory and Irvine could have reached the summit. Mallory, in all of his writings, never alluded directly to the Second Step, nor indeed to any Step on the mountain. Nevertheless, we can reasonably infer that in June 1921, scanning Everest from the Rongbuk glacier, he had become aware of the Second Step and had a plan either to climb it or to circumvent it.

The North Face

To complete the northern approach, Mallory had to see the North Face close up. To that end, on 1 July 1921 he embarked with five porters, leaving Bullock in camp. His plan was to reach the head of the Rongbuk valley, what he called 'the great cwm under the North face.' The term 'cwm' (pronounced 'coom' and rhyming with 'room') was a Welsh word, and a long-standing part of the British climbers' vocabulary, signifying a rounded hollow at the head of a valley – a three-sided basin. The party tramped for three hours on soft snow overlying the glacier, and reached 19,100 feet. The main conclusion was that the North Col could be reached from this side, but via what Mallory called 'a broken glacier', or via snow slopes which he deemed 'uninviting'.

On 3 July a second sortie reached 21,000 feet before returning to camp. Mallory then turned his attention to Ri-ring, a peak to the west of the main Rongbuk glacier. He wanted a high point from which to examine the North Face. He set 5 July as mission day: his party started at 4:15 am and reached the North Col at 9:30 am. The porters dropped out; Mallory and Bullock continued, reaching the summit of Ri-ring at 2:45 pm. They started the descent at 3 pm and were back in camp at 7:15 pm.

At the top of Ri-ring, their barometer read 23,050 feet; they had ascended 5,550 feet in ten and a half hours, with an average vertical speed of 529 feet per hour. The descent took only four and a quarter hours; the average descent rate was 1,306 feet per hour. Mallory must surely have made these calculations and filed them mentally for future reference.

It was from the vantage point of Ri-ring, with the whole of Everest's North face in view, that Mallory's view of the Northeast Shoulder began to soften. The rock slope from the North Col to the Shoulder, which he had previously called 'uninviting', he now characterized with English convolution as 'at no impossibly steep angle'.

The western approach

Mallory's next objective was to see what lay behind the Northwest Ridge.

He had noted that the Rongbuk glacier had a western branch, which looked as flat as the main valley. He expected therefore that the western glacier might curve around the Northwest Ridge and end in another cwm. Without yet seeing it, he had named it the 'Western Cwm'. On 8 July, he and Bullock moved up the West Rongbuk glacier and pitched a second camp. Later, they discovered a rocky protrusion in the middle of the glacier, which they nicknamed 'The Island'. On the morning of 13 July, they found themselves in the mist on the edge of a precipice, and judged that they were on the frontier with Nepal, where they could not trespass. More confusion followed, and false starts. Finally on July 19, as Mallory would write:

> *'We reached the col at 5 am, a fantastically beautiful scene; and we looked across into the West cwm at last, terribly cold and forbidding under the shadow of Everest. ... But another disappointment — it is a big drop about 1,500 feet down to the glacier, and a hopeless precipice. .... In any case work on this side could only be carried out from a base in Nepal, so we have done with the Western side.'*[23]

At the end of this phase of the reconnaissance, Mallory had a profound insight into the key to the ascent, which did not follow from any specific observation but rather seemed to spring fully-formed to his mind. Of his thoughts at this point, he would write:

> *'... our growing view of the mountain had been steadily leading to one conviction. If ever the mountain were to be climbed, the way would not lie along the whole length of any one of its colossal ridges. Progress could only be made along comparatively easy ground, and anything like a prolonged sharp crest or a series of towers would inevitably bar the way simply by the time which would be required to overcome such obstacles.'*[24]

Reading this passage, we sense that he would use the ridges where he could or should, and where they challenged him, he would not pick a fight but would make a detour. We may suspect that he was thinking of certain areas near the Northeast Shoulder (possibly the towers which are today known as the Pinnacles); and we may wonder if he was thinking about the Second Step.

What was clear to Mallory was that there was a viable route via the North Col. He was consolidating his position on this route:

> *'... the North arete coming down to the gap [the North col] between Everest and the North Peak, Changtse, ... is comparatively smooth and continuous, a bluntly rounded edge. We had still to see other parts of the mountain, but already it seemed unlikely that we would find more favourable ground than this.'*[25]

With the northern approach on the front burner, and the western approach eliminated. Mallory now prepared for a final foray into the valleys radiating from Everest: this time from the east.

The eastern approach

Mallory had discovered at some stage that the Rongbuk glacier had a third branch, which joined the main valley from the east, some ten miles north of Everest. The monsoon was well underway, bringing rain and snow. Mallory wanted to start the eastern approach on July 25; that was not to be, for one main reason. On 22 July, he received unwelcome news from Colonel Howard-Bury:

> '... *all my photos taken with the quarter-plate camera had failed — for the good reason that the plates had been inserted back to front, a result of ignorance and misunderstanding ... the next two days were spent in a photographic expedition. And so it came about that we saw no more until a much later date of the East Rongbuk Glacier.*'[26]

The centrepiece of this episode has become part of the Mallory legend, cited as proof that Mallory was forgetful, scatter-brained, or incompetent. There is no need for us to accept any part of this portrayal: if we wished, we could adduce counter-examples of his focus, foresight and competence. What matters for our story is that the East Rongbuk glacier did not receive the reconnaissance that it might have merited.

Mallory's team-mate Major Wheeler had identified the East Rongbuk early on, in the course of his photographic mission. Mallory, when he later became aware of it, thought it insignificant, because it produced only a trickle of water when it entered the main valley. Therefore, he did not imagine that it was ten miles long and started from the slopes of Mount Everest itself. In fact, a walk up the East Rongbuk would lead to the North Col, one of Mallory's keys to the summit; but to the eastern side of the Col.

As a result of this misperception, Mallory engaged in a long and largely superfluous journey to the village of Kharta, some twenty-five miles east of Everest. There he re-joined Colonel Howard-Bury and the rest of the expedition. At the village, the eponymous Kharta stream flowed from the west into the Bum-Chu (or Arun) River. Mallory's hypothesis was that the Kharta emanated from a glacier which in turn started at Everest; therefore, if he followed the Kharta upstream, within two days he would arrive at his North Col. As subsidiary objectives, he expected to view what he called the East Face of Everest (what is now called the Kangshung Face), and to assess access to the Northeast Ridge from the east. On 2 August, he set out on this mission.

As a vantage point for the eastern approach, Mallory chose a peak that he knew as Carpo-ri (its modern name may be Kartse). On 7 August, his party climbed a col to the east. From there, they could see the Kangshung Face. Mallory would write:

> *'We had already by this hour taken time to observe the great Eastern face of Mount Everest, and more particularly the lower edge of the hanging glacier; ... almost everywhere the rocks below must be exposed*

> *to ice falling from this glacier; that if, elsewhere, it might be possible to climb up, the performance would be too arduous, would take too much time and would lead to no convenient platform; that, in short, other men, less wise, might attempt this way if they would, but, emphatically, it was not for us.*'[27]

The Kangshung Face was thereby eliminated; and to this day, it remains the face of Everest which climbers rarely attempt. The first ascent of Everest via the Kangshung Face was in 1983.

For Mallory, it remained to be determined whether the Northeast Ridge could be approached from the east. This idea was soon laid to rest:

> '... *the distance from the North-east arete [ridge] was small enough and we were now looking almost directly up its amazing crest. If any doubts remained at this time as to that line of attack, they now received a coup de grace. Not only was the crest itself seen to be both sharp and steep, suggesting an almost infinite labour, but the slopes on either hand appeared in most places an impracticable alternative; and leading up to the great rock towers of the North-east shoulder, the final section, the point of a cruel sickle, appeared effectually to bar further progress* ...'[28]

We see that Mallory was aware of the rock towers on the Northeast Shoulder, in modern times known as the Pinnacles. These three towers are among the most lethal places on Everest. They were not climbed until 1988; and it was not until 1995 that an expedition reached the summit via the Pinnacles. If Mallory was able to eliminate the Pinnacles on first sight, we can readily imagine that he would not find the Second Step inviting.

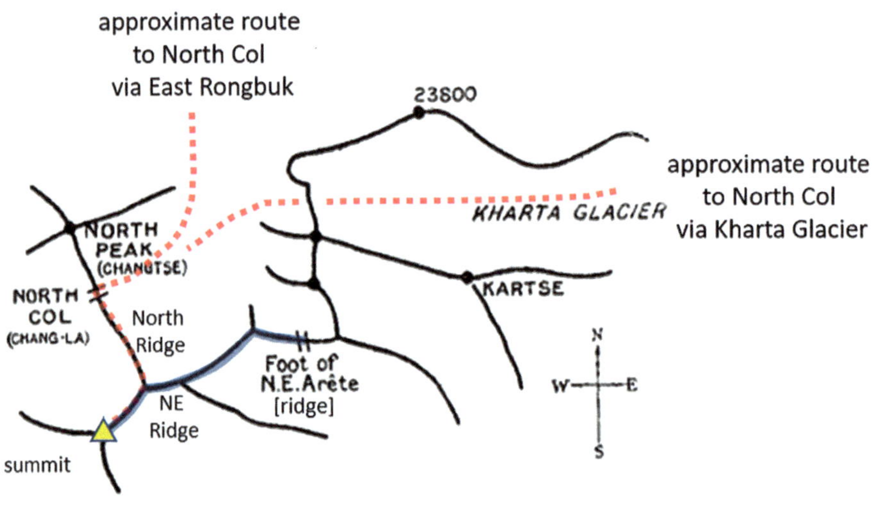

Figure 2.4. Mallory's diagram on the eastern approach. (George Mallory, public domain); additional graphics by author)

At this point Mallory would have known that the Northeast Ridge could only be approached from the north: in other words, from the North Col and the North Ridge, as he had first surmised.

The last piece of the puzzle was an eastern approach to the North Col, if such existed. Here, Mallory's narrative is beset with confusion. He admits that he received several messages affirming that the East Rongbuk Glacier would serve that purpose and that the Kharta Valley would not. One such was from his friend Bullock, above him in the Kharta glacier:

> *'... a chit [note] from Bullock: "I can see up the [Kharta] glacier ahead of me and it ends in another high pass. I shall get to the pass to-morrow morning if I can, and ought to see our [East Rongbuk] glacier over it. But it looks, after all, as though the most unlikely solution is the right one and the [East Rongbuk] glacier goes out into the Rongbuk Valley."'*[29]

For the remainder of the eastern approach, Mallory seemed to vacillate between the East Rongbuk and the Kharta glacier. His narrative conveys his confusion. As an author, he would have benefited from a good editor. But his final position must surely rest in a diagram that he included in his section *of Mount Everest, The Reconnaissance, 1921*. The diagram, although never elucidated in the text, is captioned 'Diagram showing that the Kharta Glacier does not lead to the North Col'. We reproduce it, with annotations, in Figure 2.4.

The assault

In a book that was nominally about the reconnaissance of Everest, with no mandate to climb the mountain or even to set foot on its upper slopes, Mallory did indeed write a chapter titled 'The Assault'. No-one took him to task for it. We may imagine that the mantle of leadership of the climbing party, which fell so early and so unexpectedly on him, empowered him to do whatever he judged useful and possible. It is not too difficult to imagine slightly different circumstances, perhaps no more than better weather, in which history would have recorded that Mallory and Bullock, in 1921, were the first to stand upon the roof of the world.

In the first paragraph of this chapter, Mallory did not disguise his extraordinary ambition:

> *'... we must aim at reaching the North-east Shoulder. ... could we reach the great shoulder of the arete [Northeast Ridge] we should at least be in a better position to estimate what lay between there and the summit. Finally we saw no reason to exclude the supreme object itself.'*[30]

To place this ambition in context: in 1921 the highest point reached by any climber was 24,600 feet, by the Duke of Abruzzi near K2 in the Karakoram range.[31] Mallory, if he were to reach the Northeast Shoulder of Everest, would be at about 27,300 feet; for that alone, on his first excursion to the Himalayas, he would be the most successful climber in the world. If he were (say it softly) to reach the summit, he would be ranked among the great explorers of all time.

To reach the Northeast Shoulder, Mallory had to attain the North Col. He had seen it from the west, at the head of the Rongbuk Glacier, and had not much liked what he saw.

The alternative was to climb it from the east. In this case, Mallory had received ample evidence that the East Rongbuk Glacier was the easy and obvious route. Nevertheless, he persisted with the difficult approach via the Kharta Glacier. To reach the North Col from this direction, he would have to cross a high pass which he called Lhakpa La ('Windy Pass').

On 31 August 1921, Mallory and Bullock set up a new Advanced Base Camp. Neither his narrative nor Bullock's diary make it clear exactly where this was; but it was evidently in the Kharta valley and on the bank of the Kharta stream. On 6 September, they were joined by Howard-Bury, Wollaston and Raeburn; on 11 September, by Morshead and Wheeler; and on September 14, by Heron who stayed two nights. Briefly, the whole British party was assembled.

In the course of the subsequent expedition, which Mallory would later call 'the assault', the climbing party would change composition several times. We can guess, and sometimes we can read, that there was debate as to whether the plan made any sense.

On September 20, Mallory and Morshead set off with fourteen porters for the Lhakpa pass. The others joined them later in the day. Camp was established at 20,000 feet. On 22 September, Raeburn was left in charge of the camp; the other six climbed to Lhakpa La and pitched tents in a small hollow. The following day, the party started to fragment. Bullock's diary records that Howard-Bury, Morshead and Wollaston beat a retreat. Bullock attributed their departure to the 'moderate difficulty' of the North Col; but the differences must have been more profound than that.

Mallory, Bullock and Wheeler pressed on. The following day, September 24, shortly before 11:30 am, they reached the North Col.

Here, Mallory's narrative reveals what he must have been hoping for:

> *'My eyes had often strayed, as we came up, to the rounded edge above the [North] col and the final rocks below the North-east arete [ridge]. If ever we had doubted whether the arete were accessible, it was impossible to doubt any longer. For a long way up those easy rock and snow slopes [there] was neither danger nor difficulty.'*[32]

However, if Mallory had harboured a quiet plan to push the envelope to the Northeast Shoulder, it was not to be. Here the party would for the first time encounter the violent west wind of Everest, which would weigh on the minds of all future expeditions. Bullock's diary tells the story:

> *'We proceeded to the [North] col shelf where we were exposed to the wind, which also swept the whole North buttress [North Face] and at once decided that to go on was impracticable. Wheeler had been quite against attempt all along. I was prepared to follow M. [Mallory] if he wished to try and make some height, but was glad when he decided not to.'*[33]

We now see Mallory at his most pragmatic:

> *'... the wind had settled the question; it would have been folly to go on. ... it would be bad heroics to take wrong risks; and fairly facing the situation one could only admit the necessity of retreat.'*[34]

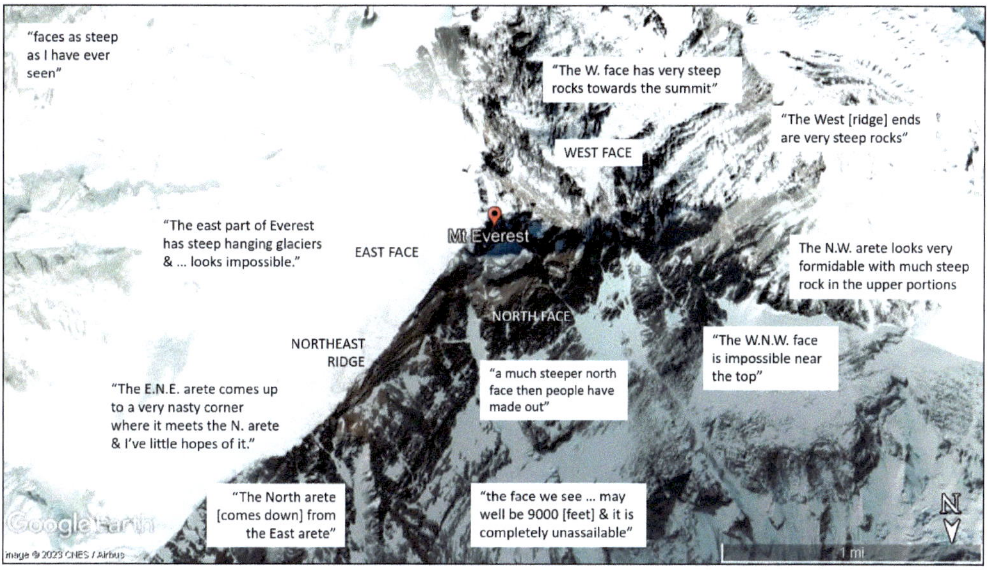

Figure 2.5. Mallory's assessment of the faces and ridges of Mount Everest in 1921. (Base image © CNES / Airbus / Google Earth; text from George Mallory's letters to Ruth Mallory and to Captain John Percy Farrar, 1921; graphics and legend by author)

With that, the eastern approach was over, and with it, the 1921 expedition. Of Mallory's perceptions of the mountain at this stage, we may be permitted two observations. Firstly, his approach was methodical, systematic and iterative. He sought an inventory of all the possibilities; and of those he found, he would opt for the easiest and safest. Secondly, there was nothing flamboyant or quixotic in his style. When confronted with an obstacle, he would circumvent it or he would retreat.

The route to the summit

In this chapter, it remains for us to summarize what Mallory felt, at the end of the 1921 expedition, regarding the best route to the top of Everest. We imagine that when writing for publication in 1922, he had had time to reflect on his experiences.

He was still ambivalent about the eastern approach, specifically the choice between the East Rongbuk glacier and the Lhakpa La. He acknowledged that his omission of the East Rongbuk had been a 'misfortune', and that the Lhakpa La had been more difficult than he had expected. He came close to saying that the East Rongbuk, although still unexplored, might eventually be the best solution.

For the rest, Mallory's vision was clear. The high climb must begin on the North Col. The ridge connecting to the North Col to the Northeast Shoulder (what we now call the North Ridge) was 'ill-defined', but smooth and continuous, with no obstacles. At the Northeast Shoulder, the climber would make a right turn, and the Northeast Ridge would point the way to the summit. Mallory was careful, or so it seems from his writing, to avoid specifying the crest of the ridge. He wrote (and here we read his only, oblique, references to the First Step and Second Step):

> *'The rise is only 1,000 feet in a distance of half a mile, but the first part of the crest is distinctly jagged by several towers and the last part is steep.'*[35]

Here, Mallory was alluding to the final ascent from 28,000 to 29,000 feet. Half a mile from the summit marks the formation which we now know as the First Step[36]. By the 'towers' he could only have meant the First Step (with a base at 27,950 feet by the contemporary calibration)[37] and the Second Step (with a base at 28,140 feet)[38]. These formations, in 1921, had no names. From the north, as they are usually depicted in modern images, they look indeed like steps. Mallory however must have viewed them predominantly from the east, from where they do look somewhat like towers.

With regard to the 'last part', Mallory surely meant what would later be called the 'Final Pyramid', which starts at about 28,400 feet, at what is now called the Third Step. It is indeed steep, with an angle of about 45 degrees, but modern climbers have generally not found it difficult.

Here, finally, we have the only real clue in Mallory's writings as to what route he would follow if he ever had the chance:

> *'Much will depend upon the possibility of escaping from the crest to avoid the obstacles and of regaining it easily. ... the sloping snow-covered ledges on the North-west [i.e., the North Face] may serve very well; the difficulty about them is their tendency to be horizontal*

Figure 2.6. The Northeast Ridge and summit of Everest, viewed from the North Col. (Michael Tracy; additional graphics by author. Altitudes are by the contemporary calibration)

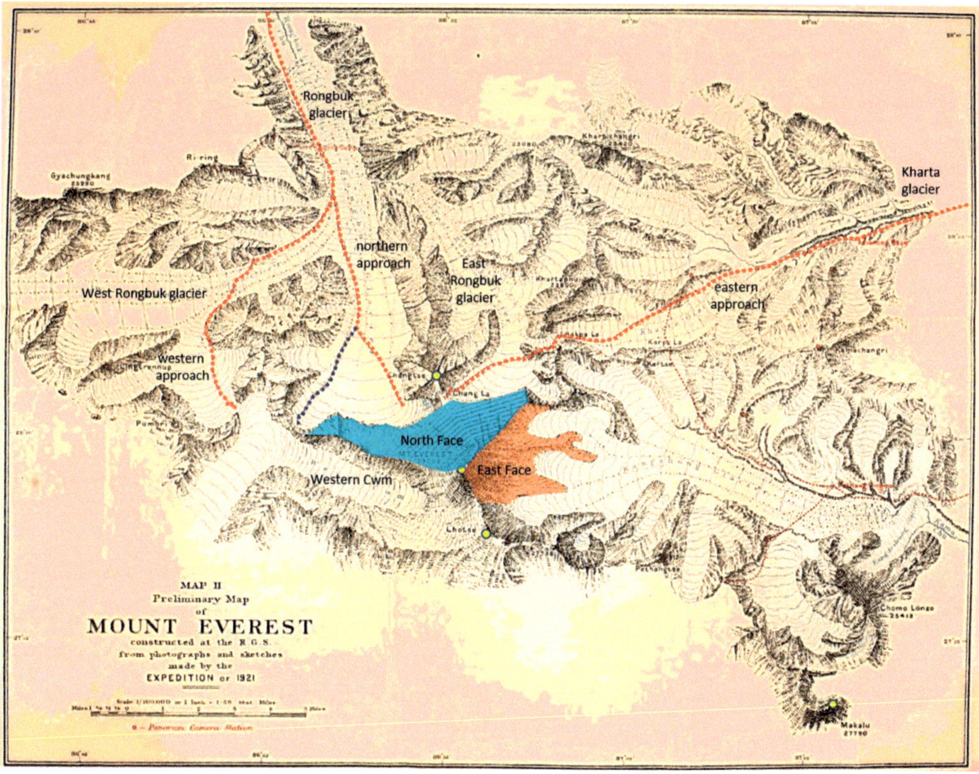

Figure 2.7. The principal approach routes followed by the 1921 reconnaissance expedition. (Base map: Royal Geographical Society, public domain; additional graphics by author)

> *in direction and to diverge from the arete where it slopes upwards, so that a party which had followed one in preference to the crest might find themselves cut off by a cliff running across the face above them. But one way or another I think it should be possible with the help of such ledges to reach the final obstacle.'*

After Mallory's disappearance, the legend would be propagated that he was a 'ridge climber'. For the moment, we may be permitted to think otherwise.

Chapter 3

1922

Following the reconnaissance of 1921, the British embarked in the spring of 1922 on a second expedition to Mount Everest, this time with the specific mission to reach the summit.

The expedition was headed by Brigadier-General Charles Granville Bruce, a professional soldier in the British army. Bruce would later be the principal author of the book *The Assault on Mount Everest 1922*, which remains to this day the most comprehensive and insightful account of the expedition. The term 'assault' conveys the British approach to the mission: it was conceived in military terms. The mountain was an adversary, to be overcome by force. Words like 'attack', 'fight' and 'epic' would appear in the titles of later narratives.

George Mallory was making his second trip to Everest. Among the other members of the 1922 party, those who would later be selected for the 1924 expedition were Colonel Edward Norton, Dr Howard Somervell and Captain John Noel, the official photographer and cinematographer. In 1924, Norton would become the *de facto* leader; he and Somervell would make the record-breaking climb that preceded Mallory's and Irvine's attempt.

We are fortunate in that in *The Assault on Everest 1922*, five of the fifteen chapters were written by Mallory. Under the broad heading 'The First Attempt', he wrote the chapters 'The Problem', 'The Highest Camp' and 'The Highest Point', totalling 106 pages. Under the heading 'The Third Attempt', he added two chapters with twenty-six pages. Together with his letters to Ruth Mallory from Tibet, and his twelve-page article 'The First High Climb', published in *The Geographical Journal* of December 1922, these writings yield further insights into Mallory's perception of Everest prior to 1924.

But first, we should allow Sir Francis Younghusband, as the author of the 'Introduction' to *The Assault on Everest 1922*, to set the scene. He wrote:

> *'During 1921, under the leadership of Colonel Howard-Bury, this reconnaissance [of Mount Everest] was most thoroughly carried out. Mr. Mallory found what was quite certainly the easiest — indeed the only practicable — way up the mountain ...*[1]
>
> *[In 1922] ... for the actual effort to reach the summit two men were specially marked out. One, of course, was Mr. George Leigh-Mallory, who had done such valuable service on the reconnaissance of the previous year; and the other was Captain George Finch ... Both of these were first-rate men and well known for their skill in mountaineering.*[2]

It is clear that at the outset of the 1922 expedition, Mallory was already recognized both as the man who had found the route to the top, and as one (and probably the leader) of those who would execute that journey.

Figure 3.1. George Mallory on the 1922 British Everest Expedition: (left) in the first climbing party; (right) at Base Camp. (Author, after photographs by John Noel)

The 1922 expedition would not reach the summit, but Mallory would emerge as a hero. General Bruce would write:

> *'It is not for me to describe in detail the great attempt on the mountain made by the party consisting of Mallory, Somervell, Morshead, and Norton, but I must point out quite clearly that as a tour de force alone it stands, in my opinion, by itself. It was the most terrific exertion, carried out during unfavourable weather and in the face of that dreadful West wind.*
>
> *... It was a tremendous effort, unparalleled in the history of mountain exploration, but it gave immense confidence to all that the mountain was not unconquerable.'*[3]

For our understanding of the evolving interaction between Mallory and the mountain, we now look to Mallory himself to take up the story.

The problem

Mallory began his account of 'The Problem' with a passage that was almost mystical:

> *'... half the charm of climbing mountains is born in visions preceding this experience—visions of what is mysterious, remote, inaccessible. ... so long as we cannot without a tremor imagine ourselves upon a mountain's side, that mountain holds its mystery for us.'*[4]

We begin to realize that Mallory needed a worthy adversary: one who would instil fear into him, and would make him conscious that he could lose. More than that, he was in some sense ambivalent about succeeding on Mount Everest:

> '*... when I say that sympathy in a mountaineer [for success] may wobble, the mountaineer I more particularly mean is the present writer. ... how can I help rejoicing in the yet undimmed splendour, the undiminished glory, the unconquered supremacy of Mount Everest?*'[5]

In this passage we may conjecture that Mallory was preparing himself for, or at least anticipating, a disappointment. The mountain, finally, might be too easy. He might succeed, and his success might turn to dust:

> '*... it has been said already of this mountain that the way to the summit is not very terrible, it will present no technical difficulties of climbing. Has it not then, after all, a character unsuitably mild? Is it not a great cow among mountains? It cannot be denied that the projected route to the summit presents no slopes of terrible steepness.*'[6]

Years later, other pioneers would experience a comparable anti-climax. Chuck Yeager, asked to recall his feelings on breaking the so-called 'sound barrier' in 1947 in the Bell X-1 rocket plane, said 'Well ... you just sit there and have a fleeting thought like: man, that wasn't as bad as I thought it was going to be.'[7]

As counterpoint to his doubts, Mallory needed a narrative of the challenge, the danger and the uncertainty of scaling Mount Everest. As other authors have well observed, Mallory had survived the Great War. He was part of an endeavour with a military character and with military imperatives. He needed the mountain to be difficult, and indeed to fight back. To conclude his analysis of 'The Problem', he wrote:

> '*Mount Everest, therefore, apart from its pre-eminence in bulk and height, is great and beautiful, marvellously built, majestic, terrible, a mountain made for reverence; and beneath its shining sides one must stand in awe and wonder.*'[8]

The solution

Mallory had defined the problem as twofold: difficulty and complacency. He now set out to delineate the solution. His approach was technical. The mountain had certain dimensions; certain ascent rates were feasible; certain timeframes had to be respected. One had to start from the objective and work backwards. He wrote:

> '*[The climber] may imagine that on the final day he might rise 2,000 feet to the summit ... We may therefore fix 27,000 feet approximately as the desirable height for the last camp.*

> *... we have another camping ground fixed for us by circumstances, approximately at 23,000 feet, the broad shelf lying in the shelter of the ice-cliffs on the North Col.*
>
> *We must ... establish an intermediary camp between these two, say at 25,000 feet.'*[9]

Mallory thereby set out the parameters for the locations of what would become, in 1924, Camps IV, V and VI. He then considered the optimum size of the climbing party:

> *'A party of two appears insufficient, for if one man should become exhausted the other will probably want help in bringing him down.*
>
> *... since an exhausted man cannot be left alone, certainly not without the shelter of a tent, nor should one man go on alone, a party of three must turn back so soon as one man is unable to go further.*
>
> *Four men would give a better chance of success in this case, for then two might go on and still leave one to look after the sick man.'*[10]

Jumping two years ahead, we might imagine that the high camp for 1924 would be modelled on Mallory's concepts for 1922. If we knew that, we would have an idea of what Mallory and Irvine had available to use or to carry on their fateful last climb. But in 1922, regarding the supplies for the high camp, Mallory had only this to say:

> *'Two tents are better than one, for it may be difficult to find a place for four men to lie side by side ... and they must have sleeping-bags, provisions for two days, fuel, and cooking-pots.'*[11]

To this author, it seems significant that Mallory mentioned provisions for two days. That implied two nights at the high camp: of which logically, one would be the night before the summit attempt, and the second, the night after. It is implicit that, as of 1922, Mallory expected to return from the summit to the high camp. He did not expect to bypass the high camp for a direct but fast descent to the intermediate camp, where there would be plentiful provisions. On the contrary, he seems to have anticipated bypassing the intermediate camp on the descent:

> *'We may assume that this camp [the intermediate camp at 25,000 feet] is to be used as a stage on the way up only and not on the way down.'*[12]

When we read Mallory's words, preserved over nearly a century, we do not hear a reckless man, an adventurer, a big hard hero. We hear a man who recognizes and evaluates risks and contingencies, who is risk-averse, who plans with care and in detail, but anticipates that things can go wrong. We hear a man who cares about his companions; one who will not abandon a climbing partner who cannot continue.

Other climbers, including some of Mallory's colleagues, would operate differently. In 1924, Norton would abandon his companion Somervell twice: once on the ascent and once on the descent. In 1960, the three Chinese climbers who reached the summit left their colleague Liu Lien-man alone above the Second Step. All parties survived; and all were duly hailed as heroes. But Mallory in his mountaineering career was never known to have left a companion behind. We shall remember this when we come to the events of 1924.

One of the rules that Mallory proposed in 1922, and broke in 1924, was to exclude the idea of a party of two. As we know, in 1924 he would climb to his high camp, and from there to oblivion, accompanied only by Irvine. When we address the events of 1924, we shall consider whether he had any choice.

The first high climb

Although Mallory wrote some splendid prose (interspersed with some stifling verbiage) about the trek to the low camp, we may re-join his narrative on what the expedition dispatches would eventually call 'the first high climb'.

Mallory knew in advance that they would not reach the summit. On 17 May 1922 he wrote to his wife:

> *'We shan't reach to the top, if we reach the shoulder at 27400 [feet] it will be better than anyone has expected.'*[13]

On 20 May at about 5 am, Mallory rose from his tent at Camp IV, located at 23,000 feet on the North Col, to wake the porters. Only four of them were fit for work. At 7:30 am, the four climbers and the four porters set out towards the North Ridge. They did not take supplementary oxygen. In the lead was Morshead, who re-enters our story briefly here and will soon depart; he was followed by Mallory with two porters; in the rear were Norton, Somervell and the last two porters. The names of the porters, as so often in these early accounts, have been lost to history.

During a break at about 24,200 feet, Norton lost hold of his rucksack, which escaped and disappeared forever down the mountainside. The significance of this event for us is both Norton's reaction (of which, more later), and that in his subsequent notes, Mallory would muse on his own habits in packing his gear:

> *'... as I never can resolve in cold blood to leave anything behind, when each article presents itself as just the one I may particularly want, I pack them all into a rucksack and then pull out this and that more or less at random until the load is not greater than I can conveniently carry ....'*[14]

Here we may conceivably gain an insight into what Mallory would carry on his last climb; on which otherwise, there is no written or oral record.

The team had planned to pitch their intermediate camp at 26,000 feet. But at 11:30 am the barometer was reading 25,000 feet; Morshead and several porters had not kept up with the group; the terrain was rising steeply. A collective decision was made to pitch Camp V; after several false starts, by 3 pm the tent was in place and the porters had been sent down to the lower camp. They were at that moment higher than any other climbers in history. They hunkered down for the night.

On 21 May 1922 at 8 am, the four climbers roped up and started the ascent. Norton was in the lead; he was followed by Mallory, Morshead and Somervell. Within minutes

(Mallory wrote: 'a few steps'), Morshead gave up. Somervell, who was a medical doctor, affirmed that Morshead was fit to descend to the camp and stay there. By mutual agreement, Morshead retreated; the other three continued.

At some point during the climb, it became clear to all (as it had been to Mallory) that they could not reach the summit. Their vertical ascent rate was, at best, 400 feet per hour. If they could maintain that, and if no obstacle intervened, the climb would take ten hours; they would be on the top at 6 pm. Mallory would later write:

> *'We were prepared to leave it to braver men to climb Mount Everest by night.'*[15]

The three climbers agreed to continue until 2:30 pm and then to turn around. In fact, they stopped at 2:15 pm. They were about 400 feet below the place known as the Northeast Shoulder, where the North Ridge joins the Northeast Ridge. Mallory later thought that they could have reached it in two hours, at the risk of compromising a safe return. Their barometer read 26,800 feet; eventually, the theodolite would show that they had reached a record-breaking 26,985 feet. They had taken six and a quarter hours to ascend about 2,000 feet; their average rate of ascent had been about 320 feet per hour.

The party started their descent at 2:30 pm and they were back in Camp V at 4 pm. Their average descent rate had been over 1,300 feet per hour: more than four times their average ascent rate.

In *The Assault on Everest 1922*, Mallory wrote of his mental state during the ascent:

> *'Looking back on my own mental processes as we approached 27,000 feet, I can find no traces of insanity, nothing completely illogical; within a small compass I was able to reason, no doubt very slowly. But my reasoning was concerned only with one idea; beyond its range I can recall no thought. ... It seemed to me that we should get back to Morshead in time to take him down this same day to Camp IV.'*[16]

We are trawling Mallory's reports and correspondence not for tales of heroism or adventure, but for insights into Mallory the mountaineer: how he approached the mountain, what he would attempt and what he would forego; and especially, what he might or might not do in 1924. In Mallory's accounts for the first high climb in 1922, we detect the first hints that Mallory could be a nervous and impulsive climber:

> *'I suppose it was stupid or careless of us to be caught like this. It is easy enough to keep one's hand warm with clumsy gloves so long as one is doing nothing in particular with them - but you may imagine what happened; as soon as it came to cutting I took the lead over from Morshead & went all out to get this job done as quickly as possible for fear the coolies [porters] would be done in by the cold & refuse to come on - & then of course I thought no more about my fingers.*
>
> *... The frost bites are nothing to worry about; of four fingers touched on the right hand only the third gives trouble. Even that one has no harm below the top joint ...*

> *It was a big strain altogether. Personally I wrecked myself with that cutting and when we were pitching tents had hardly the strength to lift a stone & the trouble is that one doesn't recover, the night at 25000 [feet] was miserable & I didn't expect to go on.'*[17]

From this passage (and nowhere else is the trauma of this climb disclosed), we learn that Mallory became impatient, took off his gloves to cut steps in the snow, contracted frostbite on four fingers, slept badly and still continued the climb the following day. He had known that his party would not make the summit; at 25,000 feet, the party had already set an altitude record; he did not have the presence of mind to propose a turnaround. Had he done so, Norton would surely have agreed (as we shall see from the events of 1924), and Somervell would have concurred.

For less than an additional 2,000 feet of altitude, the three men had put themselves out of action for any further climbing. Mallory knew this after their descent:

> *'... the trouble is that three of us appear to be out it now, Norton's ear and my finger are much the same case [of frostbite] ... I should have liked to make one more try - from a camp at 26,000ft, & nothing but this finger would prevent my going up again in a few days time.'*[18]
>
> *'Poor Norton has not been fit since we came down & there is no question of him going up again.'*[19]

The first high climb should have taught Mallory to turn around while his health and strength were intact. It was a lesson that he would fail to absorb in 1922; and would have completely forgotten by 1924.

The second high climb

On 25 May 1922, Captain Geoffrey Bruce (a cousin of General Bruce) and Captain George Finch set out from the North Col for a second attempt on the summit. Climbing with bottled oxygen, they pitched their high camp at 25,500 feet: five hundred feet higher than Mallory's party had done. On 27 May, Bruce and Finch set a new altitude record at 27,300 feet on the North Face. That is another story, well told by Finch himself.

Of Geoffrey Bruce's and Finch's climb, there can be no doubt that Mallory was keenly aware of their strategy. But he kept his cards close to his chest:

> *'I think they will certainly break our record - they have had very good weather - but I don't expect them to have reached the top at the first attempt. All depends upon whether they succeed in dumping cylinders ahead of them.'*[20]
>
> *'I shan't feel in the heart jealous of any success they may have. The whole venture of getting up with oxygen is so different from ours that the two hardly enter into competition.'*[21]
>
> *'Finch appeared done [exhausted] when he came down in spite of liberal use of oxygen, but is fit enough.'*[22]

Here, Mallory was concealing his plans. He was portraying himself as a purist, a non-oxygen climber. But he had every intention of using oxygen at his next opportunity; not only that, but he foresaw the need to cache oxygen ahead of the climb. His words give us a clue – it is no more than that – as to what he would do in 1924.

As for what, after the fact, Mallory thought of Finch's and Bruce's climb: he wrote to Ruth Mallory on June 1, 1922:

> *"They made a stout effort on the last day but in some ways managed very badly. It was an initial(?) mistake carrying up a first camp to 25500 [feet] instead of moving the one that we had established; and they put it on the wrong side of the ridge exposed to the wind. And then by some mismanagement about shortage of supplies both at the North Col & 25500 [feet] I believe – coolies were sent up from the North Col at 4 p.m.!, they did well to get back there at 11 p.m. But the idea of coolies wandering about up there in the dark with none of us to look after them fills me with horror. ... Finch seems to have an altogether different standard of caring for the coolies from mine. I'm determined we will run no risks with their lives during this next venture."*

Mallory's concern for the porters was surely genuine; but fate would decree otherwise.

Disaster

Starting on 3 June 1922, Mallory, Somervell and Crawford set off on a third attempt. Finch was initially a member of the party but withdrew, exhausted. Norton and Geoffrey Bruce were out of action. It was apparently intended that Crawford would supervise the return of the porters, and that Mallory and Somervell would go for the summit.

Mallory had by now recognized the value of supplementary oxygen. In the expedition report, he would write:

> *'... Somervell and I[,] when we went up for the third attempt this year[,] intended to use oxygen; judging from what had been said by Finch, Bruce, and others too who had used oxygen up to the North Col[,] we imagined we should go further with [oxygen] than without.'*[23]

Somervell, in his memoirs some years later, confirmed the composition of the party and the planned use of oxygen, though he said nothing about the route or the strategy:

> *'Finch, Mallory, Crawford, and I were first selected to make it [the third attempt], but ... [Finch] wisely retired while still on the glacier. ... We intended to use oxygen.'*[24]

In fact, Mallory had a specific strategy in mind. In the expedition report, he wrote:

> *'... we intended to go up to our old camp at 25,000 feet without it, perhaps use a cylinder each up to 26,000 feet, and at all events start from that height for the summit with a full supply of four cylinders [each].'*[25]

and in a letter to Ruth Mallory, he elaborated:

> *'... we should have hardly a chance of reaching the top without oxygen & in spite of Finch's absence with his expert knowledge we [presumably Mallory and Somervell] decided to carry up ten cylinders with the two apparatus used by Finch & G Bruce to our old camp established on the first attempt at 25000 ft. So far we should go without oxygen, in taking up the camp (one of the 2 Mummery tents & the sleeping sacks) another 1000 feet we might find it advisable to use each one cylinder, in any case we should have 4 cylinders each [illegible] with us next day.'*[26]

This passage is surely a forerunner of Mallory's approach in 1924. He saw the need for a final camp as high as humanly possible; in 1922, he would have been happy with 26,000 feet; in 1924, he would aim for 27,000 feet. For two climbers, he foresaw a need for eight full cylinders of oxygen on the summit day. Since two climbers could carry six cylinders at most, and possibly only four in practice, it is clear that he planned to cache two or four cylinders along the route, in advance of the climb. In a later chapter, we shall learn of an artifact that testifies to this plan.

Four days after the departure from Base Camp, the climb ended in disaster. On the ascent of the North Col, which was normally an easy climb, Somervell took the lead, followed by Mallory, one (unnamed) porter, then Crawford and thirteen other porters. They were struck by an avalanche; seven porters lost their lives. The expedition was over. That too is another story.

Morshead

Finally, the collapse of Major Morshead must have weighed on Mallory's mind. In 'The First High Climb' in December 1922, he elaborated on his concerns:

> *'At starting from the North Col[,] Morshead seemed fitter than any one; his failure was a complete surprise to all of us; and in view of it I think a party of the future should reckon that some such experience may happen to any one of them. At a high altitude even the strongest might suffer this loss of muscular power;* ***and he will not recover up there.***'[27] [Mallory's emphasis].

As it transpired, Morshead's breakdown did not materially affect the rest of the 1922 climb. The climbing party probably turned around sooner because of him; but in all circumstances, they would have turned around. Later, Mallory surely wondered what could mitigate such an event. In 1922, Morshead was thirty-nine years old. We begin to understand why, in 1924, Mallory would want to make his high climb with a companion aged twenty-two.

Lessons learned

With regard to our view of the events of 1924, our take-aways from Mallory's 1922 narrative may reasonably include the following:

- Mallory knew that he could reach 27,000 feet, and probably 27,500 feet, without supplementary oxygen. He was confident that with oxygen, he could do better.
- He had no desire to make a summit attempt that would require a descent in darkness.
- He was aware that without oxygen, his mental processes were slowed down; but he was able to make intelligent decisions. He did not become obsessed; he did not catch 'summit fever'.
- He knew that his descent rate, even without supplementary oxygen, would be easily double and possibly triple his ascent rate.
- With diminished mental capacity he nevertheless retained concern for the welfare of his companions.
- He did not see himself as imposing any course of action; the party's decisions were by mutual consent (though here, he probably understated the force of his own personality).
- However, he did not learn to keep his gloves on; nor when to save his health and strength for another day.

We might be permitted to suppose that some or all of these observations were valid in 1924, and that they informed Mallory's decisions on his last climb. To these ideas, we shall return.

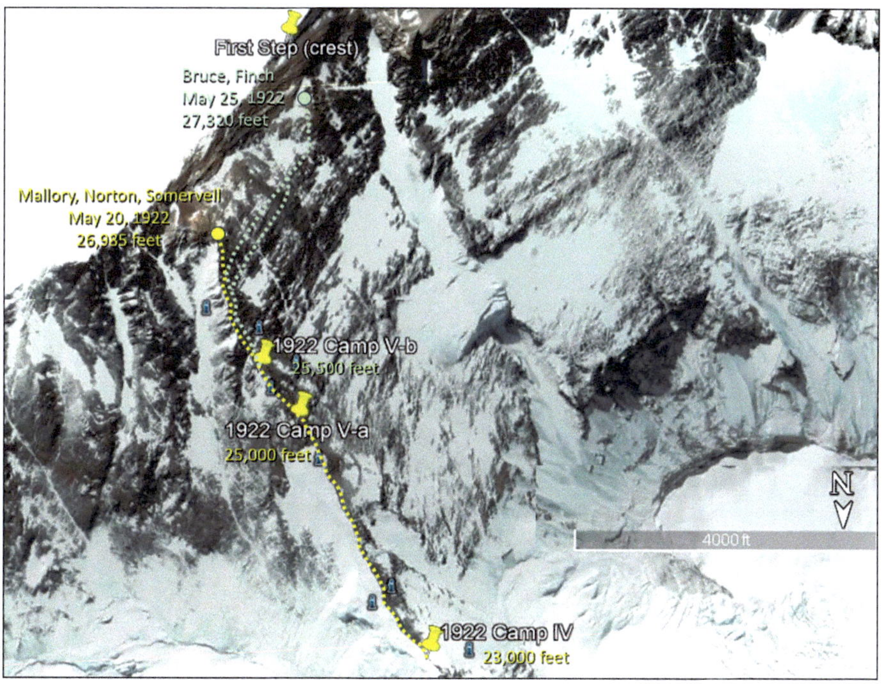

Figure 3.2. Approximate locations of the high camps, and routes of the high climbs, of the 1922 British expedition. Camp V-a denotes the high camp of Mallory, Norton and Somervell; Camp V-b denotes the high camp of Geoffrey Bruce and Finch. (Base image © CNES / Airbus / Google Earth; graphics and legend by author)

Chapter 4

'English Air'

It seems to have been the photographer John Noel who first coined the term. Writing with a mixture of admiration and condescension, of the Sherpa and Bhotia who were tasked with shifting the heavy loads of the 1924 expedition, he recalled:

> *'When they first saw our unsightly and awkward oxygen tanks, they laughed heartily and said, "The air in our country, sir, is quite good. Why do you bring bottled air from England?" ... When they tasted it they realized how wonderful it was ... Then often they would come to us and say ... "I want a little English air."'*[1]

Already in 1924, the story of 'English air' went back several years. Oxygen fell between opposing camps. The use of oxygen in mountaineering became a symbol of a dispute between sport and science. We shall start the story from the scientific perspective.

Kellas

In the British mountaineering context, the story of oxygen had its origins in an expedition to Mount Kamet in India, in the summer of 1920, by Dr Alexander Kellas and Major

Figure 4.1. Dr Alexander Kellas and an unidentified Sherpa, around 1911-1914. (Author, after a photograph by an unidentified assistant to Dr Kellas)

Henry Morshead. Kellas was later to join the Everest reconnaissance expedition of 1921, during which he would unexpectedly fall ill and die; Morshead would be a climbing member of the Everest expeditions of both 1921 and 1922.

Kellas was the leader of the 1920 expedition; his specific objectives were to assess the physiological effects of climbing at high altitudes, and to explore the use of supplementary oxygen. He had the support of the British government, via the Oxygen Research Committee and the Medical Research Committee, both under the authority of the Department of Scientific and Industrial Research.

Kellas started out from his base at Kathgodam, in Uttarakhand state, in early August 1920. From the outset, he was not optimistic about the prospects for the use of compressed oxygen, at least not in the form that had been supplied to him:

> *'On testing the weight of the oxygen cylinders at Kathgodam it became evident that they were almost certainly too heavy for high altitude work ... They are nearly three times the weight of the cylinders previously shown to me. ... Their weight (16 lbs. approx., or with pressure regulator, etc, nearly 20 lbs.) is as much as most coolies[2] [porters] care to carry as a load even at 20,000 feet.'*[3]

Kellas had obviously expected to work with lightweight cylinders, probably of about seven pounds when filled, such as had been shown to him by a Colonel Stewart in 1919. His observations on the weight of the cylinders were apposite and prescient. By 1922 it would begin to appear that, with the equipment of 1920, serious attempts on Everest would need a four-pack of cylinders for each climber. That pack would weigh in at close to eighty pounds.

Apparently, Kellas nevertheless transported some or all of his heavy cylinders to Kamet, a distance of at least 200 miles from Kathgodam. He joined up with Morshead on 19 August 1920. On 20 September, they reached their high point of 23,600 feet on the saddle of Mount Kamet, about 1,850 feet below the summit. At some point, probably on the ascent, they made unspecified trials with oxygen:

> *'Preliminary experiments at 21,000 feet on Kamet confirmed that [the cylinders] were unsuitable, but no opportunity of working out systematic experiments occurred until after reaching the camp at 18,000 feet, near the Bagini glacier.'*[4]

On 21 September, Morshead had to depart, and Kellas descended to his base camp with a view to continuing his experiments with oxygen. He apparently conducted these experiments over the course of a week, sometime between 5 and 16 October 1920, at his camp at 18,000 feet.

In all the subsequent pre-war expeditions to Everest in which oxygen was available, only the Western climbers would use it; the porters would be expected to climb and descend without oxygen. However, Kellas had no climbers on whom to experiment. He was not in good physical condition, and presumably had not the personal strength and endurance to test oxygen on himself. He therefore, evidently, chose to equip selected porters with cylinders and breathing apparatus, and he timed their climbs over designated routes. We may summarize his results as follows:

route	nature of route	vertical distance	use of oxygen	typical time	typical vertical speed
		feet		hh:mm:ss	feet/hour
long	ascent over easy snow, and return	3000	no	02:00:00	3,000
long	ascent over easy snow, and return	3000	ascent only	03:40:00	1,636
medium	ascent over rough snow; return via rock scree	600	no	00:28:00	2,571
medium	ascent over rough snow; return via rock scree	600	yes	00:39:00	1,846
short	ascent of stony ridge	200	no	00:08:20	1,440
short	ascent of stony ridge	200	yes	00:10:30	1,143

In summary, on all three routes the porters were slower with oxygen than without. Kellas inevitably concluded:

> *'... the cylinders are too heavy for use above 18,000 feet, and below that altitude they are not required. They would be quite useless during an attempt on Mount Everest. It would seem advisable in the circumstances to carry out experiments with cylinders of double the capacity filled to half the pressure ... A volume of 140 litres (i.e. 5 cubic feet) of oxygen might be helpful, if the weight of the cylinder were not above, say, 7 lbs.'*[5]

Oxylith

Kellas then turned to the idea of a chemical oxygen generator. In his eventual report to the Oxygen Research Committee, he referred to 'Professor Leonard Hill's Rubber Bag and Oxylith'. Probably, he had read of Professor Hill's invention of a portable oxygen device, based on the chemical reaction between an 'oxylith' (in this case sodium peroxide) and water. In 1909, Hill had written:

> *'The apparatus consists of a small metal box – the generator - connected with a vulcanized rubber bag - the breathing bag. The bag holds about 15 litres, and ends in a rubber mouthpiece. ... Three blocks [0.3 pounds of oxylith] make a full charge, and the oxygen yielded from this is amply sufficient for fifteen minutes' inhalation. ... it can be used wherever a pint or two of water can be obtained.'*[6]

Hill's idea was essentially the same as that used today in emergency oxygen generators for air passenger transport. If during an air journey, we have the misfortune to lose cabin pressure and to need an oxygen mask, the gas that keeps us alive for a while is generated by a chemical process.

To this end, Kellas prepared a generator on Professor Hill's model, and did two series of experiments.

In the first experiment, he asked a test subject (presumably a porter) to climb his 'short course' – an ascent of 200 feet on a stony ridge – twice, first after breathing for five minutes from the breathing bag, and fifteen minutes later without this preamble. He recorded the times for the ascent; there was no perceptible difference.

In the second experiment, he charged the generator and the subject repeated the short route, carrying the breathing bag under his arm, and inhaling from it continuously. In this case, unlike in the previous tests with the cylinders, there was an improvement in the ascent time: of the order of 25 per cent.

Kellas wrote in his report that '… a modified form of Hill's [breathing] bag, of considerably increased capacity - say, 150 to 200 litres – might be of use'. This was ten to thirteen times larger than the model that Hill had described. Kellas presumably had in mind a charge of three to four pounds of oxylith, plus water to react with it (he did not specify how much water). In any case, his idea seemed to offer an improvement in weight on the equivalent volume of compressed oxygen.

Extrapolating from Hill's early tests, Kellas's concept of an oxygen generator might have yielded a usable breathing time of 2.5 to 3.5 hours. He might have calculated that such a climb could be anticipated from a high camp to the summit of Everest. In the event, the highest British camp ever established on Everest (the Camp VI of the 1933 expedition) would be at 27,400 feet: 1,600 feet below the summit. After two unsuccessful attempts, the 1933 team would conclude that a yet higher camp was needed: probably close to 28,000 feet. At that date, no-one alive knew what ascent rates could be achieved at such a height, with or without oxygen.

As it transpired, the chemical generation of oxygen was never pursued. Oxygen cylinders became lighter, and the breathing apparatus more efficient. From 1921 onwards, the debate would be simply between compressed oxygen, and the natural lung power of sporting gentlemen.

The reconnaissance

Notwithstanding the mixed results of Kellas's experiments, there was sufficient promise in his results to warrant a continued examination of the use of oxygen on Everest. By January 1921 it was known that politically, it was possible for Europeans to enter Tibet; and preparations for an expedition to Everest were launched forthwith. Although the project would be formally known as the Mount Everest Reconnaissance, it was clear in the minds of the Royal Geographical Society that the primary objective was, if not an ascent, at least the identification of an ascent route. That is to say, scientific discoveries were secondary. In this context, it was natural to invite men who could make the greatest contributions to the climbing objective. Among them was Alexander Kellas. Sir Francis Younghusband, president of the Society, wrote:

> *'Dr. Kellas, who had made several climbing expeditions in the Himalaya and had in 1920 ascended to a height of 23,400 feet on*

> *Mount Kamet, was also invited to join the climbing party. He had been making experiments in the use of oxygen at high altitudes and was still out in India preparing to continue these experiments on Mount Kamet in 1921. It was suggested to him that he should make the experiments on Mount Everest instead, and the party would thereby have the benefit of his wide Himalayan experience. This invitation he accepted.'*[7]

Among the climbing members of the 1921 expedition, Mallory for one had an awareness of the importance of oxygen:

> *'... it is to be expected that efforts above 23,000 feet will be more exhausting than those at lower elevations ... [the climber] should be able to breathe regularly, the demand upon his lungs along the final arete cannot fail to be a terrible strain, and anything like a tussle up some steep obstacle which would interfere with the regularity of his breathing might prove to be an ordeal beyond his strength. As a way out of these difficulties of breathing, the use of oxygen has often been recommended and experiments were made by Dr. Kellas ...'*[8]

These words were published in 1922; Mallory wrote them when the expedition was over. By that time, he believed that he knew the approximate route to the summit; at least, he knew that the North Col, the North Ridge and the Northeast Ridge were markers of that route. We do not have to dwell on his reference to the 'final arete' (the final ridge); at that stage he would not have identified a specific route. In his comments on oxygen, we may detect the first intimations of his uncertainties about using it. These uncertainties would not be finally resolved until 4 June 1924.

In support of the research that was expected of Dr Kellas, some relevant equipment was shipped to him (though the contemporary accounts do not make clear exactly what it was, and whether he brought it with him on the expedition). A. R. Hinks wrote:

> *'The most important scientific work of the first year's [1921] expedition should have been the study of the physiological effects of high altitude that Dr. Kellas had undertaken ... He was prepared also to make several difficult researches into the physiological processes of adaptation to low oxygen pressure; and some delicate apparatus was prepared and sent out to him by the Oxygen Research Committee.'*[9]

But as we know, on 5 June 1921 at the Tibetan village of Kampa Dzong, Alexander Kellas died. There was no-one who could continue the work that he had planned. Charles Howard-Bury, leader of the expedition, would later write:

> *'His death meant a very great loss to the Expedition in every way, as he alone was qualified to carry out the experiments in oxygen and blood pressure which would have been so valuable to the Expedition, and on which subject he was so great an expert.'*[10]

Finch

It therefore fell to the Everest expedition of 1922 to put oxygen to the test.

In the context of that expedition, the earliest references to the planning for oxygen appear to be those of Howard Somervell, himself a medical professional, although in 1922 he would not be a user of oxygen:

> *'The winter of 1921-2 was occupied very largely with preparing, in one way and another, for the climbing of Everest. The question as to whether oxygen should be carried was discussed at length, and I as a physiologist could not help feeling — in conjunction with many physiologists much more experienced and distinguished than myself — that it was extremely doubtful whether human beings could live and move upwards at a height of anything much above 23,000 feet ...*
>
> *... the safest thing to do seemed to be to take oxygen, and my friend P. J. Unna and I had several discussions about the form the apparatus was to take. ... The apparatus weighed over 30 lb., and could not be cut down to less than this, either in 1922 or two years later.'*[11]

However, the story of oxygen in 1922 belongs to the man who championed its use, and ultimately paid a heavy price for his stance: George Ingle Finch.

In the spring of 1922, Finch was thirty-three years old. Born in Australia, he had been educated in France and Switzerland. He held a diploma in technical chemistry from the Eidgenossische Technische Hochschule in Zurich, Switzerland. Like Mallory, he had fought in France during the Great War. His mountaineering credentials were exemplified by his sometime presidency of the Zurich Academischer Alpen Club. In 1921, the Everest Committee had invited him to join that year's expedition, and had then rescinded the invitation on the grounds that two doctors had found him unfit. For the 1922 expedition, he had undergone another medical examination, had been found fit and had been selected as a climbing member.[12]

Figure 4.2. George Finch wearing the oxygen apparatus, 20 March 1922. (Author, after a photograph by John Noel)

Sir Francis Younghusband, President of the Royal Geographical Society, would later recall the central role that Finch had played in the decision to take oxygen:

> *'Captain Finch, who was himself a lecturer on chemistry at the Imperial College of Science, Mr. Somervell, and Captain Farrar, pressed so strongly for the use of oxygen, and Mr. Unna was so convinced he could construct a reasonably portable apparatus, that the Committee decided that the experiment should be made.'*[13]

Finch was therefore the natural candidate to be the oxygen officer for the expedition. General Bruce would write:

> *'... Captain George Finch ... came not only as a most important member of the climbing party, but also as the scientific expert in charge of the entire oxygen outfit.'*[14]

Finch quickly discovered that in his responsibilities for the oxygen supply, he had two problems to overcome: the physical condition of the equipment, which was somehow manageable; and less tangibly and thereby less tractably, the degree of acceptance of the whole concept.

The first problems manifested themselves on the mule train, a few days out of Darjeeling, *en route* towards Sikkim and Tibet. Loosely packed in wooden boxes, the oxygen cylinders had started to abrade, one against the other. Finch had all the boxes laboriously opened, discovered the damage, and locally purchased cloth and string to protect the cylinders, which were wrapped and repacked.[15] It was a first illustration of the expedition's haphazard treatment of the oxygen supply, and of its *ad hoc* solutions to issues of maintenance and repair.

On arrival at Camp III, on 20 May 1922, it became evident that the oxygen equipment was in bad shape. Finch would write:

> *'... not one of the ten oxygen apparatus was usable. ... most of the soldered metal joints leaked; washers had become so dry that the other joints could no longer be made gastight, and several of the gauges were out of action. ... neither of the two types of masks with which we were supplied could be used.*
>
> *[But] A few toy football bladders and glass 'T' tubes were all I needed. With these materials and odd bits of rubber tubing, I was able to construct a new mask ... The success of this simple mask pleased me greatly; without it, no really effective use could have been made of our oxygen supplies.*
>
> *Examination of the oxygen cylinders revealed that their contents were still intact; so we thereupon set to work with hacksaws, pliers, soldering iron and so forth to repair the damaged apparatus. Eventually two of these were made to function satisfactorily and, later on, two more.'*[16]

From our twenty-first century perspective, it may seem like madness to embark on a climb of the highest mountain in the world, with vital equipment cobbled together from scraps of material, using whatever tools were at hand. The 1922 expedition reads like a precursor of Apollo 13. But the rescue of the three astronauts from Apollo 13 was an emergency, and the ascent of Everest was not.

Finch's greater problem, at least as he perceived it, was in the nature of a clash of cultures.

In the first official account of the 1922 expedition, *The Assault on Mount Everest 1922*, Finch would contribute three chapters under the heading 'The Attempt With Oxygen'. Herein, he set out for the first time the nature of the intellectual, scientific and political debate that surrounded the use of oxygen on Everest. He would write:

> *'Prior to the formation of the 1922 Expedition, the oxygen problem had already been the subject of much discussion round which two distinct schools of thought had arisen. The first, headed by Professor G. Dreyer, F.R.S., Professor of Pathology at the University of Oxford, was staunch to the belief that, without the assistance of a supply of oxygen carried in containers on the back of the climber, it would be impossible for a man to reach the summit of Mount Everest. The second body of scientific opinion held that, not only would it be possible for a man to attain the summit of Everest unaided by an artificial supply of oxygen, but that the weight of such a supply would only hamper the climber in his efforts, and thus completely counterbalance any advantages likely to accrue from its use.'*[17]

In his capacity as leader of the expedition, General Bruce appeared in principle to lend his support to the idea of using oxygen. His only concern was the weight of the equipment:

> *'The one factor which renders the ascent so difficult is the want of oxygen in the air. Provide the oxygen and the ascent could be made at once. But to provide the oxygen heavy apparatus would have to be carried—and carried by the climbers themselves.'*[18]

As early as March 1921, Finch had undergone tests in decompression chambers at Oxford University, with and without oxygen. We can infer that these experiences had convinced him that oxygen was essential to the ascent of Everest[19]. Somervell had participated in the same tests, and as we have seen, he was on Finch's side. The 'oxygen school' had the backing of Captain Percy Farrar, the former president of the Alpine Club; and of P.J.H. Unna from the Oxygen Subcommittee of the Everest Committee.

Against this perspective there was, at least in Finch's view, an opposing school of thought. It was never clear who, specifically, was against the use of oxygen on Everest. Finch alluded to a 'body of scientific opinion', but there is nothing in the scientific literature of the era that expressed opposition to oxygen on theoretical or empirical grounds. Possibly Finch had in mind the early experiments of Alexander Kellas, in which Kellas's subjects had indeed climbed more slowly with oxygen than without; but Kellas had concluded that the solution was simply to be found in lighter cylinders. Finch, in the official expedition report, would never allude to any specific antagonism to oxygen. In his own memoir, published in 1924, he would elaborate a little:

> '*... there existed another force of oxygen antagonists, largely unscientific, who were willing enough to admit that oxygen might, indeed, have its uses, but condemned it on the ground that its employment was unsporting and, therefore, un-British. ... And so it came about that, by the time we reached the Base Camp, I found myself almost alone in my faith in oxygen.*'[20]

However, in all of his writings, Finch would never name a scientist or climber who explicitly opposed the use of oxygen in principle or in practice.

Mallory

At this juncture we might enquire what Mallory, that most practical of men, thought of oxygen. On the first attempt of 1922, as we know, Mallory, Norton and Somervell climbed without oxygen to 26,985 feet. Both General Bruce and Mallory explained, in different ways, why they did not take oxygen:

> Bruce: '*[May 20, 1922] ... the length of time there was left to us for our actual attack on the mountain ... decided Strutt [the deputy leader] to allow four members to make an attempt on the mountain without oxygen. Certain defects had been found in the oxygen apparatus, and Finch was employed in rectifying these difficulties, and at the same time he was not quite ready to proceed further. ... as the weather was so bad and the monsoon was evidently arriving before its time, and as at the moment the oxygen apparatus was in such a doubtful condition, it was far better to make an attempt than possibly to fail in making any attempt at all.*'[21]

> Mallory: '*General Bruce gave orders for only two of us to go forward and use the first opportunities for pushing on from Camp III. ... Without a further supply of transport there was no question of using the oxygen, for we should have more than enough to carry up without it.*'[22]

For Bruce, it seems that weather and shortage of time were the issues; and he evidently did not have confidence in Finch's maintenance of the oxygen equipment. For Mallory, the issue was manpower for carrying the cylinders; and implicitly, at that juncture, he thought that he could make the Northeast Shoulder without oxygen. After his climb without oxygen to 26,985 feet, and especially after Geoffrey Bruce's and Finch's climb with oxygen, which eclipsed his own, he would start to rethink.

The wake-up call

As we summarized in our Chapter 3, on 27 May 1922 Geoffrey Bruce and George Finch reached 27,320 feet, using oxygen. Near their high point Geoffrey Bruce had an accident with his oxygen apparatus, whereupon Finch saved the situation but chose to turn around. Bruce and Finch had bettered Mallory's climb by 345 vertical feet. That story has been told by Finch and by others in *The Assault on Everest 1922,* and in Finch's own memoirs.

Mallory must have talked to Finch and to Geoffrey Bruce; and he must have absorbed the implications of that high climb. He would have been aware that Finch had claimed an ascent rate of 1,000 vertical feet per hour in the first hour out of the North Col; and 900 vertical feet per hour in the first thousand feet from the camp at 25,500 feet[23]. Clearly, the benefits of oxygen dawned on him at once. Later, he would write:

> *'We had already resolved to use oxygen on the third attempt. ... Somervell, after Finch's explanation of the mechanical details, felt perfectly confident that he could manage the oxygen apparatus, and all those who had used oxygen were convinced that they went up more easily with its help than they could expect to go without it. Somervell and I intended to profit by their experience.'*[24]
>
> *'... there is, besides, a precaution which surely can and will be taken: to take a supply of oxygen for restorative purposes. The value of oxygen for restoring exhausted and warming cold men was sufficiently well illustrated during the second attempt [by Bruce and Finch] in 1922.'*[25]

Ever the innovator, Mallory had already worked out a strategy whereby he could not only improve on Bruce's and Finch's performance, but could do better and go for the top. It was a matter of using oxygen sparingly at first; and taking a full load in a dash to the summit:

> *'... we hoped for a further advantage in going higher than Finch and Bruce had done before [we would start] using oxygen; ... If this was not the correct policy as laid down by Professor Dryer [Dreyer], it would at least be a valuable experiment.'*[26]

In 1922, the carrying frame could hold a maximum of four cylinders. If Mallory meant to leave for the summit with four cylinders per climber (which he surely did), then there would have to be a cache at 26,000 feet. Mallory must have thought about transport for the cache; and he must have assumed that porters would be available and willing to do the job.

In the concepts of a full load for the summit dash, and of a cache at the high camp, we can detect precursors to Mallory's strategy for 1924 (of which, more later).

Aftermath

It is a matter of record that Mallory's mooted third attempt, and with it the expedition, was ended by an avalanche on 7 June 1922, in which seven porters lost their lives.

Returning to India and thence to England, Mallory had time to reflect on oxygen and what he would do on any future expedition. When he composed his contribution to the official report, *The Assault on Everest 1922*, his stance was still ambivalent. On the one hand, we sense that he had not been greatly impressed with the narrow margin by which Bruce and Finch had beaten his high point. He wanted still to allow the possibility that the ascent could be done without oxygen:

> *'... I don't think it impossible to get up [to the summit] without oxygen. The difference of atmospheric pressure between 27,000 feet and the summit is small, and it is safe to conclude that men who have exerted themselves at 27,000 feet could live without difficulty for a number of hours on the summit. As to whether their power of progress would give out before reaching 29,000 feet, it is impossible to dogmatise.'*[27]

In thinking that Everest could be climbed without oxygen, Mallory was right. He would be proven correct on 8 May 1978, when Peter Haberler and Reinhold Messner would do so.

The pragmatic side of Mallory, nevertheless, recognized that oxygen could make the difference; and that a foreseeable advance in technology might be all that was required:

> *'It is conceivable, and I believe by no means unlikely, that a different type of cylinder may be used in the future, and capable of containing more oxygen, compared with the same weight, than those of 1922. A 50 per cent improvement in this direction should alter the whole problem of using oxygen. With this advantage it might well be possible to go to the top and back with the four cylinders which a man may be expected to carry from a height of 25,000 feet or little higher.'*[28]

Mallory's ambivalence on oxygen would remain with him through 1924; and as we shall see, possibly it would only be at the last moment that he would cast his lot.

Finch redux

As for Finch, notwithstanding his feeling that almost no-one agreed with him, he was permitted to write three chapters in the expedition's official report. After the narrative of his climb with Geoffrey Bruce, his subsequent chapters were titled 'Conclusions' and 'Notes on Equipment'. Therein, he set out his views on oxygen; and since his words survived the editing of the report, we may reasonably infer that his views were in some sense officially acknowledged. He wrote:

> *'... the assumption may be made that on any further attempt upon Everest oxygen will form a most important part of the climber's equipment.'*
>
> *'Oxygen should be employed from the foot of the North Col slopes onwards, for no useful purpose can be served by tiring oneself through not using it ...'*
>
> *'From the North Col to a high camp situated at an altitude of about 26,500 feet, a slightly increased quantity of oxygen would suffice ... Between the camp and the summit there would be a vertical height of*

only 2,500 feet, and it is conceivable that with a full supply of oxygen this distance could be covered in as little as four hours.

This last part of the programme, however, would not be feasible unless a small dump of oxygen were made at a height of about 27,500 feet.'[29]

Mallory at some point must have read Finch's reports, although nowhere in his writings would he acknowledge Finch's expertise. Here we may pause, and wonder whether Mallory retained any of Finch's advice.

Firstly, as we have seen, Mallory did not want to use oxygen as low as the North Col; his idea on the contrary was to use it little, or not at all, until at or near his high camp. Finch had written that this strategy would tire a climber; and that above 23,000 feet, there would be no way to recover from exhaustion.

Secondly, Finch was implying that from a high camp, a climber could achieve an average vertical ascent rate of 625 feet per hour. Here is a number that, we may conjecture, remained in Mallory's mind. Whether he believed it, or thought that he could emulate it, we do not know.

Thirdly, Mallory retained Finch's message about a high cache of oxygen. That would be the core of his eventual strategy for the final climb. It would not be a small cache either.

Finch's last word on the 1922 expedition was that '… the most important lesson of all was that we had been taught the real value of oxygen'.[30] If the Everest Committee shared his view, then for the next expedition he was a natural choice. His trials in the low-pressure chamber at Oxford University had demonstrated his extraordinary resistance to hypoxia; of all possible candidates, he had the most experience of using oxygen at high altitude; and he, alongside Geoffrey Bruce, had climbed higher than anyone in the world. Indeed, on 16 June 1923, in the context of planning for the 1924 expedition, the Everest Committee invited him to advise on the use of oxygen.[31]

But Finch was not invited to join the expedition; nothing in the public domain shows whether he was even considered; and he never returned to Everest.

Chapter 5

Windproof

Early on in the exploration of Mount Everest, once a pathway to the summit was identified, it became evident that the cold would not be an obstacle to the ascent. The true enemy would be the wind.

Prior to the reconnaissance of 1921, it was well known that Tibet was a wind-swept country; and that more often than not, there was a violent wind blowing from the west or the northwest. No European had been within sixty miles of Everest; but an approach through Tibet would entail a climb on a presumed northern face of Everest. Such a climb would be exposed to at least some component of the prevailing wind. The Everest Committee was surely aware of the wind, as well as the cold, with which the expedition would have to contend. Sir Francis Younghusband wrote in his introduction to the expedition's official report:

> *'... the greatest trouble was taken to ensure that the most suitable and best tents, sleeping bags, clothing, boots, ice-axes, ropes, cooking apparatus, provisions, etc., were purchased and that they were properly packed and listed ...'*[1]

However, it was not until 24 September 1921, when Mallory, Bullock and Wheeler reached the North Col, at 23,000 feet, that the true and terrifying power of the wind became apparent. Mallory felt himself capable of climbing another 2,000 feet; from Bullock's diary, we know that he would have continued if asked; what Wheeler would have done, we do not know. It was a moot point, as Mallory would later recall:

> *'And higher was a more fearful sight. The powdery fresh snow on the great face of Everest was being swept along in unbroken spindrift and the very ridge where our route lay was marked out to receive its unmitigated fury. ... To see, in fact, was enough; the wind had settled the question; it would have been folly to go on.'*[2]

One of Mallory's photographs has survived from that day, to convey what his party saw from the North Col. It is reproduced as Figure 5.1.

Nothing in the accounts of the expedition can tell us to what extent Mallory's party was equipped to face the wind. The archives of the Royal Geographical Society have a couple of group portraits of the men in camp, and one of Mallory and Bullock on their mules somewhere on the journey across Tibet; we could suppose that in these photographs, they were not dressed for climbing.

In any event, one of the key messages of the 1921 expedition that carried over to 1922 was: be prepared for the wind.

Figure 5.1. The summit and part of the North Face of Everest, taken from the North Col in 1921. (George Mallory, public domain)

1922

Throughout the expedition of 1922, the climbers were keenly aware of the wind. Their recollections of its dreadful power would remain long after the expedition was over:

> General Bruce: *'What was very much brought home to us was the absolute necessity of windproof material to keep out the tremendous cold of these winds.'*[3]
>
> Finch: *'... the best clothing for a climber on Mount Everest is windproof ...'*[4]
>
> Mallory: *'... we recognized an enemy ... the devastating wind of Tibet.'*[5]
>
> Noel: *'We had had our first encounter with the Tibetan wind. It is more than a wind. It is a thousand knife-points that pierce all and any clothes you may wear.'*[6]

To be fair to the Everest Committee, the experiences of the 1921 climbing party had been registered; the need for protection against the elements was recognized. General Bruce wrote in his narrative of the 1922 expedition:

> *'Our methods had almost to be those of an Arctic expedition; at the same time our clothing and outfit in many ways had to be suitable for mountain climbing. ... one of the secrets of living with immunity [sic] high up is that the actual clothes on the men's backs should be as light as possible and as windproof as possible. Proper protection should be taken against the wind for the head also, and the greatest care must be taken and the necessity for care be understood by everybody in the protection of their hands and feet.'*[7]

With regard to wind proofing, the various accounts of the 1922 expedition do not make it entirely clear whether there was a collective solution or whether each climber made his own arrangements. Somervell in his memoirs alluded to a debate:

> *'The experience of the 1921 expedition, and of other Himalayan and Polar explorers, was as far as possible pooled with regard to many items of equipment, and the claims of a few thick clothes as against many thicknesses of thin ones were discussed again and again, no definite conclusion being reached. Personally, I was for many thin ones, and have retained my preference after half a dozen expeditions to the Himalaya ...'*[8]

As with the oxygen issue, it seems to have fallen to George Finch to define the solutions. In his 'Notes on Equipment', he wrote:

> *'Clothing is a most important matter. It would be difficult to exaggerate the intensity of the cold encountered at high altitudes on Mount Everest.*

> *Several layers — the innermost of which should be of silk, the others wool of moderate weight — form a much better protection against cold than one or two heavy layers. The chief item of clothing, however, should consist of a jumper*[9] *and trousers*[10] *made of windproof material. Two of these windproof suits should be worn one above the other, and every precaution taken to reduce the circulation of the air to the smallest possible extent.'*[11]

Finch was a man to put ideas into practice. On the 1922 expedition, he wore a windproof suit of his own design, filled with eiderdown. Over eighty years later, Dr John West would write that Finch's suit had been 'the forerunner of the down clothing that is now standard for high-altitude climbing.'[12] The best description of this suit comes not from Finch himself but from John Noel, the expedition's photographer, who never participated in the high climbs but was a keen observer of his colleagues. Several years later, Noel would write:

> *'The great idea is to get something light and windproof. On Everest the wind is worse than the actual temperature, which does not go lower than about 30°[F.] below zero.*[13] *... The freest [sic] and warmest anti-wind dress is camel-hair underclothing with plenty of air space next to the skin, topped with loose sweaters and woollen knitted jackets. Over the lot you wear a windproof blouse and trousers in the Arctic fashion. ...*
>
> *Finch, who had a scientific brain, invented a wonderful green quilted eiderdown suit of aeroplane fabric, doped*[14]*. Not a particle of wind could get through. Underneath he used to wear a suit of silk underclothes, then one of wool, then another, then a fourth of thicker wool, then a fifth of the thickest substance he could find - then he really began to dress in earnest, when he was to go up to the highest camp with the wind reaching a velocity of 100 miles an hour.'*[15]

Regarding protection for the head and hands, the best description again was that set down by Noel:

> *'Headgear must provide protection from the ultra-violet sun-rays. ... with a wide-brimmed sunproof hat, with earflaps ready to pull down, snow spectacles, woollen gloves with outer leather covers hanging by a tape round your neck, and the skin of your face and beard covered with a thick layer of white grease to deflect ultra-violet rays, you will be equipped for the day.'*[16]

Nevertheless, in the clothing of the 1922 expedition, it is easier to find divergence than uniformity. There are several widely circulated photographs of the two climbing parties, which show the heterogeneity of their dress in camp (though not necessarily how they dressed on the climbs). As to the actual climbing gear, there is one photograph of Mallory and Norton on the first attempt, nearing their high point; one of Finch in his windproof down-filled suit; and one of Bruce and Finch descending from the second attempt. From these we can form a best guess as to the typical outerwear for the climbs:

- one or more windproof jackets, extending from the shoulders to hips or knees
- (presumably) windproof trousers
- puttees (spiral cloth bindings) around the lower legs, from knee to ankle
- lined balaclava helmets (for Finch and Bruce); floppy hats (for Mallory and Norton).

We are left with the impression that each climber could dress as he saw fit; and this is somewhat confirmed by Mallory, who wrote:

> *'Apart from each man's personal supply of clothing there were large reserves of specially warm articles such as gloves, socks and helmets, and two big boxes of experimental foot-gear.'*[17]

Footwear

Here we should observe that footwear merited special attention, because it served two functions, which had to be compatible: to protect the climbers' feet from cold, and to provide grip and stability on various types of terrain, which on Everest would include rock, ice and snow.

Once again, we recognize the authority of Finch. For thermal insulation, given the materials available in the 1920s, he saw little benefit from the boot itself. Insulation would have to come from socks, and many of them. Writing after the expedition was over, Finch recommended a sole made from hinged wood, which would have been a good insulator:

> *'Boots were a source of trouble to all, but fortunately we had so many different designs which we could test out thoroughly that we are now able to form a very shrewd idea as to which kind is the most suitable.*
>
> *Leather conducts heat too well for reliance to be placed upon it for the preservation of warmth. ... A thin layer of felt should form the inside of the sole. The boots should be large enough to accommodate in comfort two pairs of thick socks, or, even better still, two pairs of thin socks and one pair of thick socks. ... The sole of the boot should be composed of a layer of thin leather attached to a layer of three-ply wood, hinged in two sections at the instep.'*[18]

The stability of the climber would be assured by the rigidity of the boot; and the grip on terrain, by steel nails. The Everest climbing boots of 1922 were what, today, we would call hob-nailed boots:

> *'The uppers of the boots should be of felt, strengthened where necessary to prevent stretching, by leather straps covered by duroprened*[19] *canvas. Toe and heel caps must be hard and strong ... Nails used in the boots should penetrate through the leather into the three-ply wood, but not through the latter.'*[20]

From the various narratives of the expedition, it is not clear whether any climber actually used the wooden hinged soles that Finch would later recommend. Noel apparently did not; his account refers to leather soles:

> *'... you get into your loose boots made with thick leather soles nailed on the rim and only stumpy nails on the sole because their iron has the property of conducting heat and cold between foot and ground.'*[21]

One device that was available in the 1920s, but was never used on the pre-war Everest expeditions, was the crampon. European mountaineers had been using various types of spike and claw, attached to their climbing boots, for decades or longer; but the English engineer Oscar Eckenstein is credited as the inventor, in 1908, of what we would call the modern crampon[22]. Eckenstein's invention was an array of spikes which could be attached to the boot by straps. It was in essence a traction device, and its function was to keep the climber upright on a steep slope of ice or snow, on which otherwise he or she would have to cut steps with the ice axe. Finch made no reference to crampons, and Mallory explained why:

> *'... anything in the nature of crampons (steel frames with spikes) would be still more dangerous because the straps binding them on the foot tend to stop circulation.'*[23]

Finally, we are indebted to Noel for explaining the use of puttees, which as photographs attest, Bruce, Finch and Norton had certainly used, and possibly Mallory also:

> *'... the windproof trousers ... themselves are bound to your ankles by puttees leaving the knees loose and free, so there is no chink by which the wind can enter.'*[24]

In summary, as of 1922 there was something approaching a consensus as to how the right clothing would defeat the wind, cold and sun of Everest. The keys were those expounded by Finch: many layers of lightweight insulating underclothing; at least one outer garment that was unequivocally windproof; and protection for every square inch of skin that might ever be exposed to the sun.

Here we should reiterate that nothing in the accounts of these early expeditions suggests a casual or cavalier attitude to climbing Everest. On the contrary, the organizers and climbers were drawing upon decades of mountaineering and Arctic exploration, and on the insights of practical and scientific minds. The climbers' clothing and their equipment were the right gear for the job.

Tejbir

If we may fault the early expeditions for any aspect of the planning, we might point to the discrepancy between the provisioning of the Europeans and that of their Asian colleagues. Among the narratives of the expeditions, this double standard is well illustrated by the story of Tejbir.

Tejbir Bura was a Nepali national. He held the rank Lans-Naik (Lance Corporal), that is, a non-commissioned officer, in the British Indian Army. He was a member of the 2nd Battalion, 6th Gurkha Rifles, the regiment in which Captain Geoffrey Bruce was serving, and which General Bruce would later command. Tejbir's participation in the 1922 expedition was arranged by Sir Henry Rawlinson, commander-in-chief of the British Indian Army; no records have survived as to whether this was Rawlinson's initiative, or Tejbir's, or someone else's.

Sometime after 20 May 1922, Geoffrey Bruce and Finch were working on the oxygen equipment at Camp III. At some juncture, they (to use General Bruce's words) 'roped in' Tejbir as their assistant. General Bruce's narrative explains the plan that they had for him:

> *'He was given extra oxygen to carry, and their intention was that, after proceeding as far as the [Northeast] ridge, he should be sent back to their camp to wait their descent.'*[25]

Neither Tejbir nor Geoffrey Bruce had ever climbed on snow or ice. Finch explains the extent of their preparation:

> *'... on the 18th [May 1922], we arrived at Camp II, where the greater part of the afternoon was devoted to giving Geoffrey Bruce, Tejbir, and several of the porters, a lesson in the elements of mountaineering and of ice-craft.'*[26]

With an afternoon's training, Finch thereupon launched Geoffrey Bruce and Tejbir on the ascent of the highest mountain in the world.

The subsequent story has been told in Finch's account of the expedition, and in his memoirs. The essence is that he, Geoffrey Bruce and Tejbir spent two nights in a camp at 25,500 feet; they survived the second night only by periodically inhaling oxygen; on the third day, they resumed the climb with the original intention of having Tejbir carry oxygen to the ridge at over 27,000 feet. But Tejbir, carrying a 50-pound load including two extra cylinders of oxygen, collapsed at 26,000 feet. The climbers relieved him of his load and sent him down; he descended to the high camp without further incident. Only later would Finch and General Bruce admit:

> Finch: *'Tejbir broke down — an unfortunate occurrence that may be largely attributed to his lack of really windproof clothing.'*[27]
>
> General Bruce: *'I think it is pretty certain that Tejbir's breakdown was largely due to his not having a windproof suit. This biting West wind goes through wool as if it was paper, and he was exposed to it for a great period of time ...'*[28]

Mallory, in a letter to Ruth Mallory dated June 1, 1922, did not mince his words:

> *"The story of the Gurkha orderly [Tejbir Bura] is pretty bad too – the plan was to take him on from 25500 [feet] carrying 6 cylinders of oxygen for 1000(?} ft(?) or 1500 ft by which time it was supposed he would be exhausted; he was then to be sent down by himself drinking oxygen from one cylinder!"*

Figure 5.2. Lance-Corporal Tejbir Bura on the 1922 expedition. (Author, after a photograph by George Finch)

On 5 February 1924 during the 1924 Winter Olympics, Baron Pierre de Coubertin on behalf of the French Olympic Committee personally presented thirteen gold medals to Colonel Strutt, who had been deputy leader of the 1922 Everest expedition. The medals were for the thirteen climbing members of the expedition; one of them was for Tejbir. His medal is not listed in the official records of the International Olympic Committee. To this day, he is the only Nepali to have earned (officially or not) an Olympic gold medal.[29]

If Tejbir had worn a proper windproof suit like the *sahibs*, he might have carried the two cylinders to the Northeast Shoulder; and Geoffrey Bruce and George Finch might have been the first to stand on the summit of Everest.

Finch took one photograph of Tejbir, wearing his trademark expansive grin (but not wearing a windproof suit), and published it in his article 'The Second High Climb', which appeared in *The Geographical Journal* of December 1922. Essentially the same article appeared the following year in the official report, *The Assault on Everest 1922*; but there was no photograph of Tejbir, nor of any of the porters.

After that, Tejbir disappeared from history. No-one knows whether he received his gold medal.

1924

When preparations were underway for the 1924 Everest expedition, the lessons of 1921 and 1922 were well understood. Once again, the wind was viewed as the greatest enemy, as Norton would write:

> *'This wind must be felt to be appreciated. Every member of the party was equipped with every device of windproof clothing [that] experience could invent. ... our kit was specially designed to exclude the wind.'*[30]

Finch had not been invited on the expedition, and we miss his meticulous notes on equipment and provisions. In his absence, Norton provided the best account of the climbers' clothing, at least of his own:

> *'Personally I wore [a] thick woollen vest and drawers, a thick flannel shirt and two sweaters under a lightish knickerbocker*[31] *suit of windproof*

Figure 5.3. George Finch on the 1922 expedition, wearing the down suit of his own design. (Author, after a photograph by John Noel)

gaberdine, the knickers[32] *of which were lined with light flannel, a pair of soft elastic Kashmir putties [puttees] and a pair of boots of felt bound and soled with leather and lightly nailed with the usual Alpine nails. Over all I wore a very light pyjama suit of Messrs. Burberry's 'Shackleton' windproof gaberdine.*

'On my hands I wore a pair of long fingerless woollen mits [mittens] inside a similar pair made of gaberdine; though when step-cutting necessitated a sensitive hold on the axe-haft, I sometimes substituted a pair of silk mits for the inner woollen pair. On my head I wore a fur-lined leather motor-cycling helmet, and my eyes and nose were protected by a pair of goggles of Crookes's glass, which were sewn into a leather mask that came well over the nose and covered any part of my face which was not naturally protected by my beard. A huge woollen muffler completed my costume.'[33]

It is worth noting that Norton's boots had leather soles, which in Finch's view would have been poor insulators.

On the other climbers' choices of outfits, the accounts of the 1924 expedition are largely silent. Geoffrey Bruce never wrote for the public. Somervell would, much later, narrate his climb with Norton, but would not describe his climbing gear. All that we know is that his preference had always been for many thin layers rather than for bulky outerwear; and that on the climb with Norton, he carried 'a few cardigans', presumably in his backpack.

In the case of Irvine, Noel's group photographs of the European expedition members, and Odell's famous last photograph of Mallory and Irvine, taken on the morning of 6 June 1924, are the sum of our knowledge.

In these last two photographs, Irvine was wearing the same clothing, consisting of an outer jacket and baggy trousers, which both look windproof; a thick muffler; puttees; and a floppy hat. He cannot have changed his outfit substantially on his last climb; except that he might, and should, have exchanged the hat for a balaclava helmet with ear flaps.

Mallory

As for Mallory, we know from his reports and letters that he favoured many layers of lightweight clothing. An illustration of his outfit (as worn in camp) appears in one of his letters to his wife:

> *'Since tea I have put on some more warm clothes & am now wearing silk and wool underclothes, a flannel shirt, a sleeved waistcoat, my lambskin coat & Burberry coat over all – below[,] plus fours*[34] *& two pairs of stockings under sheepskin boots; I am just sufficiently warm ...'*[35]

We also know that on the march or on a climb, Mallory habitually packed more clothes than he would need:

> *'... I almost invariably find that I have more clothing in reserve than I actually use.'*[36]

We may then reasonably assume that, when Mallory departed from the North Col on 6 June 1924, there was in his rucksack a store of clothing that was intended to serve him on that day's climb to Camp V; on the following day's climb to his Camp VI; and on the fateful ascent of 8 June, wherever that might take him.

Since Mallory's body was found in 1999 (a discovery which we shall elaborate in chapter 13), we have today an almost complete understanding of what he wore on his last climb. Mallory's clothing had been shredded by seventy-five years' exposure to the Tibetan wind. The climbers who found his body took samples of what remained.

In 2013, Mike Parsons and Professor Mary B. Rose, of the University of Lancaster, started the Mallory Clothing Replica Project, in which they aimed to identify what Mallory had been wearing on his last climb; to create a complete replica of his clothing, using materials and technologies as nearly as possible identical to those of 1924; and to test the resulting outfit on Mount Everest.

In the course of this endeavour, over a period of three years the universities of Derby, Lancaster, Leeds and Southampton deployed scientific instruments, including the scanning electron microscope and the X-ray spectroscope, on the fragments from Mallory's clothes. Dr George Rodway writes:

> *'The Textile Conservation Centre [of the University of Southampton] surmised that he was wearing: 'a hand-knitted jumper, two other hand-knitted fragments (perhaps one of which was part of his leggings), three pairs of socks, a blue and white shirt, a vest that is in a fibre blend with silk, and his puttees [a long narrow piece of cloth wound tightly around the lower leg] which might be cashmere rather than sheep wool.*
>
> *Further analysis of the fragments confirmed that Mallory was wearing a Burberry windproof climbing suit made of densely woven fine cotton as an outer layer. This material was considered one of the most 'high performance' fabrics of the era.*
>
> *... the Performance Clothing Research Centre at the University of Leeds ... concluded that Mallory was sufficiently well insulated to operate effectively on Everest, provided he was moving and not forced to bivouac.'*[37]

In summary, on 8 June 1924 Mallory had dressed as he usually dressed for a high climb. He had been protected against the cold, and against the wind, according to his normal precautions.

The Mountain Heritage Trust commissioned the manufacture of a replica of Mallory's clothing, which was completed by 2006. The replica was first tested in the field by Graham Hoyland, on the Rongbuk glacier below the North Col of Everest. Hoyland wore eight layers of clothing, including silk shirts, woollen cardigans and a gabardine outer coat. He reported that the inner layers were warm, the outer layers resisted the wind, and the whole permitted freedom of movement:

> *'... the layers of silk that I was wearing slid easily against the wool layers ... The patented pivot sleeve of the Burberry jacket allowed me a full reach without dragging the shirt-tails out of the breeches.'*[38]

Hoyland made these trials without supplementary oxygen, at an altitude about 21,000 feet: 6,000 feet below that of Mallory's Camp VI, and 8,000 feet below the summit. As far as is known, comparable tests have never been done at or above the altitude of the North Col, from which Mallory began his last climb.

In 2019, Dr George Havenith of Loughborough University conducted a quantitative comparative test of the replicated Mallory clothing, along with replicas of the outfits worn by the Antarctic explorers Robert Falcon Scott and Roald Amundsen in 1910, and as a control item, a modern high-altitude climbing or Arctic outfit. The comparisons with Scott and Amundsen do not greatly concern us here, since the Antarctic explorers were operating closer to sea level and with different activity rates to those of Mallory. The comparisons with modern clothing are revealing.

Figure 5.4a. Replica of Mallory's last climbing outfit (excluding boots), under test at Loughborough University in 2019. (George Havenith)

replicated clothing item	weight lb
Upper body	
silk wool vest	0.31
silk shirt, beige	0.75
pullover, Shetland	0.69
silk shirt, green	0.55
flannel (wool) shirt	1.31
jacket, Burberry	1.82
Subtotal	5.90
Lower body	
cotton long-johns	0.61
long-johns, green Shetland	0.71
long-johns, brown Shetland	0.99
breeches, Burberry	0.97
Subtotal	3.27
Footwear	
socks, blue	0.24
socks, mixed Shetland	0.18
socks, Argyle	0.18
puttees	0.23
Subtotal	0.78
Total excluding boots	9.96

Figure 5.4b. Specifications and weight of replica of Mallory's last climbing outfit. Source of data: Havenith, George (2010).

Here, the unit of reference for insulation is the Clo. One Clo is defined as follows: 'the insulating value of clothing needed to maintain a person in comfort sitting at rest in a room at 21°C (70°F) with air movement of 0.1 m/s and humidity less than 50 [per cent] - typically a person wearing a business suit [in a sheltered or interior space in a temperate climate].'[39]

Dr Havenith found that with no wind, a modern climbing outfit had an insulation value of 5.3 Clo; while Mallory's outfit had a value of 3.0 Clo. Under a wind of 10m/s (22 mph), the modern outfit dropped to about 3.8 Clo, and Mallory's outfit to about 1.9 Clo.[40] So, with or without wind, Mallory's clothes were 45 to 50 per cent less thermally efficient than their modern equivalent.

However, at the altitude of Mount Everest, the lower air density decreases the thermal conductivity of air, and therefore improves the insulating value of clothing, by about 15 per cent. In other words, on Everest, with no wind, Mallory's outfit would have had an insulating value of about 3.5 Clo; and with a wind of 22 mph, about 2.1 Clo.

We may then pose the question: given the meteorological conditions on 8 June 1924, was Mallory's clothing up to the task in hand?

Calm and close

On 7 June 1924, in a message sent down to Odell from his Camp VI, Mallory had written: 'Perfect weather for the job!'[41]

Now we must refer to Colonel Norton's diary for 8 June 1924. Norton was at Camp IV on the North Col, at an altitude of 23,000 feet. Throughout the day he described the weather as 'calm and close [humid]'. He recorded the 'air temperature' (meaning, we may presume, the thermometer reading in the shade) as 28°F at 8:30 am; 36°F at 12:00 pm; and 29°F at 4:00 pm. The 'sun temperatures' (presumably meaning thermometer readings in open sun) were vastly higher: 81°F at 8:30 pm; over 125°F (off scale) at 12:00 pm; and 48°F at 4:00 pm. We have no way to extrapolate these readings to what prevailed at the summit, 6,000 feet above the camp; but Norton made no reference to strong winds or to low temperatures.

Finally, we have Odell's account of his climb to Camp VI on the afternoon of the same day:

> *'... on arrival there about two o'clock[,] snow commenced to fall and the wind increased ... The snow continued, and after a while I began to wonder whether the weather and conditions higher up would have necessitated the [Mallory and Irvine] party commencing their return. ... [later] the squall, which had lasted not more than two hours, blew over, and before long the whole north face became bathed in sunshine, and the freshly fallen snow speedily evaporated ...'*[42]

Again, we can read nothing into Odell's narrative that conveys a violent wind or an unendurable cold.

In his article on the tests of the replica clothing at Loughborough University, Dr Havenith wrote that, even if Mallory had not been using oxygen:

> *'... for low winds ... the insulation provided by the replica clothing is sufficient down to -30°C approximately'.*[43]

In the light of Norton's and Odell's observations, and of Dr Havenith's experiments, we are surely obliged to conclude that there was nothing about Mallory's outfit that could have prevented him from reaching the summit of Mount Everest.

Postscript: Mallory's boots

The Mountain Heritage Trust did not commission a replica of Mallory's boots: for the 1999 climbers had found the right boot and part of the left boot, on his feet. Today, the boots are preserved, and occasionally placed on display, at the Royal Geographical Society in London. They have been extensively examined. Marc Koenig describes them as follows:

> *'Mallory's boots had novel hobnails attached through a 3mm calfskin leather sole but insulated from the feet by a 10mm felt. ... The weight of*

> *each boot was calculated to be 800g [1.76lb]. ... these boots are likely to be the lightest ever worn on Everest.'*[44]

This author has viewed the boots at the Royal Geographical Society. The right boot is in remarkably good condition. Only a scrap of leather, about one inch by two, has been abraded from the left side, and one nail is missing from the lateral row on the right side; all of the metal devices on the sole are in place. Of the left boot, only the leather upper has survived. The boot fragmented cleanly along the seams; the stitching held, but the body and sole are missing.

The Society confirmed to this author that it had not cleaned or renovated the boots in any way; equally, that it had not conducted scientific tests on them. It might not be too late for electron microscopy, to identify particles of rock or dust from the sides or soles. This might allow historians or archaeologists to identify the strata on which Mallory stood prior to his demise, and thereby to surmise where and how high he and Irvine might have climbed.

Figure 5.5. Mallory's right boot, as worn on 8 June 1924. (Rick Reanier/Archiv Jochen Hemmleb)

Figure 5.6. Mallory on a day when clothing was optional; Rongli, Tibet, 29 March 1924. (Author, after a photograph by Bentley Beetham).

Part II

1924

Chapter 6

Irvine

Sometime in March 1923, Eleanor Marjorie Holmes, aged nineteen, wrote to the famous mountaineer George Mallory. Marjorie was living in the small town of Bentham, in what is now North Yorkshire, England; she was teaching at a local primary school. Mallory, at that moment, was on his way back to England after a lecture tour in the United States. Holmes's letter to Mallory, we may suppose, was in the nature of fan mail. It was the start of an impassioned correspondence between Holmes and Mallory, that would continue until his last voyage to India in March 1924, from which he would not return.

As far as anyone knows, Holmes and Mallory never met. She surely saw his photograph in the newspapers; he, evidently, never knew how she looked. In one of his letters, he asked if she was beautiful; he added: 'I hope not. If you are quite ugly I will guarantee that when we meet we have the time of our lives … but if you are beautiful Heaven help me; I shall shut up like a sea anemone'.[1] What did he mean by that?

In some of his letters to Holmes, Mallory seemed to be in love with her:

> *'Why should a letter from you have [a] strange effect on me? ... after reading it I wanted to kiss you.'*
> *'... Would two sparks make a fire? Suppose the other spark were you Marjorie?'*[2]

Holmes's letters were lost to history; but she kept the letters that Mallory had sent her. After her death in 1978, those letters were discovered, and in 2015 they were sold at auction by Bonham's, for £12,500.

The correspondence between the mountaineer and his lady admirer is another story, which has been told elsewhere. But thanks to Marjorie Holmes, we have an early glimpse of one of the most improbable bondings in mountaineering history: between George Mallory and Andrew Comyn Irvine.

Enter Irvine

In a letter to Holmes, headed 'Anchor Line, T.S.S. California', and evidently written somewhere near Egypt in early March 1924, Mallory wrote:

> *'My three companions de voyage, Irvine, Beetham, & Hazard are all pleasant enough & the first I particularly like – a splendid specimen of a man; he rowed two years in the Oxford boat as a heavy weight & yet is completely modest and has a voice which reminds me strangely of Rupert Brooke's.'*[3]

Figure 6.1. The earliest known photograph of Mallory and Irvine together: on board TSS California, 12 March 1924. ((probably) Bentley Beetham, public domain)

This letter is possibly Mallory's first reference to Irvine; it is certainly the first in which he expressed his admiration for the young man who would climb with him into oblivion and legend. Rupert Brooke had been a friend of Mallory's, as well as a celebrated poet who had died during the Great War; Mallory's reference to Brooke could be read as a great compliment to Irvine.

In his shipboard letters to his wife Ruth, Mallory made several mentions of Irvine, though with greater circumspection. He was starting to convey his growing sense of partnership with this young man, while making no comparable references to his other companions:

> *'At table Irvine and I sit side by side (Hazard and Beetham at another table) ...'*[4]
>
> *'And so [very useful] no doubt will [be] Irvine - sensible, not highly strung he'll be one to depend on, for everything perhaps except conversation.'*[5]
>
> *'We sit eight at a table of whom one is Irvine & it is quite an agreeable little crowd. I am always down & have finished breakfast before anyone else arrives unless it is Irvine ...'*[6]

Irvine at this point had also noticed Mallory and had remarked on Mallory's restless energy:

> *'Mallory is far too energetic for so early in the voyage - he was up and dressed before I had even finished my morning tea & apple.'*[7]

Like most of the civilian members of the Everest expedition, Mallory and Irvine were products of English public (meaning private) schools and of elite universities: Mallory from Cambridge and Irvine from Oxford. We can assume that they shared common values that reflected their social class and the era in which they lived. It could not have been otherwise: as the Australian George Finch had discovered in 1921, the Alpine Club was a 'club for gentlemen who also climb'[8], and the Mount Everest Committee surely embodied that elitist outlook.

Apart from that, Mallory and Irvine were profoundly different men. In March 1924, Mallory was thirty-seven years old; Irvine was not yet twenty-two, younger than any other member of the expedition by at least eleven years. Mallory had fought in the Great War; Irvine had been only sixteen when the war ended. Mallory was wiry, tense and intense; Irvine, solid, stolid and amiable. Mallory was an aspiring writer; from the later accounts of the expedition, we can sense that Mallory's excursions into poetry and the classics left his young colleague politely baffled. Where Mallory's correspondence reveals his ambiguity in relationships with men, we have no such impression of Irvine.

Although Mallory's contemporaries had raved over his good looks, from a twenty-first century perspective Irvine seems the more handsome of the two. Certainly, he was a big blonde hunk: in photographs, he appeared at least three inches taller than Mallory, with the broad shoulders and powerful arms of a rowing 'blue'. He had been an oarsman for Oxford University in the Boat Races of 1922 and 1923 between Oxford and Cambridge Universities; in March 1923, he had occupied the No.3 seat in the winning Oxford team, weighing in at 178.5 pounds.[9]

In terms of mountaineering qualifications, Irvine had the least experience of any climber on the Everest team. His inclusion therefore calls for some explanation.

Spitsbergen

In 1919 'by chance' Irvine had met Noel Odell, who would be a climbing member of the 1924 Everest expedition. Odell was already a distinguished figure in the British climbing community, and a member of the Alpine Club, but at that time was not involved in any plans for Everest. Early in 1923 they would meet again, at Oxford where Irvine was preparing for the Boat Race. Odell thereupon recruited Irvine for an expedition in the Norwegian archipelago of Svalbard, which was planned for the summer of 1923[10].

In April 1923, as part of the training for the Svalbard voyage, Odell and Irvine made an ascent of the Great Gully on Craig yr Ysfa in Wales, a climb of about 800 vertical feet. The Great Gully in modern times is rated as 'severe' (roughly speaking, the highest of the 'beginner' grades: above which, the grades are for 'experienced', 'advanced', 'expert' and 'elite' climbers)[11]. Odell led most of the ascent, but delegated the lead to Irvine for the 'chockstone' section. Odell later wrote:

> *'... after 2 failures to get above chock-stone, Sandy [Irvine] got up it with great difficulty ... a fine effort for 1st lead ... a brilliant lead for a novice'.*[12]

It was probably the toughest rock climb that Irvine ever attempted in Britain.

The original plan of the Svalbard expedition had been to explore the largely unknown interior of Nordaustlandet (North East Land), the second largest island of the archipelago. An unexpected build-up of pack ice scuttled that objective. The expedition then refocused on a crossing of Spitsbergen, the largest island, by sledge

Figure 6.2. The Great Gully at Craig yr Ysfa inWales. (© Iain Johnston)

and ski from Hinlopen Strait on the east to Klaas Billen Bay on the west. The distance was approximately eighty miles; the route was primarily over glaciers and snow. Odell would be the leader; the other members of the party were Irvine, Geoffrey Milling (another oarsman from Oxford University), and Robert A. Frazer (a mathematician acting as surveyor for the expedition).

The journey took thirty days. The party disembarked from the *S.S. Terningen* at Duyn Point on the eastern shore of Spitsbergen, on 31 July 1923; they re-joined their ship on the western shore on 30 August 1923.

Of the mountaineering aspects of the journey, Robert Frazer's eventual report to the Alpine Club contained only brief mentions:

> *'By midnight August 15 [1923] we had ... reached the foot of a conical mountain, which may be that described as Mt. Hope.* ... One of the party, who views good visibility as an excellent excuse from disagreeable camp duties, stole away and climbed Mt. Hope. The summit, at 5079 feet and comparatively isolated, commanded immense distances ...'*[13] [Frazer did not say who the climber was; it does not sound like the hard-working Irvine; possibly it was Odell.]
>
> *'South of the bay stretched the undulating Loven Plateau that we had but recently crossed. An isolated domed mountain stood at its western extremity, sentinel-wise, above the Bear Bay glacier – the advance guard of the Chydenius Range. The peak* which we had latterly ascended rises to 4686 feet ...* [Frazer did not say to whom 'we' referred; the asterisk was footnoted '*Possibly Mt. Poincaire'.]
>
> *'On [16 August 1923] we separated into pairs. Odell and Irvine, fortified with instruments, disappeared for twenty hours in a westerly direction. Their reconnaissance extended for some 8 miles across the Lomme Bay glacier to the summit of a difficult rock peak† at the head of a tributary glacier ...'*[14] [Frazer added in a footnote: '†Referred to elsewhere as Mt. Irvine (see Alpine Journal)'.[15]]
>
> [On 16 August 1923] *'Milling and I, after skiing across the Bear Bay glacier, had struggled up the steep crevasse-chequered eastern slopes of Mt. Newton. ... Mt. Newton (5445 feet) is commonly accepted as the loftiest peak of Spitsbergen ...'*[16]

Frazer first read his report to the Alpine Club on 2 June 1924. He mentioned that at that moment, Odell and Irvine were on Mount Everest. His report was published in September 1924, by which time it was known that Irvine had perished.

Odell, reporting later in 1923 to the Alpine Club, included a brief mention of Irvine's climb of that peak on Spitsbergen:

> *'Irvine and [I] skied off about 13 or 14 miles from camp in a westerly direction, crossed the great Lomme Bay Glacier, and at the head of a tributary glacier ascended a fine rock-summit situated in the abovementioned group. The ascent by the S.E. ridge gave 3000 ft. or more of magnificent climbing on hard metamorphic rock ... We descended from our peak by the steep N.E. ridge which gave a sporting*

> *way off over alternate rock and sharp snow crest, and then traversed round beneath the great eastern precipice to the point where we [had] left our skis ...'*[17]

In 1935, Odell would also write to the Norges Svalbard- og Ishays-undersokelser (forerunner of the Norwegian Polar Institute) to preserve the memory of his departed young friend and protégé:

> *'[Mt. Irvine] Named by me after Andrew Comyn Irvine, who was one of my sledging party on the Oxford Expedition of 1923. Irvine and I made the ascent of this mountain on 16th August from a camp near the head of Bear Bay Glacier.'*[18]

Irvine was memorialized in 1942, when the mountain that he had climbed was inscribed in *Place Names of Svalbard* as Irvinefjellet.[19]

Irvine's own diaries of the Spitsbergen trip have survived; and his grand-niece Julie Summers, in her book *Fearless On Everest*, drew upon his diaries and letters. These sources add detail and colour to Frazer's and Odell's accounts:

> *'They stopped at Lodingen and then Svolvaer, where Sandy [Irvine] and Odell climbed the highest peak southwest of the town ...'*[20] [This would be Tjeldbergtind, an easy hike with a high point of 1,070 feet.]
>
> *'Whenever they had a moment to themselves during one of their frequent stops up the coast, Odell, Sandy [Irvine] and sometimes the two Geoffreys (Summers and Milling) would leave the main party and climb some rock, crag or glacier bank in the immediate vicinity. The climb they made on a glacier on 28 July [1923] was the first time Sandy [Irvine] had experienced ice climbing ...'*[21]
>
> *'... we reached the foot of the peak which we intended to ascend [now named Irvinefjellet] by a pinnacle ridge running S.S.E. as the*

Figure 6.3. Andrew Irvine on Spitsbergen, August 1923. ((probably) Robert Frazer. Images by courtesy of Merton College, Oxford / Sandy Irvine Trust)

Figure 6.4. The approximate routes of Irvine's sledge party across Spitsbergen, 1923. (Base map from Norwegian Polar Institute, *Svalbardkartet*; graphics and legend adapted by author from *Spitsbergen Retraced*, map on p.12)

fine precipice face some 2000 ft high showed too great difficulties to attempt in the time we could afford. We started up at 1240 [pm] and had a very fine rock climb up the crest of the ridge some pitches being of considerable difficulty. The rock gave very good climbing being hard melamorphine[22] *rock & Odell declared the whole character of the climb, very reminiscent of the Tower Ridge of Ben Nevis. It gave about 2800ft climbing.'*[23]

[About 8 September 1923] *'Odell had planned to tackle a serious rock climb on Jaegerrasstind, a peak in the Lyngen Alps [probably Store Jægervasstinden, 5062 feet]. ... When they arrived at the foot on the rock face, 1000 feet above sea level, they were presented with a fifty pitch climb to the 5500 feet summit. ... After twelve hours of strenuous climbing over difficult and sometimes treacherous rock, they were forced to concede defeat and turned to descend, only three hundred feet from the summit.'*[24]

Finally, thanks in no small measure to a recreation of the Spitsbergen journey in 2016, by a team of undergraduates from Oxford University, we have today a greater understanding of Irvine's journey than the contemporary reports, or even his own diaries, ever permitted.

The expedition was named 'Spitsbergen Retraced'. It had the specific objectives of following, as closely as possible, the route of the 1923 expedition; and more ambitiously, to reproduce up to twenty of the photographs taken in 1923, from the same

Figure 6.5. Irvinefjellet; and Odell's and Irvine's possible route in 1923. (Base image © CNES / Airbus / Google Earth; additional graphics by author)

Figure 6.6. Store Jægervasstinden. (© Sondre Kvambekk @500fjell)

vantage points. The four students – James Lam, Will Hartz, Jamie Gardiner and Liam Garrison – disembarked near Duyn Point on 30 July 2016 and returned to their boat at Klaas Billen Bay on 29 August 2016. They had covered 180 miles and had largely retraced the route that Odell and his colleagues had taken in 1923.

In terms of reproducing the mountaineering of their predecessors, the 'Spitsbergen Retraced' team summited all six of the peaks that were known to have been climbed in 1923. These were as follows:

- Poincaretoppen (4751 feet) – *'no major difficulties ...'*
- Irvinefjellet (5121 feet, climbed by Irvine and Odell) – '*The rock was indeed very compact in places and we roped up to protect the steeper sections. With the sun out and warm temperatures, fast progress was made up the ridge.'*
- Laplacetoppen (a.k.a. Mount Hope, 5197 feet) – *'Trying to ski up a couloir on the west face of the mountain we soon found it too icy and steep[,] so reverted to scrambling up a buttress to the summit ridge.'*
- Newtontoppen (5617 feet, climbed by Frazer and Milling) – *'The rock itself was compact red Granite, being both extremely solid and textured it made for fantastic climbing. A number [of] steep steps added some complexity to the route ...'*
- Makarovtoppen (5033 feet) – *'The snow was very wind-blown and icy, making progress quite tricky ... The descent was icy and required a great deal of attention.'*
- Cernysevfjellet (a.k.a. Mount Chernishev, South East shoulder, 4003 feet) – '*ascent via a snow field on the west side of the mountain. With a slope of around 30 degrees and a particularly cold spell, the snow field was extremely icy ...*'[25]

Of these six mountains, only Irvinefjellet is documented as having been climbed by Irvine himself. It is not described as a difficult climb.

We can conclude that Irvine had reached 5,121 feet at the summit of what we now know as Irvinefjellet, and about 4,800 feet on Store Jægervasstinden. These were probably his highest and most difficult climbs prior to Everest.

In summary, the contemporary and modern accounts present the voyage to Norway and Spitsbergen as a test of endurance and strength, but not as a preparation for technically difficult climbs, nor as training for high altitudes. Possibly the attempted ascent of Store Jægervasstinden was as close as Irvine would come to a foretaste of Everest.

The selection

At the beginning of May 1923, the high command of the 1924 Everest expedition was already in place: General Charles Bruce as leader and Lieutenant-Colonel Edward Norton as deputy leader. On 2 May 1923 the Mount Everest Committee made its initial selection of the climbers. Bentley Beetham, George Mallory, Noel Odell and Howard Somervell were approved.

In the autumn of 1923, Odell recommended Irvine to the Committee as an additional climbing member of the 1924 expedition. Odell's proposal was endorsed by Dr Tom Longstaff, who had been on an Oxford University expedition to Spitsbergen in 1921, and had been the chief medical officer on the 1922 Everest expedition. Evidently in the face of some opposition, the Committee agreed to invite Irvine's participation.

Given the unorthodox nature of the Committee's decision, we could argue that Everest, even in 1923, was considered a straightforward climb. In December 1924, presenting a severely technical paper to the Alpine Club, Colonel Norton would state that: 'above the N. Col the mountain is an easy rock peak, with no ice or crevasses.'[26] Nevertheless, the same paper recorded that the climb from Camp I to Camp IV on the North Col had involved an ascent of 4,900 vertical feet on ice and snow: a climb which had no parallel in Irvine's experience prior to Everest. Irvine also would surely have been expected to climb above Camp IV, which was at 22,700 feet, having never climbed above 3,000 feet in Britain or much above 5,000 feet on Spitsbergen. The Everest expedition was predicated on the use, or at least the availability, of supplementary oxygen; but Irvine had never used or needed to use it.

Furthermore, there was at least one other candidate for the expedition, with undisputed achievements on Everest itself, and with demonstrated experience in using oxygen. His name was George Ingle Finch. In 1922, he and Geoffrey Bruce had reached 27,320 feet on the North Face of Everest, both using oxygen, and setting a world altitude record. Just before reaching their high point, in all probability Finch had saved Bruce's life after a malfunction of the oxygen apparatus, upon which he had quickly shared his oxygen with Bruce and had restored the equipment to order. At that point, in view of Bruce's condition, the climb was over. In short, Finch knew how to use oxygen, he could handle emergencies, he could climb, and he knew when to turn around. In 1924, he was available and he wanted to be part of the expedition. But Finch was Australian.

With hindsight, the Everest Committee's selection of Irvine, especially in preference to Finch, makes no sense. We might conjecture that if Finch had been selected, he and Mallory, and possibly two other climbers, might have stood on the summit of Everest in 1924. The decision went another way; and perhaps we shall never know why.

Irvine the engineer

Here we should mention that at the time of his selection for Everest, Irvine was studying for a degree in engineering. This in itself might not have been relevant; but we may conjecture that Odell, who had been designated as the oxygen expert for the 1924 expedition, saw Irvine as a practical hands-on assistant. Irvine's engineering perspective would soon become apparent, on the sea voyage from Liverpool to Kolkata, as Mallory would write:

> *'We have got up an oxygen apparatus from the [ship's] baggage room and have been playing about with it. Irvine finds fault with it ...'*[27]

By the time that the expedition was ashore in India, Irvine had at least a few weeks' experience with the oxygen equipment and had been casting a critical eye upon it:

> *[30 March 1924] '[I] found all but one of the oxygen frames had been more or less damaged in transit, so spent afternoon and evening repairing them with copper rivits [sic] and wire.'*[28]
>
> *[17 April 1924] 'I have my work cut out with the oxygen! Every apparatus tested yet leaks more gas than are breaths. None were tested before leaving England.*
>
> *34 cylinders out of 90 had to be refilled at Calcutta because they had leaked. So far we have tested 16 and found 6 empty.*
>
> *I am at present completely redesigning the apparatus and trying to make up a serviceable design before we reach the base camp.'*[29]
>
> *[18 April 1924]: 'Weighed eight oxygen cylinders at random. One had 30 Atmos [atmospheres, meaning about 30 per cent of a full charge], one had 10 pounds only'.*[30]

Impressions

Irvine was now to meet the high command of the expedition. Joining the team with the unequivocal backing of Odell and Longstaff, he could not fail to make a good impression. Equally, the two leaders, neither of whom had been involved in the selection of Irvine, would now be obliged to acknowledge or to ignore his minimal experience for the task ahead.

In case we should imagine that General Bruce was not greatly concerned with climbing experience, we only have to look at his descriptions of the other three new arrivals: John de Vars Hazard 'who had a great mountaineering record'; Bentley Beetham 'a born mountaineer, and - how shall I describe him? - a mountaineering *Ghazi* [warrior]'; and Mallory 'the Bayard of the Mountains - '*sans peur et sans reproche*' - the only member of the Expedition who was making his third journey'[31]. Bruce's reference was to the medieval French military leader Pierre Terrail, *seigneur de Bayard*, who had been known as *le chevalier sans peur et sans reproche* 'the knight without fear and beyond reproach'.

In the case of Irvine, Bruce would necessarily focus on Irvine's personality and practical bent. He wrote:

> '... *'our splendid experiment' [is] Irvine, bringing with him magnificent recommendations from Longstaff and Odell after Spitzbergen experiences, and, further, bringing his own great personality. He rapidly ceased to be an experiment, for we soon found that with a young body he possessed a mature judgment, combined with a very remarkable handiness and adaptability as a practical working engineer. All these valuable qualities, combined with infinite stamina and infinite unselfishness, made Irvine a very great asset to our party.* '[32]

Norton, who would assume the *de facto* leadership of the expedition after General Bruce fell ill, was likewise obliged to judge Irvine differently from the others. Of himself and the other older men in their thirties and forties, he wrote:

> *'Mallory, Somervell, Geoffrey Bruce and myself had all been high [on Everest] in 1922, while Mallory had carried out the climbing reconnaissance in 1921 as well. Odell, Beetham and Hazard were Alpine climbers of notable speed and endurance and of great experience.* '[33]

Norton could only admit that Irvine was not a climber at the same level, and had to search for other qualities:

> *'Young Irvine's record was somewhat different, for his mountaineering experience was limited (though sufficient to guarantee him a safe member of any climbing party); but he had rowed two years in the Oxford [University] boat, and if further proof of the essential qualities of endurance and courage were necessary, he had given them amply while sledging in Spitzbergen with Odell the previous summer, and later ski-ing in Switzerland.* '[34]

Norton's endorsement of Irvine seems unconvincing; it was not self-evident to equate the Boat Race, sledging and skiing with climbing Mount Everest. He could have cited Irvine's climbs of the unnamed peak that would later be known as Irvinefjellet, and of Store Jægervasstinden; perhaps he did not know about them. In any case, the decision had been made for him.

Oxygen

Having entered the enterprise on Odell's and Longstaff's endorsement; having earned the undoubted respect of Mallory; and having gained the acceptance of the leadership: Irvine's role in the expedition coalesced around what he did best: fixing things. Above all, he took ownership of the problems of the oxygen equipment.

In this respect, Odell was a natural partner for Irvine. They were a close-knit pair; they had shared the experience of thirty days on the ice and snow of Spitsbergen, as well as the almost successful climb on Jægervasstinden. Although Odell had been designated, and remained, the nominal oxygen officer, he and Irvine quickly formed a team. Norton started to call them 'the experts':

> [Shekar Dzong, Tibet, 24 April 1924] *'It was here that Odell and Irvine, the oxygen experts, definitely ascertained that the apparatus supplied us had some very serious defects; a large proportion of its numerous valves were found to leak. Many of the cylinders were partially - some completely -- empty, and various other defects came to light. The two experts, who had for days been working every afternoon, and often late into the night, put in a regular field-day, and finished by evolving a new and simplified arrangement of the apparatus, which was satisfactorily tested the same evening by Mallory and Somervell ...'*[35]

Mallory saw Irvine's role in the same light, though in his view, Irvine was doing all the work:

> *'Odell is in charge of the gas [oxygen], but Irvine has done the principal engineering work on the [oxygen] apparatus - what was provided was full of leaks and faults and he has practically invented a new instrument, using up only a few of the old parts and cutting out much that was useless and likely to cause trouble ...'*[36]

The old firm

Before his final and fateful bonding with Mallory, one further evolution would occur in Irvine's role. As the real climbing got underway, Irvine and Odell would morph into 'supporters', charged with the maintenance of the climbers' comfort and morale by whatever means were necessary. This was a role which evidently had been identified in 1922, and was now put into practice. After Mallory's and Bruce's unsuccessful summit attempt on 1 June 1924, Norton described the 'supporter' role as follows:

> [North Col, 2 June 1924*] 'Odell and Irvine ... were fulfilling, for the first time in the history of Everest climbing, the official role of supporters. ... For over a week those two lived on the North Col (23,000 feet), and cooked every meal ... They went out day and night to escort and succour returning parties and climbers over the intricate approaches to the camp, carrying lamps and drinks, and even oxygen to restore the exhausted ... or, not infrequently, descending to Camp III for more stores, while more fortunate climbers passed through and disappeared in succession up the mountain. ... never again shall we enjoy such support as we were given by the 'old firm'.'*[37]

From 'young Irvine', the genial broad-backed tinkerer and handyman, he had risen to the status of a partner in the 'old firm': a very English phrase reserved for those institutions of the most unquestioned probity and longevity. These words were written after Irvine was gone forever. Probably, nowhere in the accounts of the 1924 expedition were warmer words ever said of him.

This was Irvine's penultimate role on Mount Everest, and one that he would fulfil until 6 June 1924. To that transition, we shall return.

Who was Irvine?

Finally, we are entitled to ask: so, who was Irvine? Who was this hunky smiling fellow who would march into the unknown with a high-strung and moody man whom he had known for barely three months? What was it about Mallory – his mystique, his courage, his intensity? – that made Irvine put his life in Mallory's hands?

This author will admit to trawling the expedition reports, the memoirs of the climbers, and the journals and correspondence of Mallory and Irvine themselves; and coming up with little more than hints and clues. If Mallory and Irvine ever had a conversation about anything other than the matter at hand – about strategy, routes, risks, friends, poetry, women, life itself – no trace remains.

Irvine began his journals and letters with references to 'Mallory' and ended with 'George'. But there is nowhere a sign that he liked or disliked Mallory, or even had any view about Mallory, other than as the leader and decision-maker.

For Mallory, conversely, Irvine was always 'Irvine', never 'Andrew', and never 'Sandy'. For Mallory, this author believes, Irvine was the man of steel. Irvine was the man who, physically, would not break down, as Morshead had in 1922. Irvine would not become ill or exhausted, as Geoffrey Bruce, Norton and Somervell had become, in succession, on the first two climbs of 1924. Irvine did not need to be a good or inventive climber; he just needed to be strong, and to stay the course.

As to what Irvine thought of his colleagues and climbing partners on Everest: we have no idea. He was evidently a man of few words; he had little in the way of anecdotes. He said nothing that anyone later could quote or remember. Even in his diaries and letters, he recorded his colleagues' state of health and strength, but wrote nothing that could be considered praise or reproach.

With regard to the Sherpa and Bhotia porters, and the Gurkha officers, Irvine never learned a word of their languages, and knew perhaps two of them by name. He recorded it dispassionately in his diary when one or another of them fell sick, or broke a leg, or died. In this, he was not different from most of his English colleagues.

As for Everest: Irvine was the antithesis of Mallory. Where Mallory loved and feared the mountain, Irvine simply had no idea of the dangers. His writing nowhere conveys any concern that the mountain had killed seven men in 1922 and at least two so far in 1924. The expedition was for him, what Englishmen of his time might have called a 'lark'. Some comments in his letters may convey his insulation from the hard reality.

> *'It will be great fun if we all 4 get to the top at the same time!'*[38]
>
> *'... I'd sooner get to the foot of the final pyramid without oxygen than to the top with it.'*[39]
>
> *'I hope they [Norton and Somervell] got to the top but by God I should like to have a whack at it myself.'*[40]

A 'whack', for an Englishman of the 1920s, would have conveyed the idea of a swing with a cricket bat. If you miss the ball, no big deal; if you're stumped, you walk like a gentleman to the pavilion, where tea and biscuits await. It would be hard to imagine Chuck Yeager, in 1947, allowing as how he was not averse to breaking the sound barrier; or Neil Armstrong in 1969, proposing a whack at the moon.

Irvine's misfortune was that he did not recognize the magnitude of the enterprise. Mallory knew that magnitude exceedingly well; and its enormity overcame whatever fears or doubts he had. But as far as anyone knows, he never shared that perspective with Irvine. The rest, as we know, is history.

Chapter 7

Brainwave

Notwithstanding the lessons learned in 1921 and 1922, when the third Everest expedition departed from England for India in February 1924, there was no formal and specific plan on the physical and logistical nature of the climb. That is to say: it was agreed that the approach would be via the North Col; from there upwards along the North Ridge; and thence by some as yet undefined route on the North Face or the Northeast Ridge, to the summit. It was foreordained that the attempt on the summit had to be made before the breaking of the monsoon: in other words, not later than early June. Where the camps would be, how many climbs there would be, who would climb and in what order, and whether or not they would climb with oxygen, were questions unresolved.

The published accounts of the expedition are circumlocutory on the nature of the debate. Referring to 'our programme for climbing the mountain', Edward Norton wrote that he had launched the discussion as early as 1923:

> *'As long ago as the previous Christmas [1923] in England I had circulated a paper containing my ideas on the subject, and with these Mallory had by correspondence disagreed in certain respects.'*[1]

Norton had been writing to Mallory around Christmas 1923 despite the fact that Mallory was not yet a member of the expedition. The Everest Committee had already appointed Norton as chief of the climbing party. Mallory would join the expedition at the 'eleventh-hour'[2], as Norton would put it later. However, Norton evidently had assumed that Mallory would join sooner or later, and in his inclusive way, attempted to elicit Mallory's thinking.

Mallory indeed joined the expedition at the latest possible moment. His letter to the Mount Everest Committee, accepting its invitation, was dated 13 February 1924. On that date, General Bruce and Colonel Norton were already on a steamship, on their way to India; they would disembark at Mumbai on 16 February. Mallory agreed to join the expedition as a 'member', with no designated role. He undertook to observe 'all directives and orders' issued by General Bruce as leader, or by any other leader *pro tem*, or by any person or persons authorized by them.

But as of Christmas 1923, the strategy for climbing the mountain rested with Norton. It was natural for Norton to seek Mallory's views; for all we know, he may have sought the views of other climbers. Mallory was free to disagree with Norton. However, at that stage he had no formal authority within the expedition.

As far as this author can determine, the correspondence between Norton and Mallory has been lost. If so, we have no way to know what plan Norton had had in mind, and with what aspects Mallory had disagreed. Norton's accounts make it clear that the debate had been resumed after the party's departure from Darjeeling in the direction of Tibet:

> *'At Darjeeling [India], and again at Phari [Tibet], we had held lengthy discussions - Mallory, Somervell, Geoffrey Bruce, and myself - and, failing to agree altogether, had decided to continue our arguments across the endless plains of Tibet.'*[3]

Around 11 April 1924, on the occasion of an unavoidable four-day layover at Kampa Dzong, Norton recorded: '... we had so far reached something of an impasse.'[4] That Norton considered there to be an impasse, and that implicitly it was between Mallory and himself, illustrates the uncertain or fragile chain of command within the party.

This was about to change.

Passing the baton

On 8 April 1924, Norton and the others in his party learned that General Bruce, in a following party, had contracted a fever and had stopped in the village of Tuna, Tibet, about twelve miles north of Phari. On 13 April, they received the bad news that General Bruce would not re-join the expedition; he would be carried on a stretcher to Phari and thence back to Darjeeling, India.

Norton wrote:

> *'... we lost from April 13th something of that lighthearted atmosphere which the General alone could maintain.'*[5]

Here there began a polite and very English struggle for power, which Norton would lose and Mallory would win. With the departure of General Bruce, Norton became by default the leader of the expedition; there was no need, even if it had been possible, to seek confirmation from the Mount Everest Committee. But Norton was also the leader of the climbing party; he was authorized and entitled to make climbing decisions. He was not obliged to delegate that authority.

Nevertheless, that is what happened. Norton would write later:

> *'... owing to [Mallory's] eleventh-hour decision to join this year's Expedition, I had been appointed leader of the climbing party, a role to which his previous record on the mountain might well have entitled him, and which he assumed as soon as I became leader of the Expedition.'*[6]

From our twenty-first century perspective, saturated as it is with Mallory's fame, this might seem logical. But Norton was now the leader of the expedition. Mallory, under the terms of his participation in the expedition, was required to accept Norton's orders. There was nothing in those terms which designated Mallory as the chief of the climbing party. Formally, Norton had every right to retain that role.

Norton's words convey to us that he deferred to Mallory's climbing experience on Everest. But Norton's own was comparable. In 1922, he, Mallory and Somervell together had reached 26,985 feet on the North Ridge without oxygen; Geoffrey Bruce and Finch on the same expedition had slightly bettered that altitude, but Mallory had made no further high climb. True, Mallory had the expedition of 1921 to his credit; but that had been defined as a reconnaissance expedition, not a climbing expedition. In 1921, Mallory had reached 23,000 feet on the North Col; so had Bullock and Wheeler. In short, Norton's track record on the mountain was as good as Mallory's.

From Norton's own writings, from contemporary photographs of him, and from others' descriptions of him, we sense that he was a kind, humble and mild-mannered person. An anecdote by Mallory himself, from the 1922 expedition, in fact from their high climb together, conveys something of Norton's personality.

> *'I must have communicated to the other rope some small jerk — sufficient, at all events, to upset the balance of Norton's rucksack. He was unprepared, made a desperate grab, and missed it. Slowly the round, soft thing gathered momentum from its rotation, the first little leaps down from one ledge to another grew to excited and magnificent bounds, and the precious burden vanished from sight. For a little interval ... no one spoke. "My rucksack gone down the kudh!"*[7] *Norton exclaimed with simple regret.'*[8]

In any event, whether for reasons of personality, protocol or politics, on 13 April 1924 Norton ceded the role of climbing chief to Mallory. Whether he did so explicitly, or whether the two men simply assumed that there had been a change in roles, no record remains. It was in the nature of a repeat of 1921, when Mallory had become the *de facto* leader of the expedition after the death of Dr Kellas and the illness of Raeburn.

Whether, given an earlier opportunity to choose, the Everest Committee would have made Mallory the climbing chief, we cannot say. Norton seemed to think that they might have done so; he did not say that they would have done so. There was no doubt that Mallory could climb at the altitudes, and on the terrain, in question; but as it had been demonstrated, so could Geoffrey Bruce, Finch, Norton and Somervell. Where Mallory had shown his genius was in route-finding; he alone had identified the North Col and the North Ridge as waypoints on the road to the summit.

In effect, if *Everest* (1924) had been a precursor of *Predator* (1986), Mallory was cast to play Billy, the taciturn and inscrutable Native American. Billy can do all the things that a soldier should do, but he has a unique talent: he is a tracker; he can read the terrain. General Bruce was cast as the genial, cigar-chomping, muscle-bound Major Dutch; and Norton was the stand-in. Now the lead and the stand-in had both dropped out, and Mallory had the chance to play Dutch. He accepted the role with alacrity. He wanted to be the last man to fight the Predator, *mano a mano.*

None of the other members of the expedition seemed to be aware that there had been a shift in the balance of power within the expedition. John Noel, the chief photographer, was not part of the climbing party; his impression was that General Bruce's authority had passed to Norton and to Geoffrey Bruce:

> *'When we had the misfortune to lose General Bruce we found in Norton and Geoffrey Bruce two successors who understood the natives and could also hold and enthuse them. Colonel Norton, a distinguished*

> *soldier with the D.S.O. and Military Cross, with a brilliant staff and fighting record in the European War, a mountaineer of tried capacity, became our sound and careful leader.'*[9]

Somervell, writing some years later, would recall:

> *'[General Bruce's] mantle fell upon Norton, who was just about the best man that could be found to wear it. He was humble enough to ask our advice freely, especially as regards the climbing of the mountain, sensible enough to know when to take it, strong enough to see that what he decided upon was done, and splendid with the porters — a born leader of men ...'*[10]

If anyone else realized that Mallory was henceforth the chief climber, no record of it has survived.

For at least a couple of days after it was known that General Bruce would not return, the debate continued about how best to climb the mountain. Referring probably to the days between 13 and 17 April, 1924, Norton would recall:

> *'Now was the chance, and each day we went at it, sometimes Mallory and I, sometimes he and I with the addition of Somervell and [Geoffrey] Bruce, and once in full committee of all the climbers. But we were to leave Kampa [Dzong] with our plan still in the air; Mallory's and my points of disagreement were much narrowed down, but enough remained to preclude a final decision. I cannot now remember the exact points on which we split ...'*[11]

Mallory's extraordinary promotion should have been an occasion to share the news with his wife, to whom he wrote every few days. But uncharacteristically, Mallory appears to have told her nothing. At least, if he wrote to her between 12 and 17 April 1924, his letters have not been preserved. It is in his letter dated 17 April that we first learn of his new role as the chief climber.

Brainwave

Mallory's plan for climbing Mount Everest is worth reproducing in full (with this author's annotations for clarity):

> *'... I've had a brain-wave — no other word will describe the process by which I arrived at another plan for climbing the mountain: -*
>
> *(a) [Climbers] A & B with fifteen porters (about), starting from [Camp] IV (North Col), establish [Camp] V, building emplacements for four tents at about 25,500 [feet], and descend.*
> *(b) [Climbers] C & D, gasless [oxygen-less] party, go to [Camp] V with another fifteen porters, of whom seven carry loads, and descend, the other eight go up without loads, practically speaking, and sleep.*

(c) *[Climbers] C & D proceed to establish a Camp VII at 27,300 [feet] (about) with these eight porters carrying up 6 loads.*

(d) *[Climbers] E & F, gas [oxygen] party, on the same day as (c) start with ten porters (about) from [Camp] IV, go without loads to [Camp] V and from that point [climbers] E & F using oxygen they take on the stores and gas previously dumped at [Camp] V about 1,000 feet higher to [Camp] VI at 26,500 [feet].*

(e) *Then the two parties start next morning and presumably meet on the summit.'*

In a letter to his friend Tom Longstaff, dated 19 April 1924, Mallory would add one crucial detail, which gives us an insight into what he would do on his fateful last climb:

> *'The two parties start an hour or more before daylight in full moonlight & windless air, we hope & meet on the summit ...'*[12]

In this respect, Mallory must have been supposing that at the moment of departure towards the summit, there would be a moon. If he was counting on that attempt to be made in May or early June, he was right. Supposing that his watch was set to Darjeeling time: throughout May and June the sun would rise at 4:41 am. But the time of moonrise would advance by about 36 minutes every day. Until 2 June 1924, the moon would rise before the sun. On 8 June 1924, moonrise would be at 9:25 am; there would be no moonlight before dawn.

We can see that the essence of Mallory's plan was that four climbers, in two parties of two, would attempt the summit on the same day. One party, without oxygen, would leave from a Camp VII at 27,300 feet; they would have 1,700 vertical feet to climb. The other party, with oxygen, would leave from a Camp VI at 26,500 feet; their climb would encompass 2,500 vertical feet.

Mallory's letter to Longstaff seemed to imply that the two parties would start at the same time, namely 'an hour or more' before dawn; in other words, not later than about 3:45 am. The two parties would not be able to communicate with each other; but separated by only 800 vertical feet, given good visibility, they should be able to see each other. The departure of one party could be a signal for the other to set off. If the visibility was not good, it would surely be reason to postpone the attempt to the following day.

Likewise, Mallory's letters did not explicitly say whether he thought that the two parties would arrive simultaneously at the summit. But we may reasonably conjecture that he expected to be in the party with oxygen; and it would be no more than a reflection of his ambition if he expected that party to arrive first.

This allows us to make an educated guess about Mallory's ideas on climbing rates. The oxygen party would gain 2,500 feet in less than the time for the non-oxygen party to gain 1,700 feet; so the members of the oxygen party would be climbing at least 47 per cent faster than their colleagues. From his experiences of 1922, Mallory had an idea of what could be done. He, Norton and Somervell, climbing without oxygen, had averaged 318 feet per hour from their high camp to their turnaround point at 26,985 feet; Geoffrey Bruce and Finch, with oxygen, had averaged 315 feet per hour in the comparable section of their climb to 27,320 feet. Accordingly, Mallory would have

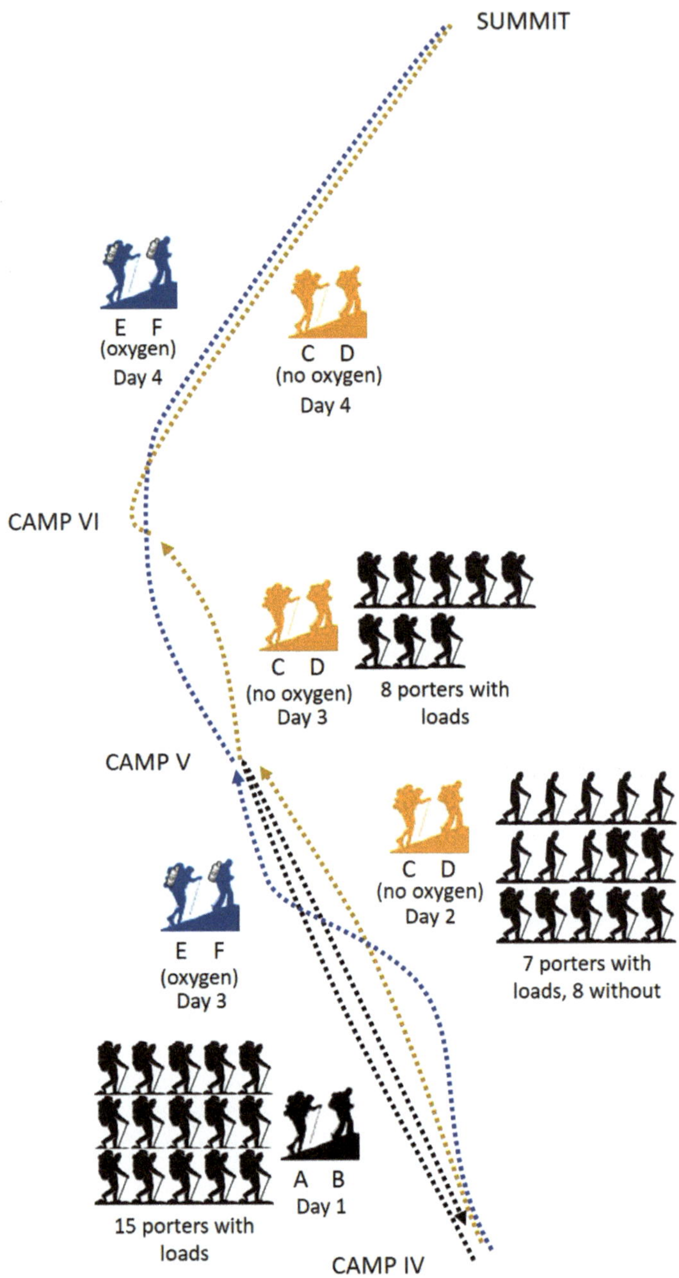

Figure 7.1. Mallory's Plan A of 17 April 1924, for simultaneous summit attempts by an oxygen and a non-oxygen party. Data from Mallory, George: 'Mallory's Letters', in *The Fight For Everest 1924*. Climber icons by courtesy of NicePNG. Distances between camps and summit are approximately to scale. (Author)

expected oxygen to yield no advantage up to that altitude. Above that point, he would expect the non-oxygen party to slow down. In the light of his plan, we can conjecture that he anticipated around 200 feet per hour for the non-oxygen party and at least 300 feet per hour for the oxygen party.

Finally, Mallory said nothing about the route; not even whether the two parties should follow the same route. His plan allowed for the non-oxygen party to take one route, and the oxygen party, another. He must have assumed that the oxygen party's Camp VI would be on or near the North Ridge, as it had been in 1922. As for his imagined Camp VII for the non-oxygen party, no record remains as to where he expected it to be; we might conjecture that it would be somewhere off the ridge, in a westerly direction, in the direction of the summit. His plan expressed no necessity that the Camp VI party should pass by Camp VII on their way to the summit. Perhaps he expected that each party would make its own route-finding decisions.

Later, when the expedition was over, Norton would feel obliged to defend Mallory's plan, and in so doing, to recognize its flaws. These were, as identified by Norton, the following:

- It was too complicated. (Here we sense the mind of Norton the officer, thinking about deploying unpredictable soldiers at precise times and places on the battlefield; and most of his climbers were not even soldiers.)
- The porters might not be willing or able to carry loads above 27,000 ft (and if they did not, there could be no Camp VII).
- He had doubts about whether the oxygen party could make it from the North Col at 23,000 feet to the proposed Camp VI at 26,500 feet in a single climb. (Here we can imagine him pondering the rise of 3,500 vertical feet, assuming an average climb rate of 300 feet per hour and wondering if anyone could climb for close to twelve hours.)
- Mallory's plan required at least twenty porters to climb above 25,500 feet. Norton saw this as forty per cent of his entire manpower. (Like a good officer, he expected attrition of his army.)
- Finally, Norton had eight climbers available, including himself; Mallory proposed to gamble four of them on a single climb.[13]

Such were Norton's reservations after the fact. We can only record that notwithstanding his doubts, Mallory's plan was approved. Norton would write, of the events of 16 April 1924:

> *'... we finally settled the outline of our plan of campaign. To Mallory goes all the credit of evolving, from the conflicting views held up to date by him and me, a plan which combined all the good points of both, and which was that evening unanimously approved by all the climbers in conclave.'*[14]

If on that day, any climber expressed any of the doubts or reservations that Norton would later enumerate before the Alpine Club, we shall never know. With that, Mallory's plan was the plan.

Plan B

However, Mallory had left one element unaddressed. There were eight climbers; we can hardly doubt that all eight wanted to stand on the summit of Everest. Mallory's plan provided for a single attempt in which four climbers would, more or less simultaneously, reach the summit. If they succeeded, surely the expedition would be over; that would leave four men who would return to England with, at best, the North Col on their resumés.

Here, it appears that Norton exercised his leadership and made a provision for a second attempt. If the first four climbers – the 'A team' – for any reason did not succeed, the second four – the 'B team' would have a chance. Norton would write:

> *'Four more climbers would support [the first] attempt or remain in reserve, and in the event of an initial failure, these four would repeat the attempt with any modifications dictated by the experience of the first attempt. ... [although] most of us felt the odds were against a second attempt being necessary ... '*[15]

Here began the jostling for position. We can imagine the eight climbers as forerunners of the seven brave Mercury astronauts, lining up for the first shot in 1961. Among the Mercury Seven, there would be pilot aristocracy – men like Al Shepard and John Glenn; there would be hard-tack fighter jocks like Gus Grissom and Wally Schirra; and there would be outsiders who did not fit the pattern, like Scott Carpenter. Among the Everest Eight, we can also see social stratifications. The aristocrats were surely Mallory and Norton. The fighter jocks included Geoffrey Bruce, Odell and Somervell. The outsider was undoubtedly Irvine.

To his credit, Norton set out his criteria for assigning climbers to the four climbing parties, as follows:

- A member of each party must have some competence in Nepali or Hindi. Norton wrote 'must know something' of those languages; he was not even dreaming of a few words in Sherpa or Tibetan. Here, we may suppose, Norton was thinking of the porters' willingness to push the envelope, and the climbers' ability to motivate them.
- The parties should have an even distribution of the more experienced climbers. That would refer to everyone except Geoffrey Bruce and Irvine; so this criterion would exclude a party of those two men.
- The parties should have an even distribution of climbers with previous knowledge of Mount Everest. That would mean Geoffrey Bruce, Mallory, Norton and Somervell. On the face of it, that should have excluded a party consisting of any two of those men.
- The two parties for the first attempt should include the men who were most fit or acclimatized. At this stage, Norton would not know who those men would be; but he must have expected that he and Somervell at least would qualify.
- Each of the two oxygen parties must include one of the oxygen experts (who were now recognized to be Irvine and Odell). If therefore, Irvine was on the first attempt, Odell would have to be on the second, and vice versa.

Those were the overt criteria; but there was an inside track. Norton had already ceded part of his authority, including his own role as a climber, to three other men:

> *'... it will be guessed how keen was the competition - unexpressed though it was - to take part in the earlier attempt. ... not that I kept the decision in my own hands; on the contrary, I had discussed it exhaustively with Mallory, Somervell and Bruce - the three veterans of 1922 - for some days. ... My own position I left to Mallory and Somervell to decide.'*[16]

The result of these discussions bears the unmistakable stamp of Mallory's pre-eminence in the hierarchy of power:

- first attempt, oxygen party: Mallory and Irvine
- first attempt, non-oxygen party: Norton and Somervell
- second attempt, oxygen party: Geoffrey Bruce and Odell
- second attempt, non-oxygen party: Beetham and Hazard.

It was at this point that Irvine knew that he would be climbing with Mallory. We do not know whether he learned it from Mallory himself, or from Norton:

> *'I have provisionally been chosen to do the first Oxygen climb with Mallory. Norton & Somervell doing Non Ox. [non-oxygen] on the same day. ... The Non Ox start a day earlier from the North Col stopping at [camps at] 25,500 & 27,300 [feet]. While we [oxygen party] stop only [at a camp] at 26,500 [feet]. This gives 3 camps as refuges on the way down in case of exhaustion or bad weather.'*[17]

One aspect of the hierarchy was never explicitly expressed; that was the leadership of each party. Above, we reproduced the order of the parties, and for each party, the order of the climbers' names, as Norton later would record them. The order of the names is not alphabetical. Implicitly, in each case the first name was the leader of the party. The four climbing leaders therefore were Mallory, Norton, Geoffrey Bruce and Beetham (in that order).

Again we can imagine, on the announcement of these names, the reactions of the four men who were relegated to the second attempt. As Tom Wolfe would write so eloquently in *The Right Stuff*, the true fighter jock had to keep climbing the steps of the mighty ziggurat of flying achievement, or he would be left behind. On the real ziggurat of Mount Everest, Geoffrey Bruce, Odell, Beetham and Hazard had been *left behind*.

Norton well understood the consequences of creating an 'A team' and a 'B team':

> *'I explained this decision, with the reasons that led to it, at a conference of all the climbers the night before we left Shekar Dzong ... there was not a word of protest or dissatisfaction from any of the disappointed climbers.'*[18]

We recall these words from 1856, by the poet Alfred, Baron Tennyson, who well understood, or at least believed in, the stoicism of the English soldier:

> *'Was there a man dismay'd?*
> *Not tho' the soldier knew*
> *Some one had blunder'd ...'*[19]

Even if no-one said so: the selection of the climbers was not entirely in conformity with the criteria that Norton had enunciated.

Mallory and Irvine, who by using oxygen would make the most demands on the porters, were probably the least able to communicate with them. As Norton himself would acknowledge, 'Mallory had learnt a sufficient smattering of Hindustani [Hindi] to communicate with these men to a certain extent'[20] (though none of the porters, being Sherpa or Bhotia, would have spoken Hindi as a native language). Of Irvine likewise, Norton had to admit: 'not a word of [the porters'] language could he speak'.

Norton could have added that Mallory and Odell would have been a better pairing than Mallory and Irvine; later, he would make this exact point, in an effort to salvage Mallory's fateful last climb, but too late. Mallory was, at this early stage, committed to Irvine.

Reading between the lines, we sense that Mallory had not only assured his place on the 'A team' but had also appropriated the oxygen party for himself and Irvine. By default, if Norton wanted to be on the 'A team' (and one feels that he did), he would have to be in the non-oxygen party.

Norton and Somervell, having both been on the 1922 expedition, and having made a high climb together, were not a logical choice to pair up for the second time. Such a party would be strong (as they would soon demonstrate), but at the expense of the strength of the other parties. Their respective experience and knowledge could have been shared with, for example, Beetham or Hazard.

Geoffrey Bruce and Odell were not a self-evident pairing for the second oxygen party. In 1922, through no fault of his own, Bruce had had an accident with his oxygen apparatus, which had derailed his climb with Finch. He had, in any case, reported little personal benefit from oxygen. Bruce had evidently been on the inside track as far as the discussions were concerned; but once the 'A team' was defined, he was destined for the 'B team'.

Of the unsung Beetham and Hazard, all that we can infer is that they were never really in the running, and that their roles fell to them as residuals, after the favoured climbers had been assigned their respective positions.

In any case, this too was about to change. Neither Mallory's original plan, nor Norton's interpretation of it, would survive the forces of nature or of chance. As Norton would later put it, '... the Fates ruled that it should never be put into execution ...'[21]

The rescue

Firstly, on 15 May 1924, Beetham suffered an attack of what Norton described as sciatica, and was forced to descend to the Base Camp. That reduced the climbing team to seven men.

The second twist of fate was the change in the weather. The story has been well told by Norton in his chapter 'The North Col' in *The Fight For Everest 1924*. The essence is that on 21 May 1924, Hazard, Irvine, Somervell and twelve porters established Camp IV on the North Col. Irvine and Somervell returned to Camp III the same evening, leaving Hazard and the porters on the North Col. On the night of 21 May, and most of the day of 22 May, snow fell heavily. The climbers suspected the onset of the monsoon. On 23 May, Hazard evacuated Camp IV and returned, but arrived at Camp III with only eight of the porters. The other four had turned back and were stranded on the Col.

Norton's account assigned no blame. Mallory recognized that Hazard had put the whole expedition in jeopardy. He wrote an account to his wife on 27 May, with a frankness that was, for him, unusual:

> *'Hazard had bad luck to be left alone in charge of the porters at [Camp] IV, only for one night according to our intentions, but the snow next day prevented Geoff [Bruce] and Odell from starting – the following day he [Hazard] elected to bring the party down ... evidently he didn't shepherd his party properly at all & in the end 4 [porters] stayed up [at Camp IV] & one of these badly frostbitten. Had the snow been a bit worse that day we went up to bring them down[,] things might have been very bad indeed.'*[22]

Mallory was right. The disaster of 1922, when seven porters had died on his watch, must have seemed about to be repeated. If the four porters perished at Camp IV, the expedition would be over. However, Mallory's reading was not to be shared with the British public. His letter to Ruth Mallory was eventually published in the official account; the entirety of the foregoing passage was excised and was replaced by the phrase '[Unfortunately on the next day four porters were left on the North Col.]' It was left for the reader to guess that some text had been deleted and that the phrase within the square brackets was not Mallory's.

As for Hazard, after his dereliction of duty nothing more was said. He continued to participate in the activities and discussions of the expedition, but evidently joined Beetham on the peripheral 'C team', with no prospect of a high climb.

It is a matter of record that Mallory, Norton and Somervell set out for the North Col and rescued the four porters. They did so at great cost to their own physical well-being. Norton realized immediately that the summit attempts were in peril. He describes the climbers' condition at the outset:

> *'We were about to send three of the four climbers detailed for the first [summit] attempt on what must be a severe test of endurance, and this would still further diminish our chances of success if a change in the weather permitted a resumption of the attack. ... We were all distinctly the worse for wear; both Mallory and Somervell had very bad coughs and sore throats, which hampered them badly in climbing ...'*[23]

On Norton's account of the nearly disastrous, but ultimately successful, rescue, we cannot improve. However, the rescue of the porters was a turning point for the expedition.

John Noel, the photographer, writing three years later, painted a picture of the state in which the rescuers and rescued made it back to the base of the Col:

> *'When we met, the whole lot of them sank down in the snow. They were absolutely done! The porters were like drunken men, not knowing what was happening. Norton, Somervell and Mallory hardly spoke. ...*
>
> *... during the next days there was a general exodus from Snowfield Camp [Camp III] of everybody who was not up to the mark. It developed into a sort of renewed retreat. Mallory remained a great deal in his tent and sleeping-bag. He looked ill and in my opinion he was 'an unfit man' when, some days later, he started for the mountain with Irvine ... Mallory's end began from this time. His strength was sapped.* ***He made his last climb on his nerves.****'*[24] [emphasis in the original]

Plan C

At this juncture, Mallory's original plan, with or without Norton's refinements, was dust. Norton started the process of conceiving a new one:

> *'Several facts made it obvious that if the Fates were to give us one more chance, we must be prepared to put into operation some simplified plan.*
>
> *... For the moment things looked a little better, and we again began to doubt if the weather we had experienced was really anything to do with the monsoon.*
>
> *... not more than fifteen ... out of our original fifty-five porters could now be counted on to reach Camp IV [on the North Col] ...*
>
> *Our plan must obviously be such as would enable us to stage a serious attempt on the summit with the least possible delay ... '*[25]

In short, there might be a few days of good weather remaining; the monsoon might break around 2 June, as it had in 1922. The attrition of the porters, which Norton had anticipated, had happened; there could now be no question of a massive upload of stores and equipment to high camps. Several climbers, including Mallory, Norton and Somervell, were in less than good shape. The seven remaining climbers, plus Shebbeare the transport officer, held two consecutive 'councils of war' on 26 and 27 May 1924. On the latter date, they arrived at a new plan, as Norton relates:

> *'In the end the simplest possible plan carried the day and was adopted nem. con. [no-one dissenting] ... We decided to scrap oxygen altogether and to assault the mountain in a series of attempts, each of two climbers: the parties to leave Camp IV on consecutive fine days and to sleep twice above that point, once at Camp V, at about 25,500 feet, and once at Camp VI, at about 27,200 feet, or as near to those heights as we could induce porters to carry for us.*

> *... I insisted on a supporting party of two climbers to be at Camp IV always, and this seemed to indicate that not more than two attempts could be made, for we could hardly believe that, after what we had already undergone, anyone would be found to do more than one really high climb.'*

After the expedition, writing for *The Geographical Journal*[26] and *The Alpine Journal*[27], Norton would elaborate on the decision to abandon oxygen. He gave three reasons, which we paraphrase as follows:

- There was no stock of oxygen in place, even at Camp IV on the North Col. There were not enough porters to carry the oxygen required, even to Camp IV; a further uplift to a presumed Camp V and Camp VI seemed out of the question.
- As of the last days of May 1924, the monsoon was expected to break any day; and when it did, the accompanying snowfall would make climbing impossible.
- Geoffrey Bruce and Odell, the only climbers who at that point in the expedition had tried climbing with oxygen, were unconvinced of its benefits. For his audience at the Alpine Club, Norton put this more strongly: 'We had very little faith in the very imperfect [oxygen] apparatus at our disposal.' (Norton did not remind either of his audiences that Finch, the man who had had such faith, had not been invited to join the expedition.)

In early June 1924 the new and simplified plan was, more or less, executed in two high climbs. As to how it was executed, and what lessons were learned, we shall return in a later chapter. However, it was not the final plan. Mallory would have the last word.

Resurrection

On the evening of 4 June 1924, Norton and Somervell returned from their high climb to over 28,000 feet. They were dehydrated and exhausted; Somervell had lost the lining of his throat; Norton was snow-blind. It had been the expedition's second attempt at the summit. According to the plan on which everyone had agreed, no further attempts were envisaged. Norton presumably expected to break camp and start the long journey back to England. He would now learn that Mallory had other plans.

It happened that on 4 June, Mallory and Norton were sharing a tent. Of that evening, Norton would recall that their conversation began as follows:

> *'As Mallory and I lay in our tent, he explained that he had decided that if we two [Norton and Somervell] failed to reach the summit, he was determined to make one more attempt, this time with oxygen ...'*[28]

Here was the clearest evidence that Norton was no longer the leader of the expedition. Without consulting Norton, Mallory had deployed the resources of the expedition for a plan that was exclusively his own. It was in some sense a resurrection of Mallory's original plan; it assumed a Camp V and a Camp VI, a supply of oxygen, and two climbers. The main difference now was that there would be no backup party; above Camp IV on the North Col, the two climbers would be on their own.

We can reconstruct in our imaginations the tense and guarded exchange that must have followed Mallory's revelation. Norton had done the math and had put his core transport team at fifteen men – whom he called the 'tigers' – men who were ready and willing for any mission. Norton surely asked Mallory what had happened to the shared perception, that there were no porters available for an uplift above the North Col. Mallory would have anticipated that question. He had a ready reply:

> *'... he had been down to Camp III with Bruce and collected sufficient porters to enable the attempt to be staged. ... two or three porters who had returned from Camp V after the abortive attempt*[29]*, were employed again; two extra volunteers over and above the fifteen 'tigers' were found ...'*[30]

In short, Mallory had calculated that he could mobilize nineteen or twenty men; and he proposed to use every one of them.

We may suppose that Norton also asked about what camps Mallory would use, and how he proposed to stock them. Mallory again had a ready response. Camp V was already in place, at 25,500 feet. As a Camp VI, Mallory must have said or implied that he would use Norton's and Somervell's last high camp, which they had left in place, with bedding inside. And since the two camps were available and habitable, Mallory could plan on a massive uplift of oxygen:

> *'... nearly every available porter could now be used for carrying oxygen cylinders.'*[31]

Given that a porter's maximum load was thirty pounds, equivalent to two oxygen cylinders, Mallory could conceivably uplift forty cylinders of oxygen at least to Camp V, and some proportion of that to his Camp VI. With that, we might suppose that Norton could not disagree. In his own plan, up to that point, he would have anticipated no further tasks for the porters, beyond evacuating Camp III and packing for the return to England. If he thought that Mallory's plan might compromise a safe evacuation, there is no record that he said so.

Bearing in mind Norton's later reports in *The Geographical Journal* and *The Alpine Journal*, one might wonder whether he asked Mallory about the sanity of climbing with 'the very imperfect apparatus' as he would describe the oxygen systems. There is no record, however, that Norton objected to Mallory's proposed use of oxygen *per se*.

At some point in the conversation (we do not know whether early or late), Mallory dropped his bombshell. He intended to climb to the summit of Mount Everest with Andrew Irvine.

Trying to imagine the interchange between these two very English but very different gentlemen, in a tent in the Himalayas, over the distance of a hundred years, we can guess that Norton must have been dumbfounded. That Mallory wanted to make a third attempt at the summit (and Mallory's second of the expedition), perhaps would have come as no great surprise. As for the necessary climbing partner, Geoffrey Bruce, Norton himself, and Somervell, were in no condition for another climb. Beetham was out of the picture. Hazard and Odell were capable of the climb; back in the already-forgotten conclave of 16 April, they had been assigned to the 'B team'. But Irvine was far from fit; and his wafer-thin climbing experience must surely have returned to the forefront of Norton's mind.

What Norton actually said to Mallory, we shall never know. What he wrote later, with the understatement of which only the English are capable, was this:

> *'I differed with him in his decision to take Irvine as his companion - for two reasons: firstly, that Irvine was now suffering from the prevalent throat trouble ... secondly, that he was not the experienced climber that Odell was, while Odell was obviously fit and strong, and, acclimatizing very slowly as he had done, was now beginning to show unmistakably that we had in him a climber of unequalled endurance and toughness.'*[32]

Odell would shortly prove Norton correct, but in circumstances that Norton could not have wished for. What we see in Norton's words is that Odell was the right man for the job, and Irvine was not. But Norton was exhausted and snow-blind; he was not up to the task of fighting Mallory's persistence. He had already read Mallory's proposal as Mallory's 'decision'. He caved in. He would later put the following spin on the narrative:

> *'I entirely agreed with his decision ...'*[33]
>
> *'I was entirely in favour of the plan, which now represented our last chance of success.'*[34]

Later, Norton circulated (and indeed set down for the record) an unconvincing story of Mallory's argument. Mallory had argued for the inclusion of Irvine, rather than Odell, on the grounds that Irvine had a knack, even a genius, for fixing the oxygen apparatus. That Irvine possessed this skill, was widely acknowledged; we can imagine that Norton did not dispute it. That it should be the criterion for climbing Everest, Norton had the right and the authority to disagree. Norton could have said that if the oxygen apparatus needed fixing, the climbers should turn around.

Finally, Norton could have said that what Mallory needed was a climbing partner, not a handyman. Mallory had never done a high climb with Irvine, and could have had no idea how Irvine would perform above the North Col. But Norton said nothing.

Privately, Norton believed that Mallory would not succeed. Writing three years later, John Noel the photographer, who had never considered himself a climber and had no axe to grind, would recall:

> *'Norton said: "There is no doubt Mallory knows he is leading a forlorn hope."'*[35]

To whom Norton made this remark, we do not know. We may suppose that Norton expected Mallory and Irvine to give it their best shot, and to return defeated. He could not have expected them to die.

Such was the resurrection of Mallory's plan. The execution of that plan remains to this day a mystery. Clues have survived, as to what happened on Mallory's and Irvine's last climb. Those clues may permit us to reconstruct a narrative of the climb. To that narrative, we shall return.

Chapter 8

Tigers

The reader will have observed that as we travelled in time from the reconnaissance of 1921, through the first serious attempts at the summit in 1922, to the ill-fated expedition of 1924, we have seen a proliferation of narratives.

In 1921, the official account was set down by Lieutenant Colonel Howard-Bury, in his capacity as leader of the expedition, in the book *Mount Everest, the Reconnaissance, 1921*, which was published the following year. To this book, Mallory contributed six chapters, comprising 100 pages or almost one-third of the text. Our understanding of the events is enhanced by Mallory's meticulous letters to his wife, which have been preserved by Magdalen College in Cambridge; and by Bullock's dry but perceptive diary.

The narratives of 1921 are essentially consistent. They paint a uniform picture of a small and determined group of men, working their way methodically and in unison towards an unknown destination. They reveal that through events outside their control, the group lost the operational leadership of Dr Kellas and Raeburn, and that Mallory emerged as the *de facto* leader in the field.

In 1922, the expedition had a different character, marked by sustained military leadership from start to finish. General Bruce, as leader, was the principal author of the official report, which was published as *The Assault on Mount Everest 1922* (here again, we see the prevalence of military terminology: Everest was an enemy, to be vanquished). On the title page, the authors other than General Bruce were credited only as 'other members of the expedition'. Nevertheless, Mallory was again a major contributor, with five chapters comprising 132 pages; the undervalued outsider Finch authored 46 pages, including the all-important 'Notes on Equipment'; and Somervell wrote just twelve pages relating to climbing.

In *The Assault on Mount Everest 1922*, Mallory's first chapter was titled 'The Problem'. His third was 'The Highest Point' (readers would have to peruse Finch's section to learn that Geoffrey Bruce and Finch, not Mallory, had reached the highest point on that expedition). Mallory's Chapter XI (which was not the final chapter of the book) was titled 'Conclusions'. In short, by 1923 Mallory was the alpha and omega of Everest: the man who knew what had to be done and how to do it. Mallory in the eye of the British public was the authority on the physical business of climbing Mount Everest. He was to Everest what Chuck Yeager would be to the sound barrier.

The 1922 expedition would produce other fine narratives.

Writing in 1936 in *After Everest*, Somervell would devote three chapters to his experiences on the climb of 1922. Somervell saw himself primarily as a medical doctor and as a Christian missionary; he accepted that he was a mountaineer, but not a public figure. His words, set down with humility and after the passage of time, give us a counterpoint to Finch's nuts-and-bolts approach and to Mallory's heroic narrative.

John Noel was the chief photographer on both the 1922 and the 1924 expedition. He did not see himself as a climber, although he and his porters carried cameras to 23,000 feet. He was never a candidate for a high climb above the North Col. When he wrote *Through Tibet To Everest*[1], published in 1927, he was writing from a perspective of relative neutrality, in terms of the strategic and operational decisions of the expeditions. In that book he devoted six chapters to the 1922 expedition. As we have seen already, he was capable of blunt commentary that other authors preferred to circumscribe with English correctness.

Arriving at the events of the spring and early summer of 1924, we have seen how the departure of General Bruce created a vacuum of authority, in which Norton and Mallory would become the principal, if very English and very polite, rivals. We can imagine that among the other members, diverging perspectives of the wielders of authority would create competing narratives of the events.

There are at least six authors of accounts of the 1924 expedition.

The official account was, as per protocol, that of the *de facto* leader, Colonel Norton, who became the principal author of *The Fight For Everest 1924* (again we see the bellicose terminology that had become common currency in discussions of Everest). Norton also was the prime channel for the communications with *The Times* of London, the Royal Geographical Society, and the Alpine Club. In *The Geographical Journal*, he was the lead author of the 'Everest Dispatches' which appeared in the issue of August 1924, as well as 'The Climb with Mr. Somervell to 28,000 feet', published in December 1924. In *The Alpine Journal* of May 1925, he published a long and technical paper titled 'The Problem of Everest'. In the aftermath of the expedition, Norton owned the narrative.

Norton authored five chapters of *The Fight for Everest 1924;* but protocol, or tradition, required that the official account make space for 'other members of the expedition'. General Bruce, as was his right, contributed the opening chapter on the early part of the journey up until his enforced departure. Beetham, Geoffrey Bruce and Odell each contributed a chapter; we can assume that their words were vetted by Norton and by the Mount Everest Committee. Mallory was gone; he was represented only by selected letters to his wife, which she had made available to the Committee. These letters were edited in some respects (as we have seen; and of which, more later).

Here we have to observe that the official account of the expedition is subject to issues of what, in the movie business, is called 'continuity'.

Observant or pedantic moviegoers will sometimes catch that, between two shots, the cowboy's gun has switched from his left hand to his right, or that someone's shirt has changed colour. On the internet, there is a cottage industry of enumerating 'continuity goofs'. If the movie is good, most of us do not notice. Likewise, in reading the accounts of 1924, we see that at one moment the porters are in no shape to take one more step; days later, they are raring to climb the mountain. One day a climber is too ill to move; the next, he is fit for any mission. In movie parlance, we are seeing 'jump cuts'.

Later, Noel's *Through Tibet to Everest* would devote five chapters to the 1924 expedition. He would describe Mallory's and Irvine's last climb as 'The Culminating Tragedy'. We may wonder if he chose the word 'culminating' to convey that the climb had been an accident waiting to happen. Somervell, when writing *After Everest*, had no further ambitions to climb the mountain; he would have four chapters on the 1924 story. His final chapter would be titled 'Disaster – and Retreat'.

Irvine too was gone; he had kept diaries, which were never widely circulated, and were not assembled and partly published until 1979[2], but fortunately have been preserved and digitized by Merton College, University of Oxford. His entries were largely brief and factual; they conveyed little of his perceptions, neither of his colleagues nor of the mountain.

Odell never wrote a full and independent account of his experiences. His brief and famous sighting of Mallory and Irvine, on 8 June 1924 at 12:50 pm, is central to the mystery. After 1924, he was still a candidate for future expeditions to Everest; we conjecture that there were limits to what he could say. He would eventually join the 1938 expedition, which would only reach the North Col. What he saw in 1924 (if he saw anything), and where Mallory and Irvine were when he saw them (if he saw them), have been subjects of debate for a century.

The purpose of this long preamble is to acknowledge that, as we search for an understanding of the events on Everest in June 1924, diverse voices will be competing for our attention. We hope to weave together, from the disparate and sometimes contradictory accounts, a coherent narrative of the whole.

With that, we return to Mount Everest in the closing days of May 1924. There would be three attempts at the summit. Mallory himself would be on the first attempt. The first two high climbs would constitute Mallory's last chance to assess the possibilities of victory or defeat.

Odell and Irvine

On 27 May 1924, according to the official account, the climbers of the Everest expedition unanimously agreed on Norton's simplified plan. Yet the narratives leave us in uncertainty about how many attempts there would be.

According to Norton, there were two 'councils of war'. Norton would write:

> *'May 26, Somervell and I reached Camp I. The party was now disposed as follows: Odell, Noel and Shebbeare remained at Camp II with some twenty porters; Mallory, Somervell, Bruce, Irvine and I with another twenty porters were at Camp I. ... On this same afternoon we held a council of war at Camp I. ... The council of war was long and undecisive, and I summoned another for next day ... They were resumed next day with the addition of Odell and Shebbeare.'*[3]

Somervell had a different story. In his later account, he recalled explicitly that at some point, three attempts were under consideration. He quoted his own diary for 26 May 1924 as follows:

> *'Council of war, seven of us ... So M [Mallory] and B [Geoffrey Bruce] start with five porters, make a camp at 25,000 feet, and sleep there. Next day they take a tent on to 27,000 feet, while Norton and I start from the Col to camp (taking one tent with us) at 25,000. The following day, M [Mallory] and B [Geoffrey Bruce] hope for the top, Norton and I for 27,000 feet, and Odell and Irvine start to go to 25,000. Sounds all right on paper; it gives us three simple two-camp non-oxygen attempts in succession.'*[4]

This diary entry constitutes one of the most profound omissions from the official account. Firstly, it establishes that as of 26 May, the composition of the climbing parties was in some sense agreed. Mallory and Bruce would be on the first climb; Norton and Somervell would be on the second. That was, in the event, what happened. But, according to Somervell's diary, the third climbing party would be, not Mallory and Irvine, but Odell and Irvine. Somervell made no record of any discussion about Mallory's being in more than one party.

The two accounts do not reconcile; according to Norton, the first 'council of war' was on May 26 with five participants; the second was on 27 May with seven, who agreed on two attempts. Somervell tells us that on 26 May, seven men agreed on three attempts.

Irvine recorded with simple regret that he and Odell were relegated to the reserves:

> *'We have now reorganized our plans & I hope to be in the 1st or second party. Geoff [Bruce] is considered the fittest & I'm next but neither being experienced climbers we can't make a simple party between us. So George Mallory & ["one of us" is struck out in original] Geoff [Bruce] & Somervell & Norton will probably make the 1st 2 parties. Odell & I have to be reserve.'*[5]

From the outset of the expedition, it should have been clear that Odell and Irvine were a natural climbing party. Odell personally had recommended Irvine to the Everest Committee; he was Irvine's sponsor and mentor. More than that, the two men were friends. They had climbed together on Craig yr Ysfa in Wales; Irvine had led the climb on the difficult chock-stone section. Odell would later describe Irvine's performance as 'a brilliant lead for a novice'. On Spitsbergen in 1923, they had climbed together to the summit of the rock peak that would later be named Irvinefjellet. Two men with such shared experiences would trust and help each other on the mountain.

On the expedition itself, Odell and Irvine had been a team – repairing the oxygen apparatus, cooking, fixing drinks, looking after the other climbers' comfort. Norton called them, in writing and more than once, 'the Old Firm' – a very English term both of praise and of enduring rectitude.

From Norton's narrative, we understand that at some point, he insisted on two climbers being stationed at Camp IV at any given time[6]. If that stipulation held, then since seven climbers were available, only five could climb. That meant two parties of two, with one climber in reserve. Mallory exercised his authority to ensure his inclusion in the first party; Norton exercised what remained of his own to salvage a place in the second. Possibly it was at this point that the Odell-Irvine party was consigned to oblivion.

In short, at this juncture, Mallory probably expected just one chance at the summit.

Mallory and Bruce

Here the pairing of Mallory and Geoffrey Bruce appeared for this first time. This decision merits further scrutiny. From the outset of the planning, Mallory had been paired with Irvine. We can imagine that on 17 April, when Mallory wrote to his wife about his 'brainwave', he had himself and Irvine in mind as the first party. On 24 April, when Mallory's plan was approved and the four climbing parties were named, Mallory and Irvine were confirmed.

By 27 May, Mallory's plan had been scrapped and oxygen had been abandoned. Certainly, that removed one of the criteria for the original assignments – namely, to include an 'oxygen expert (meaning Irvine or Odell) in each of the first two parties. But it was not self-evident that it would remove any of the other criteria – namely, to spread the climbing experience, and the specific Everest experience, among the parties; and to include in each party someone capable of communicating with the porters.

On the question of languages, the expedition members appeared to assume that a few words of Hindi or Nepali would be sufficient to communicate with, and to motivate, the porters. To this author, that should not have been a self-evident assumption. The porters' native languages were Sherpa or Tibetan.

Mallory's place in the first party was assured. Norton and Somervell, from the beginning, had agreed to be partners on the second climb. The decision that remained was: who would climb with Mallory?

There were two arguments that favoured Geoffrey Bruce over Irvine:

- Geoffrey Bruce had climbed with Finch, in 1922, to over 27,000 feet: a remarkable achievement considering that it had been the first climb of his life on a snow mountain. Irvine's best, prior to 1924, had been 5,121 feet on Spitsbergen.
- Geoffrey Bruce was said to be fluent in at least one of the porters' languages (probably Nepali).
- As regards physical fitness, according to Norton, 'Bruce was now palpably the strongest; he had been strong all along …'.

Given that the plan was to climb without oxygen, the principal argument in favour of Irvine was that for over a month, Mallory had conveyed that Irvine was his preferred partner. This was not a stance lightly to cast aside.

As to what Irvine thought about seeming to fall from Mallory's favour, no record has survived.

Tigers

We must now introduce the three most important men on the expedition: the men who could make or break any climb. Their names were Narbu Yishe, Llakpa Chede and Lobsang. If these names do not resonate in the annals of Everest history, it is because these three men were Sherpa.

The English recruited all of their locally hired employees in Darjeeling, India. For the tough job of carrying loads across the plains and up the mountain, they selected mainly, and intentionally, men from two ethnic groups: the Sherpa (meaning Tibetans from Nepal), and the Bhotia (Tibetans from Tibet itself). The Sherpa and Tibetan languages are closely related. In modern parlance, the term 'Sherpa' has come to embrace all of the ethnicities who work with climbers on the Himalayan mountains; in this book, we shall use it in that sense.

Figure 8.1a. Llakpa Chede on the 1924 expedition. (Author, after a photograph by John Noel)

Figure 8.1b. Narbu Yishe on the 1924 expedition. (Author, after a photograph by John Noel)

Figure 8.1c. (above) Semchumbi on the 1924 expedition. (Author, after a photograph by John Noel)

Figure 8.1d. (right) Lobsang on the 1924 expedition. (Author, after a photograph by John Noel)

Like Tejbir the Gurkha on the 1922 expedition, the Sherpa and Bhotia were assigned to the preconceived narrative of the hardy, happy, carefree men whose languages few white men spoke, and who carried loads up and down the mountain.

Narbu Yishe was from the Solukhumbu district of Nepal, the Sherpa heartland. We can infer that he spoke both Sherpa and Nepali. He had been a porter on the 1922 expedition. The English had a nickname for him - Purana Miles[7] – which meant 'old soldier' and was not a compliment. To the English mind, and especially the military mind, an old soldier was one who knew all the tricks – 'every handout in every town, and every lock that ain't locked when no-one's around'[8]. Norton described him as 'a plausible rogue', 'ruffianly but stout-hearted', and 'addicted to the flowing bowl', that is, alcoholic. Nevertheless, Norton respected Narbu's strength and stamina, and wrote that Narbu was 'capable of great things high up [on the mountain]'[9].

Llakpa Chede had been born in Darjeeling. His father was from Solukhumbu, but Llakpa had never been there. He would certainly have spoken Sherpa, but not necessarily Nepali. In 1922, he had been invited to join the expedition but had been unwell at the time. He had worked at one time for General Bruce, who described him as 'my former porter and henchman'[10]. Norton had a high regard for Llakpa: 'quiet … but with the quietness of complete self-confidence; independent, sturdy, of irreproachable character, and a brilliant man on the mountain'[11]. Somervell would describe Llakpa as 'stoutest-hearted of our porters … a real sportsman with guts'.

Llakpa Chede would return in 1933, to join the British expedition of that year. Ruttledge, the leader of the expedition, had the highest of praise for him:

> *'Llakpa Chedi, the old tiger of 1924, was a tower of strength at Camp III. ... His influence over the men was very great; he announced his resolve to try and reach Camp VI, overrode all timorous objections from the "old soldiers", and conveyed much of his own gallant spirit to the young thrusters.'*[12]

Much later, as Somervell recollected with sadness, Llakpa ended up as a waiter in a café in Darjeeling, frequented by posh English ladies[13].

Lobsang (or Lobsang Bhotia as he was sometimes known, though Bhotia was just his ethnicity) had been on the 1922 expedition. In 1924, he was one of six porters who carried loads to Camp VI at 26,800 feet. Over the next seven years, he would work with several European expeditions in the Himalayas. In 1931 he passed away. Norton would write in Lobsang's obituary:

> *'Lobsang was not only a good porter, mountaineer and sirdar[14], he was a good man, with the accent on the "good", ... brave and straight, strong and true as steel, ... maintain[ing] through every trial and adversity his own self-imposed standard of achievement and his own high principles ... [of] unimpeachable character and fine example ... high courage and stern devotion to duty.'*[15]

The three men's role in the expedition had originated in a discussion between Norton and Geoffrey Bruce, on 13 May, during an enforced pause in the climbing. They both perceived a need to reinforce the morale of the porters, and their solution was to create what, in military terms, would have been called platoons:

> *'Norton and I ... decided to make them up into three definite parties, each to be led by a selected porter, with the next best as his second-in-command to take charge if anything happened to the leader. These leaders and seconds-in-command would be given extra pay, and be generally treated as non-commissioned officers ... [we] had little difficulty in selecting six as leaders'*[16]

The daily ration allowance for a porter was six annas, or six-sixteenths of a rupee. In the 1920s, the Indian rupee converted to about 24 British pence. The porters were therefore receiving about nine British pence per day. Norton and Bruce evidently planned to pay more than that to the platoon leaders. How much more, the official record does not say.

The English would later refer to these six men (and others of comparable strength and reliability) as 'the Tigers'.

At this juncture, it appears that Narbu Yishe, Llakpa Chede and Lobsang were the obvious leaders, and were so designated. They were among the six Sherpa depicted in *The Fight For Everest 1924*, in a photograph titled 'Porters Who Went Highest'.

Alongside the three leaders, there were Bom, Semchumbi and Angtenjin, whom we may suppose to have been the three deputies. Of Bom and Angtenjin, we know nothing. Regarding Semchumbi, Geoffrey Bruce characterized him as 'a loafer, a cadger … and a ne'er-do-weel'[17]; Norton described him as 'gallant'.

These six men, whose names have never passed into legend, held power over the expedition. What they were willing to do, would determine what the expedition could do. In order to make sense of the three high climbs that were attempted in 1924, we have to understand the relationship between the English and the Sherpa.

From the English viewpoint, this was a relationship between master and servant. The English, in their various accounts of the expedition, referred to themselves unselfconsciously as *sahibs* (sometimes capitalized) – a Hindi word of Arabic origin, meaning something like 'lord' or 'master'. They generally referred to the Sherpa as 'porters', but occasionally and without apparent malice, lapsed to the term 'coolie', meaning a day labourer, a term that modern dictionaries describe as derogatory.

In any case, the English attitude to the Sherpa was a mixture of acknowledgement of their strength and endurance, and astonishment at their indifference to what the English saw as achievement. Sir Francis Younghusband, in his 'Introduction' to *The Fight For Everest 1924*, could not hide his disdain for people who did not want what the English wanted:

> *'These men are born and bred in the mountains below Everest ... they are sure-footed and owing to the rigorous climate of their homes can withstand more than average exposure and fatigue. ... So there, right on the spot, must be dozens of men who could, as far as bodily fitness goes, reach the summit of Everest any year they liked. Yet the fact remains that they don't. They have not even the desire to. They have not the spirit.'*[18]

A variant of this attitude was the perception that the Sherpa were somehow not adult, but more like children under the stern paternal care of the white man. Norton wrote of them:

> *'To deal with individually and en masse these men are singularly like a childish edition of the British soldier, many of whose virtues they share. They have the same high spirit for a tough and dangerous job; the same ready response to quip and jest.'*[19]

Mallory had somewhat the same attitude: the Sherpa were like little children who had to be chivvied out of lethargy by the energetic Englishman:

> *'It is an extraordinary thing to watch the conversion of men from listlessness to some spirit of enterprise; a very little thing will turn the scale ... these rather tired children were persuaded to do something for their comfort; without persuasion they would have done nothing to make life tolerable.'*[20]

What the Sherpa thought of the English, we shall never know.

Languages

The English attempted to engage the co-operation of the Sherpa across an immense barrier of language.

The Sherpa naturally spoke among themselves in the Sherpa or Tibetan languages. Those who had been born or raised in Solukhumbu most probably also spoke Nepali, at least sufficiently to communicate with Nepalis. All of them had been recruited in Darjeeling, which we suppose was well known as a place to find work with the English. Men who travelled from Nepal or Tibet to Darjeeling in search of work would probably go on foot or on animals; there were no trains or buses, and therefore no need to speak Indian languages; but some of them must have spoken or understood Hindi.

Among the English, those who were serving or had served as officers in the British Indian Army, like General Bruce and Colonel Norton, would have been expected to know Hindi. Norton wrote that he himself had 'learnt something of four Oriental languages'[21] (he did not say which ones; Hindi and Pushto seem probable). Officers from Gurkha regiments might know Nepali, the *lingua franca* of the Gurkhas; one such was Captain Geoffrey Bruce. Indeed, Norton wrote that 'Bruce talks their [the porters'] language fluently'; he did not say which language, but Nepali would be a good guess.

Norton's command of languages is illustrated by an anecdote relating to the return journey. With climbing duties over, Narbu Yishe was assigned to Odell as a personal servant. Odell attempted to explain his requirements to Narbu; following which Narbu asked for Norton's intervention, along the following lines:

> *'"Please ask the Sahib," said he, "to give me his keys and leave the rest to me; I quite understand the duties of a bearer, and he will find that his kit will be looked after and all his work perfectly done."'*[22]

Norton does not tell us in which language Narbu had spoken; but for sure it was not English, of which Narbu knew only the word 'Yes', usually followed by 'Sahib'. Probably then, Narbu had spoken either Hindi or Nepali; and Norton had understood perfectly.

Other than Norton and Geoffrey Bruce, there is little evidence that any English member of the 1924 expedition could communicate in any Indian or local language. Somervell would later be a medical missionary in South India, where he eventually became quite fluent in Tamil; but in the summer of 1924, as far as we can surmise from his memoirs, he spoke not a word of any Asian language. Norton's account confirms that Beetham and Odell were in the same boat:

> *'Beetham adopted the ordinary methods of John Bull*[23] *on the Continent: he talked good simple English rather loudly and slowly and produced surprisingly successful results. Odell adopted a more sonorous style, and addressed the Sherpa porter in rolling periods worthy of Doctor Johnson.'*[24]

Mallory had a 'smattering' of Hindi. Irvine, as he cheerfully admitted, knew no word of any applicable language:

> *'I have 2 porters of my own neither of which can understand a word I say[,] so I forsee [sic] much fun in talking in signs & pictures.'*[25]

No wonder then that Norton and Geoffrey Bruce, in appendices buried in the official report, felt compelled to argue for the minimum of linguistic, and what we would now call interpersonal, skills on the part of any future expedition:

> Norton: *'... the first essential is that they [the climbers] must learn at least something of their [the porters'] language. ... much can be done between leaving England and arriving at Rongbuk; ... every climber should know every porter by name ... Without these fundamentals the small amount of leadership required is impossible ...'*
>
> Geoffrey Bruce: *'Every climber coming to join an Expedition should make himself acquainted with a stock of useful phrases in either Hindustani [Hindi] or Nepalese [Nepali]. He should know the name of every man in the Expedition - it is the first step towards creating an understanding between the sahibs and the porters. ... On the voyage out[,] I would urge everyone to study either Nepali or Tibetan - or else polish up Hindustani. The importance of every one being able to talk to porters cannot be exaggerated.'*[26]

We do not have to look too far between the lines to suspect that Norton and Bruce were thinking, without wishing to speak ill of the dead, of Mallory, who in letters to his wife had written:

> (Rongli Chu, 29 March). *'I'm spending a certain amount of time and effort as we come along learning Hindustani; it is very unsatisfactory because the coolies themselves are so bad at it.'*[27]

> (Kampa Dzong, 14 April). *'I read little[,] what with Hindustani words and Sherpa names to learn, but I have occasional hours with Keats' letters or the Spirit of Man*[28] *...* '[29]

These letters were published in the official report: ostensibly as a tribute to the man who had written them, and who was no longer there to tell the tale. As we have seen, the Everest Committee took it upon themselves to redact Mallory's letters when they thought fit. We might wonder if they let these extracts stand, to convey to the reader that the deceased hero had not quite done all that he could to assure his survival.

Mallory was surely correct in observing that the porters spoke little Hindi; after all, it was not their native language. But it seems never to have occurred to him to devote his 'occasional hours' to learning, as Norton would later urge, 'something' of the Sherpa language, and the porters' names. On their goodwill and their strength, his life could depend.

The first high climb

The story of the first high climb of 1924 has been well told elsewhere. The essence is as follows.

On 1 June 1924, the weather was described as 'perfect'. Mallory and Bruce had camped at Camp IV on the North Col. They were accompanied by nine of the 'Tigers'. By now, the name 'Tiger' was applied to any porter who showed stamina and a willingness to climb; these nine may have included some of the original six platoon leaders and deputy leaders.

At 6:10 am, Mallory and Bruce started the climb up the North Ridge, with eight of the porters. Of the porters, we know only that one was named Lobsang; he may have been Lobsang the platoon leader. Another was Dorje Pasang, one of those who had reached the high camp at 25,500 feet in 1922[30]. The names of the others have been lost to history. The climbers' objective was to establish, for the first time, two high camps. Camp V was to be pitched that same day, at about 25,300 feet on the eastern side of the North Ridge, somewhat sheltered from the west wind. Camp VI was intended to be pitched on 2 June, at 27,300 feet; this would be within 100 vertical feet of the crest of the Northeast Ridge.

On 2 June, the diary for Camp IV recorded that it was a 'clear fine morning'. Norton and Somervell set off at 6:45 am for Camp V, on what was to be the second high climb. They presumably expected that Mallory and Bruce would have vacated Camp V and would be on their way upwards to the planned Camp VI. Somervell would write later of his surprise when, somewhere between Camp IV and Camp V, they met Mallory and Bruce coming back down the mountain.

Mallory would never write about what had transpired at Camp V, or on the way there. His last letter to his wife was dated 27 May. Geoffrey Bruce, the career army officer, would never write for the public about his experiences on the mountain. It fell therefore to Norton to piece together what had happened.

Norton's conversation with Mallory or Bruce was brief; we can conjecture that, preoccupied as he was with his own climb with Somervell, he did not give their story his full attention. They told him that approaching 25,200 feet, some of the porters had given up and had dropped their loads. Four had made it with their loads to the site where the camp had been planned; the other four had arrived without. Bruce had descended with Lobsang, and had retrieved the abandoned loads; Bruce related that he personally had carried the loads a short distance. The camp had been pitched. Mallory and Bruce had selected the best three porters to stay with them, had sent the other five down to Camp IV, and had slept one night. In the morning, one or more of the three porters had refused to continue.

Recalling this extraordinary incident, Norton would write of his astonishment:

> *'... nothing - not even Bruce's command of the language and well-known influence over these men - would induce any of the porters to go higher ... the porters who failed were the pick of the 'Tigers,' presumably among the best men we had. Yet these picked men, under the one Sahib of all our party [Geoffrey Bruce] who knew best how to lead the Sherpa porter and on a day which at Camp IV appeared 'quite perfect,' ... couldn't be induced to advance beyond 25,200 feet.'*[31]

Other members of the expedition heard the story in the same light. Yet the story makes no sense. It is one of a number of anomalies or discontinuities in the official narrative, on which we remarked earlier. On this particular climb, the Tigers refuse to continue; on the next high climb, as we shall see shortly, the Tigers (possibly the same ones, or possibly others) are ready and able to go as high as the Englishmen want to go; and as we have learned, for the unplanned third climb, fifteen to twenty porters are ready to go higher than anyone has been before.

In the official narrative, we often find that the porters are not named, and indeed are nameless. On the first high climb, Geoffrey Bruce must have known the porters' names. It would be logical for Norton to ask for those names, to avoid assigning those individuals to subsequent climbs. If he did so, there is no record of it.

Norton would write later that Geoffrey Bruce, in the course of the climb, had strained his heart. Herein we might detect a sign of the true course of events. We might infer that Bruce, on the morning of 2 June, was physically unable to go on, just as in 1922, he had been unable to continue the climb with Finch.

We have seen that the official narrative permitted no Englishman to be at fault. As Tom Wolfe would tell us over fifty years later, in *The Right Stuff*, the true fighter jock will never admit to having *screwed the pooch*. And if the fighter jock is also a public hero, the establishment will back him up. It must have been something wrong with the machine; something that the engineers will have to figure out. For the Everest Seven, the porters were the convenient fly in the ointment, the gremlin in the airplane, the hatch on the Mercury capsule. 'I didn't do anything. The damned thing just blew.'[32]

Geoffrey Bruce, in an appendix to the official report, would obliquely refer to the kind of situation in which a climber might fail to motivate the Sherpa: exactly the situation that he had experienced with Mallory on 2 June 1924:

> *'... failure to visit their tents and enquire after their well-being will almost certainly result in loss of moral [sic], and even in their refusing to go on the next morning.'*[33]

Was he half admitting that he had *screwed the pooch*?

If the problem at 25,300 feet had been only the strength or willpower of three porters, the remedy would have been to dispatch them down to Camp IV with a request for three others to take their place. As we know from Somervell's later account, the snowy shoulder of the North Ridge was an easy place, where porters could descend without supervision[34]. Three more Tigers would surely have been found; if they needed an escort to Camp V, Odell or even Hazard could have done the job; Mallory and Bruce would probably have spent an unplanned night at Camp V and could then have resumed their programme. That did not happen; and we may never know why.

The second high climb

Norton's and Somervell's high climb – the second high climb of 1924 – would be the one great success of the expedition. Norton would claim to have reached an altitude of 28,126 feet – less than 900 feet below the summit - which was a world record for mountaineering. After the expedition, Norton would acknowledge that Mallory and Irvine might have climbed higher; there were references to Odell's sighting, which seemed to have put them above 28,200 feet. But the sighting itself came into dispute; some doubted that Odell had really seen the climbers, and if he had, there were arguments about where exactly they had been. So the confirmed world record still belonged to Norton. Somervell would reach around 28,000 feet, and thereby stake a claim to the second highest climb in mountaineering history. Both men would hold those honours until 1952, when a Swiss expedition would narrowly surpass their altitude[35].

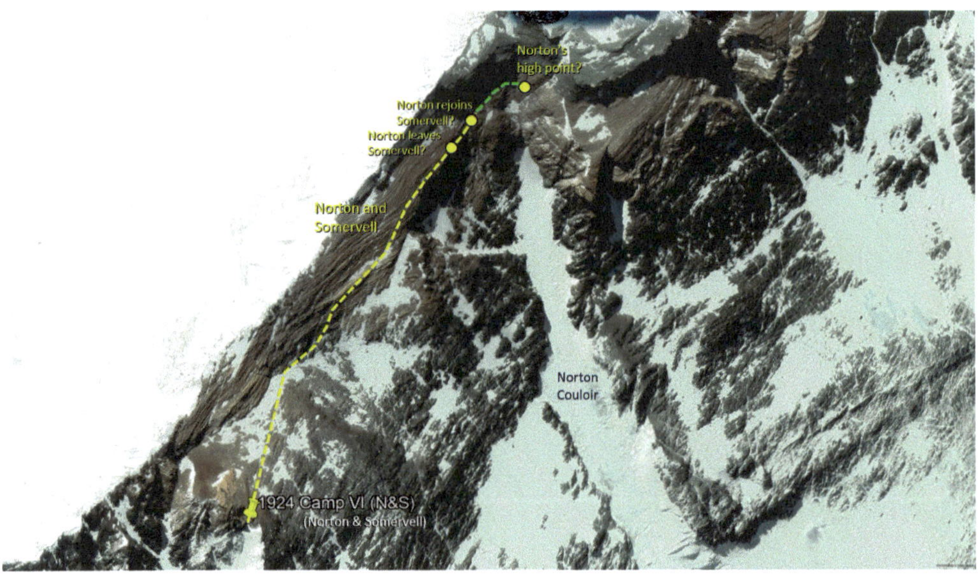

Figure 8.2. The approximate route taken by Colonel Norton on 4 June 1924 from his and Somervell's Camp VI to his high point. (Base map © CNES / Airbus / Google Earth; additional graphics by author)

The story of the second high climb has been narrated elsewhere, by Norton in *The Fight For Everest 1924* and later by Somervell in *After Everest*. Here we are interested in the essence of the climb, and in the role of the Tigers in the story.

We learned that Norton and Somervell set out on 2 June 1924. They were accompanied by six porters. As we know, on the way they met Bruce and Mallory who were coming down defeated. They continued upwards, found Camp V, and settled in. Here they sent two porters down and retained four. From the accounts of both men, we know these porters' names: Llakpa Chede, Lobsang Tashi, Narbu Yishe and Semchumbi. Llakpa and Narbu were two of the original platoon leaders, both with the status of non-commissioned officers. Semchumbi was probably one of the deputy platoon leaders. Lobsang Tashi was what Norton described as a 'simple giant'.

Somervell, perhaps spooked by Bruce's and Mallory's story, was already having doubts about whether the porters would be willing to continue. On the morning of 3 June, indeed, Norton spent the best part of four hours on a motivation session. His account of that session gives us an insight into the English incomprehension of the Sherpa:

> *'I talked for a long time to these men, pointing out the honour and glory that they would achieve if they would but carry their loads another 2,000 feet ... I remember saying, 'If you put us up a camp at 27,000 feet and we reach the top, your names shall appear in letters of gold in the book that will be written to describe the achievement.'*'[36]

Good soldier, linguist and Orientalist though he was, it seems never to have occurred to Norton that the Sherpa could not be expected to have any interest whatsoever in honour, glory or the book of the expedition. They had come to Darjeeling to find work. They were being paid around nine British pence per day – maybe a bit more, as platoon leaders. The work was hard and dangerous. In the night, rocks had been dislodged from the Englishmen's higher platform and had fallen on the Sherpas' tent. Lobsang Tashi had a head wound, and Semchumbi's knee was bleeding profusely; the Englishmen wanted them to keep climbing.

We can imagine the Sherpa thinking: 'The Englishman is talking about letters of gold. What did they give to Tejbir when they made him carry fifty pounds up the mountain? When will he start jingling some gold coins in his pocket?' As far as we know, Norton did not come up with an offer of tangible reward.

Somervell would recall:

> *'Our start even then was due entirely to one man, Lhakpa Chedi ... without whose lead it is probable that the other three would all have refused to go on.'*[37]

In the event, Lobsang Tashi could not, or would not, go on. Llakpa, Narbu and Semchumbi continued with Norton and Somervell. Semchumbi, despite his injury, kept climbing. The party pitched Camp VI at 26,800 feet, about 200 feet lower than the Englishmen had hoped. They sent the three Sherpa down to Camp IV: evidently, a journey that the porters could do without an escort. Finally, the Tigers had done for Norton and Somervell what the Tigers would not do for Geoffrey Bruce and Mallory.

Figure 8.3. The return of Norton (far right) and Somervell (third from left, on porter's back), 4 June 1924. (Author, after a frame from *The Epic of Everest*, filmed by John Noel)

The rest of the record-breaking climb, including Norton's final 100 feet of climbing alone, and Somervell's near-death experience, is recorded in the annals of Mount Everest.

Llakpa Chede, Narbu Yishe and Semchumbi had climbed higher than any Sherpa in history. Norton would publish an article in *The Geographical Journal* titled 'My Climb to 28,000 feet with Mr. Somervell'. To his credit, he did record the names of the three Sherpa who had climbed to 26,800 feet; and he mentioned Semchumbi's injury. Later, the book of the expedition would be written. But the Sherpas' names would never be inscribed in letters of gold. To this day, they do not appear even in the Himalayan Database, which was intended to record the name of every person, whether *sahib* or Sherpa, who set foot on Everest.

Lessons for Mallory

As for Mallory, he would have done the math. On 4 June 1924, Norton and Somervell left their Camp VI, at 26,800 feet, at 6:40 am. At the point where Somervell stopped and Norton continued alone, the time was about 12:00 pm, and they were around 28,000 feet. They had ascended around 1,200 feet in five hours and twenty minutes: an average of 230 vertical feet per hour. In Norton's final hour of climbing, he had ascended just 100 vertical feet, maybe less. Neither man had carried oxygen. Mallory must surely have thought: oxygen is the key, or one of the keys.

Knowing Norton's and Somervell's climb rates, and remembering Finch's performance with oxygen from 1922, Mallory could conservatively estimate his climb rate with oxygen at 300 feet per hour. There were 2,200 vertical feet between Camp VI and the summit; assuming no time lost on route-finding, that would be over seven hours' climbing; say eight. The descent rate would be well over double the ascent rate: say three hours for the return to Camp VI, a total of eleven hours. The sun would set around 7 pm; the start from Camp VI should not be later than 8 am.

Sunrise would be at 4.41 am. Mallory could not have failed to observe that by this date, there was no moon before sunrise; therefore, sunrise would be about the earliest start time. That would still leave a cushion of about three hours for delays and diversions. In terms of time and speed, the climb was doable.

The other key would be the route. Ten years later Frank Smythe, writing of his experiences on the 1933 Everest expedition, would recall Norton's ideas for a route to the summit:

> *'... below the second and first steps ... there appeared to be no feasible route through the two [rock] bands. Norton has suggested the possibility of breaking through the lower of these two bands east of the great couloir, and traversing along the slabs between it and the upper band until it is possible to break through the latter.'*[38]

We may conjecture that on the evening of 4 June, sharing his tent with the snow-blind Norton (as well as his bombshell plan for a third attempt), Mallory grilled Norton on his ideas for the route; and Norton might have shared with Mallory what he would later tell Smythe. Mallory knew that Norton's route was good to within 900 vertical feet of the summit. No other route had been tested. In that moment, Mallory might have conceived a variation on Norton's route, that would take him to the top.

Chapter 9

Pyramid

Our story has reached the morning of 6 June 1924, when Mallory and Irvine left Camp IV on the North Col, on the climb from which they would not return. The five days from 6 to 10 June encompass the mystery of their last journey.

Shortly before their departure, Odell took the famous photograph of the two, suiting up outside their tent, which has appeared in practically every book about their climb, and has been represented as the last image of them alive. (It was not: John Noel recorded them on the second stage of their climb, at or above 26,000 feet on the North Ridge, somewhere between Camp V and their Camp VI, with his cine-camera and telephoto lens.)

From that point on, they spoke to no-one, except presumably to the accompanying Sherpa in Mallory's pidgin Hindi, which the Sherpa probably barely understood. Mallory sent two letters back to the lower camps: one to Odell and one to Noel; both have been scrutinized for the best part of a century. Between 6 and 10 June, the climbers kept no journals and drew no maps, of which we are aware. As we shall elaborate in chapter 10, Odell believed that he saw them fleetingly, at 12:50 pm on 8 June, through a clearing of the clouds. Otherwise, almost everything that we know, or that we think we know, about their last climb is based on assumption and inference.

There are diverse and to some extent competing narratives of their climb. There were at least five British members of the expedition, and at least eight Sherpa, who were at the scene and could have made first-person contributions to the story. As to what the returning Sherpa recalled, no record remains, except Norton's and Noel's paraphrases of their reports, in whatever fragments of language they had in common. Among the British, Geoffrey Bruce and Hazard never set down their stories.

Norton, as *de facto* leader of the expedition, was compelled to construct a narrative that was acceptable to the Mount Everest Committee, the Royal Geographical Society, the Alpine Club, the British press and the British public. In the moment, he delegated the substance of the narrative to Odell, who surely wrote under Norton's supervision. Odell likewise was probably mindful of his future opportunities to join other Everest expeditions.

The photographer John Noel published his account in 1927. For some aspects of his narrative, he drew upon his remembered conversations with Odell. Somervell, who did not return to England after the expedition and chose to settle in India, wrote his memoirs in 1936.

Of all the narratives, in this author's mind the recollections of Noel are the most dispassionate and somehow also the most empathetic. He did not see himself as a climber and did not need the favours of any institution. As we have seen already, he respected the climbers but was capable of a frank and clear-eyed assessment of them, at moments when other observers felt obliged to add a noble or heroic spin. In our reconstruction of Mallory's and Irvine's last climb, we shall often look to Noel for authenticity.

We therefore invite Noel to set the stage for the last climb. He wrote the following words sometime after the evening of 4 June, when Norton and Somervell staggered back from their high climb, but before the morning of 6 June when Mallory and Irvine departed Camp IV:

> *'Norton and Somervell had shot their bolts*[1]*. Mallory and Irvine now took up the fight ...*
>
> *... I had an opportunity of observing Mallory closely, as I was at Snowfield Camp [Camp III] during this time, and I formed the positive opinion that physically he had become an unfit man. ... His bitter but suppressed disappointment over the continual setbacks and the ill luck of the weather this year, was manifest, ... He was throwing his last ounce of strength into this fight.*
>
> *... Irvine ... was anxious and worried about the [oxygen] machines; ... he also was far from being in good condition. He breathed heavily and with labour.'*[2]

The stage was set: two exhausted and desperate soldiers were about to go into battle against the demon mountain.

The high camps

When Mallory and Irvine departed Camp IV, two higher camps were already in place, pitched by Norton's and Somervell's parties of 3 and 4 June, and presumably provisioned with food, bedding and at least some items of equipment. It was therefore feasible for Mallory and Irvine to carry the maximum quantity of oxygen, and the minimum of food and personal items, as Odell would testify:

> *'At 8.40 [am] they were ready to start, and I hurriedly 'snapped' them as they were loading up with the oxygen apparatus. Their personal loads consisted of the modified apparatus with two cylinders only [each] and a few other small items such as wraps and a food ration for the day, amounting to not more than perhaps 25 lb [each].*
>
> *... The eight porters, who accompanied them from Camp IV, carried provisions, bedding, and additional oxygen cylinders, but of course [sic] no breathing apparatus for their own use.'*[3]

Although we can never know for sure, it is reasonable to infer that Mallory and Irvine uplifted at least twelve cylinders of oxygen to Camp V: four on their own backs and at least eight carried by the porters. Odell would later write, in the official report of the expedition:

> *'The weight of three charged cylinders alone amounted to about 25 lb., giving a total oxygen content (at 120 atmospheres) of about 1,605 litres. ... at a consumption of as much as two litres per minute - a rate found to be by no means necessary, even at 27,000 feet - that amount would sustain the user for a period of at least 12 hours.'*[4]

With a minimum of twelve cylinders, Mallory and Irvine each had enough oxygen uplifted to Camp V for at least 24 hours' climbing: proportionately more if they reduced the flow rates (which, as we shall see, they did).

For the climb from Camp IV at 22,700 feet, to Camp V at 25,300 feet, Norton's accounts would later list three timed ascents without oxygen. One would have been his own with Somervell, on 1 June; the other two were probably Odell's. In Norton's records, the fastest time had been three hours fifteen minutes; the average had been five hours ten minutes.[5] Mallory and Irvine, with access to oxygen even if not using it much, would probably have arrived at Camp V between 12 pm and 1 pm on 6 June. They might well have had to wait for the porters to catch up with them.

The rules of the diaries at the lower camps were to record all movements of personnel, including times of arrival and departure, and loads uplifted or returned. At Camp IV on 6 June, this was not done. The diary entry for that day, annotated by hand with the name 'Odell' reads as follows:

> *'Min. night temp. -9°F. Calm and cold.*
>
> *Midday. Air temp. 36°[F]. Sun temp. 110 °F. Brilliant, clouds in valley and to east.*
>
> *4.45 [pm] Air temp. 23°F. Air still, thick mists all around obscuring summits, including Everest; light mists hanging around Camp V (25,000 ft.)'*[6]

It was, at least in the early afternoon when Mallory and Irvine arrived at Camp V, a bright sunny day. Odell received one further communication from Mallory in the course of that day,

> *'That evening [6 June], soon after 5 o'clock, four of Mallory's porters returned from Camp V, where his party was spending the night, and brought me a note saying, 'There is no wind here, and things look hopeful.'*[7]

To Camp VI

On the morning of 7 June, at a time that was never recorded, Mallory, Irvine, Llakpa (probably the 'Tiger' Llakpa Chede), and three other porters set off for their Camp VI; and at an equally unknown time, they arrived. Here again, we are indebted to Norton's meticulous book-keeping for an idea of their ascent rate. Norton made notes of two ascents from Camp V at 25,300 feet to Camp VI, for which his final estimate was 26,800 feet; one of these ascents would have been his own with Somervell, and the other, again probably one of Odell's. Both ascents, without oxygen, had taken four hours fifty minutes. We can infer that Mallory and Irvine would have matched or bettered that time, and would have arrived at Norton's Camp VI in the early afternoon; and that the porters would have followed later.

In the course of this climb, Noel captured the last image of the two climbers, 700 feet above Camp V:

Figure 9.1. John Noel's last telephoto image of Mallory's and Irvine's party on June 7, 1924, between Camp V and Camp VI. Noel estimated their altitude as 26,000 feet. They were not on a skyline; the apparently empty space behind them was a bank of mist. (Author, after a frame from *The Epic of Everest*, filmed by John Noel)

> *'The longest distance picture I actually got was that of Mallory and Irvine at 26,000 feet at 2 miles range. Above that point I never saw them, the mist concealed them.'*[8]

At this juncture, we need to re-introduce Odell: the man who could have saved Mallory's and Irvine's lives. This was the man who had mentored Irvine and had brought him onto the expedition; who was a vastly more experienced climber than Irvine; who knew the oxygen apparatus less well than Irvine but well enough not to rely on it; and whom Mallory had turned down in favour of Irvine. He was also immensely fit, strong and acclimatized. In the words of John Noel:

> *'Odell [with]stood altitude, and acclimatised perhaps better than anybody else on the Expedition. He was never ill, never seemed tired; always kept an even, placid temperament unruffled by any event whatsoever. ... He had been slower than any other of the men to acclimatize, but eventually he appeared to become inured to a greater degree than any other.'*[9]

At 10 am on 7 June, with Mallory and Irvine presumed to have moved up to their Camp VI, Odell departed from Camp IV for Camp V. He climbed with Nema, one of only two porters remaining at Camp IV. His mission was to act as a support or backup climber for the summit team. This was a task that he had evidently agreed in advance with Mallory. We can also read into this mission the possibility that Mallory had a Plan B; that in the event that Irvine was not up to the climb, Mallory would send him down to Camp V with a message for Odell to take his place (a course which Norton, unsuccessfully, had counselled on 4 June). Odell would surely and gladly have agreed; and history might have been different.

In other circumstances, Odell would have climbed together with Mallory and Irvine and would have remained at their Camp VI on the summit day. But, in his account of events, there were not enough porters to carry an extra tent. Why that should be so is not self-evident.

Mallory and Irvine had left Camp IV with eight porters; one of them could have carried a tent and provisions for Odell. Then Odell would have been based at their Camp VI on 8 June; on that morning, there would have been a briefing and a set of agreed signals and fallback actions for various eventualities. Again, history might have been different.

Odell's account leaves the impression that Mallory and Irvine had left at least one cylinder of oxygen at Camp IV; and that Odell found it but could not use it:

> *'I had expected on my way up to Camp V to find a spare oxygen-breathing set that had been left there [at or above Camp IV?] earlier, but discovered that Irvine the previous day had taken the mouthpiece from it for a spare, and so rendered it useless to me. However, I carried it on up to Camp V in case another mouthpiece were available there; but this was not so, though it did not bother me, since I found I was able to get along as well without its aid, and better without the bulky inconvenience of the whole apparatus.'*[10]

Odell would demonstrate later, and twice, that he was fit and mobile without oxygen as high as 27,000 feet. But that demonstration would come too late.

Back at Camp IV, Hazard had duly registered the departure of Odell and Nema, and made the following observations of the weather:

> *'12.00 hrs. Max. sun temp. = above 125°F (ceases to register). Air temp. = 35°F. Calm, very close, clouds and mist on mountain. Camp IV in sunshine.*
>
> *16.00 hrs. Air temp. = 30°F. Sun temp. 123°F. Calm, very close, clouds and mist.'*[11]

In short, it was another day that posed no problems for climbing.

Odell probably reached Camp V at about 15:00. Shortly after his arrival, a cascade of small stones heralded the arrival of Llakpa and the other three porters who had been with Mallory and Irvine at their Camp VI. They brought the following message, one of the last two that Mallory ever wrote:

> *'DEAR ODELL, We're awfully sorry to have left things in such a mess - our Unna Cooker rolled down the slope [from Camp V] at the last moment. Be sure of getting back to [Camp] IV tomorrow in time to evacuate before dark, as I hope to. In the tent I must have left a compass - for the Lord's sake rescue it: we are without. To here on 90 atmospheres for the two days -- so we'll probably go on two cylinders - but it's a [bloody] load for climbing. Perfect weather for the job! Yours ever, G. MALLORY.'*[12]

This letter yields the following insights:

- The Unna cooker (which was used for warming meals) was missing, but was evidently not a critical loss; otherwise, Mallory would have asked Odell to bring a replacement to his Camp VI[13]. That would be a normal task for a support climber. In that event, Mallory could have delayed the summit attempt to 9 June.
- The compass likewise was not a critical item (again, if it were, Mallory would have asked for it to be brought to his Camp VI that same day). We infer that

Mallory was not planning to navigate by compass, and therefore planned to climb and descend in daylight.

- The '90 atmospheres' referred to his (and presumably also Irvine's) consumption of oxygen on 6 and 7 June. It was equivalent to 75 per cent of a full tank. If they had left with twelve full cylinders, they had ten and a half remaining.
- The 'two cylinders' surely meant two for him, and two for Irvine, to be used on the summit attempt.
- Mallory wanted Odell to evacuate Camp V before dark on 8 June, in order for himself and Irvine to be able, if necessary, to re-occupy the camp on their descent from the summit.
- Mallory did not see any need to inform Odell of the route that he and Irvine planned to take, or of his expected times of departure and return. He either did not want, or did not expect, any kind of help from Odell. If things went wrong, there was nothing that Odell could do.

We can read the letter to the effect that Mallory was planning, or retaining as an option, a route of descent bypassing his Camp VI, direct to Camp V. If that were so, it would be a large step towards an explanation of why his body was found at the approximate altitude of Norton's Camp VI, but well to the west, on a line in the direction of Camp V.

The second Camp VI

There was one aspect of Mallory's climb to Camp VI that Odell must have known; and Noel also possibly knew, or learned later from Odell. Mallory had pitched his high camp above Norton's and Somervell's Camp VI. Noel would later write:

> *'Mallory and Irvine succeeded in three stages in establishing their highest bivouac at the [Northeast] shoulder, 500 feet higher than any of the previous parties had done. From 'Eagle's Nest' [above Camp III] I photographed them on the way up at 26,000 feet. I then went for one afternoon to Ice Cliff Camp [Camp IV]; the same day [7 June] they went up to 27,000 feet ...'*[14]

Noel's reference to 'three stages' could only mean the following:

1. Camp IV to Camp V
2. Camp V to Norton and Somervell's Camp VI
3. from the old Camp VI to a new and higher Camp VI.

Norton would eventually calibrate his own Camp VI at 26,800 feet, probably by means of a theodolite at Base Camp. For Mallory's Camp VI, Noel eventually came up with an estimate of 27,000 feet:

> *'It was hoped, however, as actually did happen, to get two light tents and sleeping-bags, and a supply of food and fuel, up to the North-East Shoulder, 27,000 feet above the sea.'*[15]

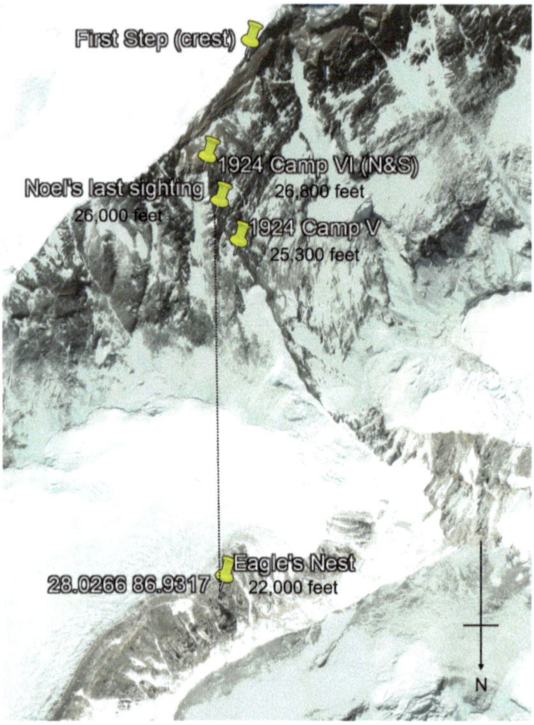

Figure 9.2. John Noel's sightline at the moment of his last telephoto image of Mallory's and Irvine's party on June 6, 1924, between Camp V and Camp VI. (Base image © CNES / Airbus / Google Earth; additional graphics and legend by author)

In all of the accounts of the 1924 expedition, Noel's is the only reference to two tents at a high camp. As we shall see later, Odell would find Mallory's and Irvine's high camp, but with only one tent. Possibly Noel was referring to a tent at Norton and Somervell's site and another at Mallory's and Irvine's, and retained in his mind a rounded altitude of 27,000 feet for both of them. We have no way of knowing.

In any event, we may now follow a clue as to where Mallory pitched his high camp. On 29 April 2001 on a climb on the North Ridge, Jake Norton (no relation to Edward Norton) found the remains of a 1924 camp.

> *'Choosing a path of logical feasibility upward at about 26,900 feet, I spied a pointed gendarme of rock not high above; ... [it had] the right altitude, and a flat-ish spot at its base somewhat protected from the wind. ... I looked down, spotting a bit of wood poking from the black-rock rubble: it was a tent pole, lying for 77 years in the rubble of what we now understood to be a largely collapsed tower.'*[16]

In the debris of that camp, he found an old sock bearing the laundry label 'Norton', for which he received a ribbing from his colleagues. The sock could only be Colonel Norton's.

In the report of the 1924 expedition report, Colonel Norton wrote that his Camp VI had been in 'a narrow cleft in the rocks facing north and affording the suggestion - it was little more - of some shelter from the north-west wind.'[17]

Figure 9.3. The probable location of Norton's and Somervell's 1924 Camp VI, and of the 'pointed gendarme' observed by Jake Norton in 2001. (Base image © CNES / Airbus / Google Earth; location of Colonel Norton's Camp VI by courtesy of Jake Norton; graphics and legend by author. North is at bottom of image)

Figure 9.4. The probable location of Mallory's and Irvine's Camp VI on 7 June 1924; and a possible climbing line from Norton and Somervell's Camp VI. (Base image © CNES / Airbus / Google Earth; graphics and legend by author. North is at bottom of image)

By courtesy of Jake Norton, this author has made an approximate geolocation of the "pointed gendarme" on Google Earth. According to Google Earth, the "gendarme" is at about 26,560 feet and Camp VI is at about 26,621 feet by the modern calibration. They are shown in Figure 9.3.

It is a fair bet that what Jake Norton found was the remains of Colonel Norton's and Somervell's Camp VI (but not Mallory's and Irvine's).

If this is the site of Norton's and Somervell's Camp VI, we have to look for places 500 feet higher on the North Ridge, and we should find Mallory's and Irvine's Camp VI. On Google Earth we see a place which is at the right altitude, and has a spot which looks sufficiently flat and sheltered for a tent. It is at latitude 27.9990°, longitude 86.9345°, for which Google Earth gives the altitude as 27,309 feet (27,279 feet by the 1924 calibration). It is nestled under the cliffs which define the Northeast Shoulder. Surely this is the site of Mallory's and Irvine's high camp.

Rockband and skyline

The other letter which Mallory's porters brought down from his Camp VI on 7 June, and which Odell possibly did not see at the time, was addressed to John Noel. The porter who carried it was Llakpa. Noel would later refer to it as 'the last letter Mallory ever wrote'. In fact, the same group of Sherpa carried the letters to Odell and to Noel, and we do not know the order in which Mallory had written them. Llakpa also had some news about the climbers; presumably both Llakpa and Noel spoke enough Hindi to understand one another:

> *'He said that the Sahibs were well and the weather was good, and that they had successfully reached the higher level. After building the camp, the Sahibs had sent the porters down.'*

In the phrases 'the higher level' and 'building the camp', probably filtered through Llakpa's and Noel's rudimentary Hindi, we have one more sign that Mallory and Irvine had made their last camp, not at Norton's and Somervell's Camp VI, but somewhere above.

The contents of Mallory's letter to Noel justifiably passed into legend:

> *'Dear Noel, We'll probably start early tomorrow, in order to have clear weather. It won't be too early to start looking out for us either crossing the rockband under the pyramid, or going up skyline at 8.0 p.m. [sic] Yrs ever, G. Mallory'.*[18]

Noel read the reference to 8 pm to mean 8 am. It was an extraordinary error on Mallory's part; in hundreds of pages of letters to his wife and friends, he had never made a comparable slip, but no other explanation was possible.

Readers of Mallory's letter universally made an additional assumption: that Mallory had planned to be at the final pyramid at 8 am. Undoubtedly they believed that his high

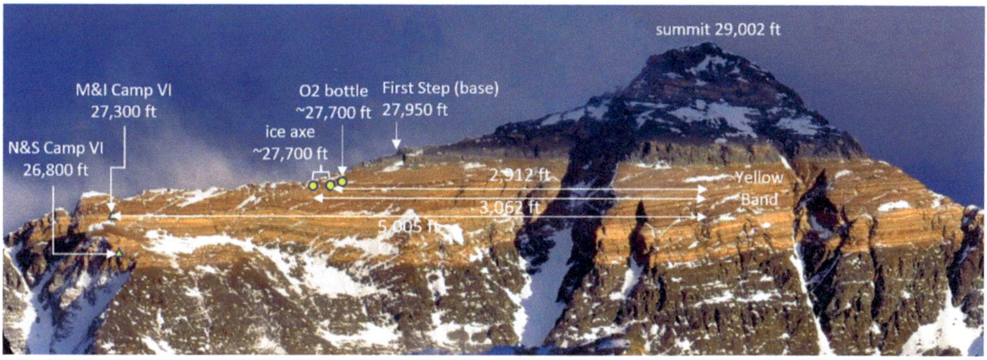

Figure 9.5. A possible interpretation of Mallory's references to "rockband" and "skyline" in his note of 7 June 1924 to Noel. (Base image © Vlado Cuchran; graphics and legend by author)

camp had been the same as Norton's and Somervell's, at 26,800 feet. The base of the final pyramid was at around 28,400 feet; and they would know that, with no moonlight, Mallory and Irvine could not have departed much before 5 am. They would have had to average over 500 vertical feet per hour: which, at such altitudes and with the route unknown, was unheard of.

However, there is a much simpler interpretation.

Mallory's letter to Noel made no reference to the final pyramid. His "rockband" was not qualified or elaborated in any way; he had never before used this term in any report or correspondence. He surely assumed that Noel could have no doubt as to what he meant. There was one rock band which was universally known to the British expeditions since 1921; that was the Yellow Band, the conspicuous stratum of light brown or yellowish limestone which underlies the dark rock layers of the summit of Everest. The Yellow Band is about 1,000 feet thick and encircles the entire mountain; one way or another, Mallory and Irvine would have to cross it to reach the summit.

Likewise, we can reasonably assume that Mallory's 'skyline' was the same 'sky line' to which he had referred in his report in 1921. That is, it was the silhouette of the Northeast Ridge against the southern sky. For Mallory to say that he and Irvine might be 'going up skyline' simply meant that at some point, they might be somewhere on the crest of the ridge. That crest is over a mile long.

Therefore, there is no need for us to read an impossible ambition or a quixotic enterprise into Mallory's letter. With a judicious appeal to Occam's Razor, we can infer that Mallory anticipated something like three hours climbing to a point where Noel would see him and Irvine though the telescope. At that point, they might have ascended around 1,000 feet; and they would be either within the Yellow Band, or above it on the crest of the ridge. Neither option excludes the other, nor necessitates the other.

Mallory was not deranged. He did not expect to be at the final pyramid by 8 am. He simply expected to be visible through the telescope at that time. He expected to be at the final pyramid at some later time. We can never know what his expectations were; but as to what really happened, we shall learn more when we turn to Odell's sighting.

The final pyramid

If Noel ever had a specific interpretation of Mallory's last letter, he never said or wrote what it was. However, in *Through Tibet to Everest*, he set down his understanding of the last section of Mallory's route, which would be on the 'final pyramid'. Since Noel here referred to two alternative routes, it would be natural for the reader to correlate these two options with the 'either ... or' of Mallory's last letter; but Noel did not refer to that letter, and we are not obliged to make that correlation.

> *'Mallory told me himself, when he talked to me of his possible routes up the final pyramid and told me where to watch for him, that he expected to go up the North-East Ridge of the final pyramid, but if he found the gully particularly difficult or if the west wind were particularly bad[,] he would take the Eastern Ridge, missing the gully by passing across the head of it and gaining better protection from the west wind. Such a route would bring him along the knife-edge of the Eastern Ridge.'*[19]

This commentary, in turn, requires its own disentanglement of the vocabulary.

The 'final pyramid' is not in doubt. John Noel took a celebrated telephoto of the summit of Mount Everest, which was reproduced in *The Fight For Everest 1924* with the caption 'The Final Pyramid'. It is referenced in figure 9.6a. The pyramid has a north-eastern face which forms a well-defined triangle, perpetually covered in snow; the side of the triangle to climber's right is what Noel called the 'North-East Ridge' (not to be confused with the Northeast Ridge of Everest itself); the side to climber's left is what he called the Eastern Ridge. These seem to be terms of Noel's invention; he had already created his own vernacular for Camp III ('Snowfield'), IV ('Ice Cliff'), V ('Windy Ridge') and VI ('High Bivouac'). The 1924 climbers did not use Noel's terms for the camps or the elements of the pyramid, nor are they in the modern climber's vocabulary.

We can reasonably assume that what Noel recorded with his telephoto lens, Mallory had also seen many times through binoculars, and approximately from the same angle and with a similar resolution. He would be aware of the triangular snowfield with its two distinct ridges, offering a choice of terrain. We can conjecture that from Mallory's point of view, the ridge to climber's right would be preferable, since he could skirt the snowfield, stay largely on rock, and thereby avoid cutting steps in snow.

Conversely, Noel was correct in understanding that what he called the Eastern Ridge offered better protection from the prevailing and often violent west wind. On that ridge, the whole vast bulk of the pyramid would shelter the climber from the wind. Mallory's note to Noel seemed to imply that he would make that decision *in situ*.

At this point, we may understand that Mallory, once he reached the final pyramid, had a Route 1, whereby he would work up and along the right-hand margin of the snowfield. Modern climbers typically go up the centre of the snowfield, but before the crest, they make a detour to the right (to the north), followed by a sharp left turn towards a feature now known as the Dihedral, which is the easiest pathway to the summit. A straight climb to the top of the snowfield would also work, but it would be more difficult. Mallory would not have known of the Dihedral, though given time, he might have found it.

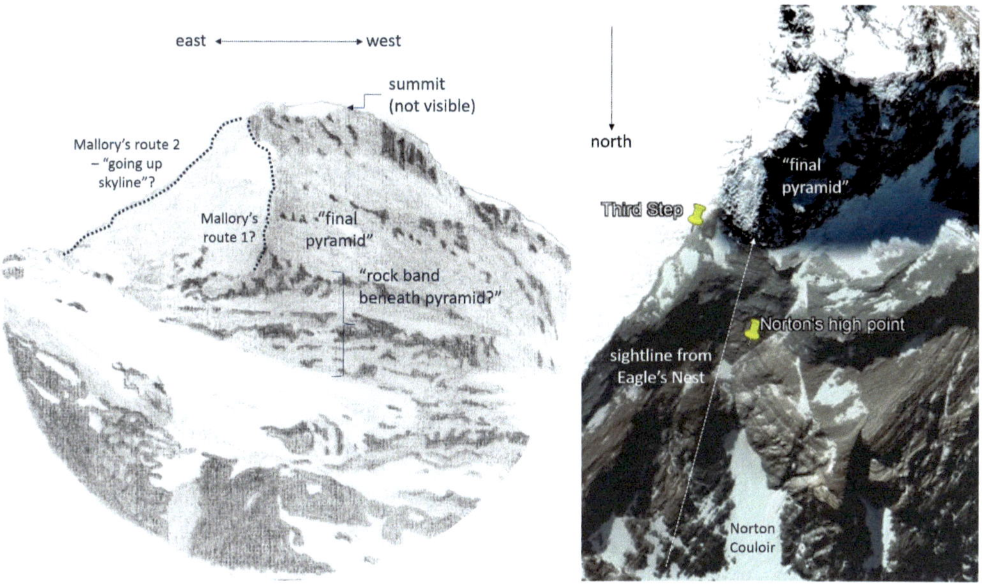

Figure 9.6a. The 'final pyramid' of Mount Everest, as defined by the 1924 expedition. (left) Author, after a photograph by John Noel; (right) base image © CNES / Airbus / Google Earth, 2021. Graphics and legend by author)

Figure 9.6b. The 'final pyramid' of Mount Everest, viewed from the plateau between the Second and Third Steps. (Stuart Holmes. Graphics and legend by author)

Mallory's note to Noel said nothing *per se* regarding the route whereby he would arrive at the snowfield.

However, Mallory also referred to the 'gully'. This was emphatically part of the 1924 climbers' vocabulary; they also knew it as the Couloir. It is the immense gully which can be seen on every photograph of Everest from the north; it runs from just below the summit pyramid down to the Rongbuk Glacier, a drop of around 9,000 feet.

Later, the gully would be universally known as the Norton Couloir, after Colonel Norton who entered it on his high climb on 4 June 1924, and could find no safe way up and out. The Norton Couloir was outside the frame of Noel's telephoto; Norton's high point was about 500 feet horizontally from, and about 350 feet below, the closest point on the final pyramid. When Norton reached his high point he was alone, and he was faced with a section of steep and crumbly rock that he could not attempt; he made the decision to turn around.

As Noel understood him, Mallory was clearly considering a route through the gully, but he surely did not want to reach the same impasse as Norton. His plan seemed to anticipate a way up and out of the gully at a different point from where Norton had run out of options.

Summit day

With that, our story resumes on summit day, 8 June 1924.

The camp diary for that day, maintained by Hazard, reads in part as follows:

> *'Min. night temp. = Ther [Thermometer] removed. Cloudy, occasional gusts of wind.*
> *08.30 [8:30 am] Air temp. = 28°F. Sun [temp] = 81°F. Mist, mountain almost entirely obscured, calm and very close.*
>
> *12 noon. Air temp. = 36°F. Sun [temp] = over 125[F.] (ceases to register). Calm, very close, mountain mist. ...*
>
> *16.00 hrs [4:00 pm]. Air temp. 29°F. Sun [temp] = 48°F. Calm, clouds inclined to lift, patches of dew etc.'*[20]

In short, a cool, calm and misty day at Camp IV: no cause for alarm.

In the tent at their Camp VI, Mallory and Irvine were alone on the mountain. The nearest human being was Odell, some 2,000 feet below; they had no means of communication with him. There is nothing on the record as to what Odell was supposed to do in case of any setback or emergency.

If the climbers' watches were still set to Darjeeling time (and there would have been no reason to reset them), the sun rose at 4:41 am. On that day, the moon would not rise until 9:25 am by Darjeeling time; they had no compass and probably no torch; therefore there was no reason to depart before sunrise. As a working assumption (and it is no more than that), we might place their departure at around 5 am.

When they emerged from their tent, Mallory and Irvine would have seen a panorama something like that in figure 9.7. From our foregoing analysis, we have reason to believe that the two climbers were at 27,300 feet. If so, their ascent to the summit constituted a

Figure 9.7. A view of the North Face (including part of the Yellow Band), part of the Northeast Ridge and the summit of Everest from the approximate position of Norton's and Somervell's Camp VI. (Michael Tracy)

climb of 1,700 vertical feet. We might reasonably expect that Mallory had allowed for an ascent rate of 300 feet per hour, with judicious use of oxygen and some provision for route-finding; therefore he would expect a climb of under six hours.

As for the descent: sunset by Darjeeling time would be at 6.29 pm.

Mallory would be aware that on 4 June, Norton had descended from his high point, in the gully, to Camp VI in two and a half hours, in a very weak physical condition (as Norton himself would later testify)[21]. The descent from the summit to the level of the gully might need an hour. Mallory might have judged himself and Irvine to be in better condition than Norton and Somervell had been; if so, he might have planned on a descent of three hours from the summit to his own Camp VI, if that was where he planned to spend the night of 8 June.

In this case, the turnaround time at the summit should not be later than 3:30 pm.

We might ponder whether at this juncture, Mallory had to make a strategic decision on the route to the summit. From everything that Mallory ever wrote about the route (as distinct from what others attributed to him), we would have to say no: that he had made his strategic decision long before. To reconstruct Mallory's strategy for summit day, we have only to read what he had set down on paper about the route to the summit.[22]

On the back of a postcard that he sent to Marjorie Holmes, probably sometime in 1923, Mallory had written:

> *'This was taken on one of the great days of discovery 1921 when we decided that the east face & N.E. ridge were alike impossible.'*[23]

In the official account of the 1921 reconnaissance expedition, Mallory had written:

> *'If ever the mountain were to be climbed, the way would not lie along the whole length of any one of its colossal ridges. Progress could only be made along comparatively easy ground, and anything like a prolonged,*

sharp crest or a series of towers would inevitably bar the way, simply by the time which would be required to overcome such obstacles.'[24]

In 1922, relating the story of his high climb with Norton and Somervell, he had written:

> *'... it will readily be understood that there was no question for us of gymnastic struggles and strong arm-pulls, wedging ourselves in cracks and hanging on our finger-tips. We should soon have been turned back by difficulties of that sort. We could allow ourselves nothing in the nature of violent struggle. We must avoid any hasty movement.'*[25]

Finally, in his hundreds of pages of contributions to official reports, lectures, interviews and letters to his wife and friends, Mallory never once used the term 'First Step' or 'Second Step'. The modern term 'Third Step' did not exist in 1924; Mallory would have seen that formation through binoculars, and would have considered it part of the 'final pyramid'.

From the documentation in the public domain, there is no evidence that Mallory ever contemplated climbing the First Step or the Second Step, or in taking any prolonged route along the crest of the Northeast Ridge.

Conversely, there was one tangible obstacle in Mallory's mind: and that was the summit pyramid, or as Noel would call it, the 'final pyramid'. In 1921, Mallory had observed it; he had this to say:

> *'The summit itself is like a thin edge of a wedge thrust up from the mass in which it is embedded. The edge of it, with the highest point at the far end, can only be reached in the northeast by climbing a steep blind edge of snow. ... it never looked anything but steep.'*[26]
>
> *'... the projected route to the summit presents no slopes of terrible steepness. ... [but] the snow slope which guards the very citadel will prove ... as steep as one would wish to find the final slope of any great mountain.'*[27]

In short, in the course of hundreds of observations of the mountain, from afar and from close up, and from surely hundreds of hours of discussion and debate with his colleagues, Mallory had no doubt that he could reach the pyramid. Only the pyramid gave him pause.

When he spoke about the 'blind edge' on the northeast, he surely meant what Noel would later call the 'eastern ridge', which is perpetually corniced with snow. Through these treacherous cornices, an unwary climber could fall fourteen thousand feet down the eastern face of Everest: what modern climbers call the Kangshung Face. It would be logical for him to tell Noel to look for him on a route to climber's right (to the north): one more exposed to the west wind, but offering a climb on rock rather than snow.

The Norton route

We may then ponder whether there was a specific route in Mallory's mind. Here we can only reconstruct what Mallory knew for sure on the morning of 8 June: that Norton had taken a route that led to within 900 vertical feet of the summit; that no-one else had found a viable route; and that at the end of Norton's route, a lone climber could go no higher and no farther.

On the evening of 4 June, alone with the snow-blind Norton in their tent at Camp IV, Mallory would have absorbed, and surely would have memorized, every step of Norton's route: every slab, every buttress, every obstacle, every landmark. It would have been either a template, or an exclusion, for his own climb.

We can be sure that at some moment in time, Mallory or Irvine was up to 200 feet above Norton's route. We know this because, as we shall relate in chapter 11, during the 1933 expedition Percy Wyn Harris found an ice axe, Mallory's or Irvine's, either 200 or 250 yards north-east of the First Step and some sixty feet below the crest of the ridge. When Norton passed those points, he was about 250 feet below the crest.[28] What we do not know is whether the person who had carried the ice axe, and who had dropped it or set it down at that point, was Mallory or Irvine; and whether he had passed that point on the ascent or the descent (or even on the day before summit day).

We can probably exclude the idea that Mallory would wish to converge on Norton's route and follow it to Norton's high point. Where Norton had been unable to climb alone, we can reasonably surmise that Mallory would not want to try, alone or with Irvine. He had already, in his letters, ruled out heroics, gymnastics and finger-holds.

We can probably also exclude Mallory's following the Norton route for some way, but with a view to breaking out and upwards before the couloir. We can surely suppose that on the night of 4 June, Mallory had interrogated Norton for every possible exit

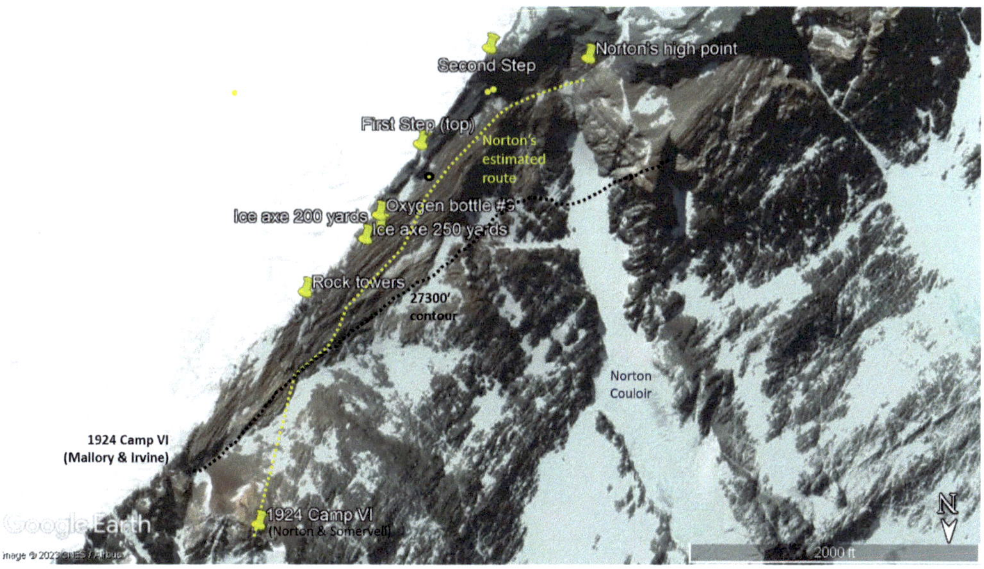

Figure 9.8. An approximation of Colonel Norton's ascent route from his Camp VI to his claimed high point of 28,126 feet on 4 June 1924; and a hypothetical traverse from Mallory's and Irvine's high camp along the 27,300-foot contour. (Base image © CNES / Airbus / Google Earth; contour line by author from Contour Map Creator; graphics and legend by author. The author acknowledges Michael Tracy's inspiration for this image)

from the route; and Norton would have said that there was none. Norton would be proved right in 1933, when Wager, Wyn Harris and Smythe would all follow his route to the bitter end, and would turn around approximately where he had turned around.

We can still imagine, on behalf of Mallory, at least two tactical alternatives to Norton's route:

- He could choose to remain parallel to Norton's route but higher, in order to avoid the Couloir completely and to reach the final pyramid above the point where Norton had been blocked.
- He could choose to parallel Norton's route but lower, which would take him into the Couloir below Norton's point of turnaround.

To this author's knowledge, no climber has ever attempted the first variant. Modern climbers with few exceptions, and all of those on commercial expeditions, follow the crest of the Northeast Ridge; they bypass the First Step, climb the Second Step via the 'Chinese ladder', scramble easily over the Third Step, and traverse the snowfield on the pyramid, to the Dihedral and the summit.

As we shall see later in this chapter, the second variant is an approximation of Reinhold Messner's climb of 1980, which began with a shallow traverse across the North Face, and ended with a successful exit from the Couloir. If Mallory had had the inspiration that Messner would have in 1980, he and Irvine would have started out with a horizontal traverse from their high camp; they would have followed the contour at 27,300 feet all the way across the North Face, keeping to the foot of the Yellow Band; and they would have entered the Couloir close to the point where Messner, fifty-six years later, would find the exit.

This route would have taken an extraordinary act of inspiration on Mallory's part. At every point on the traverse, there would have been the temptation to climb leftwards and upwards, as Norton had done and as all three climbers in 1933 would do. Yet Mallory might have known, just as Messner would know, that such a course was wrong; he had to stay low down on the North Face.

If Mallory and Irvine did this (and to be clear, on the evidence that exists, we have no way to know), they would have found the exit from the Couloir, as Messner would do; they would have circumvented the crumbly Yellow Band and arrived at the grey band above it; and once there, a leftward traverse to the Third Step would have placed them briefly in Odell's field of view.

Odell's sighting

Odell would later relate that he had seen Mallory and Irvine at 12:50 pm on 8 June, in a fleeting interval when the clouds cleared around the summit. Odell's sighting is central to the mystery of Mallory and Irvine. What we make of his sighting is crucial to our interpretation of the story. His narrative deserves and requires a chapter of this book, and it will follow.

Here we shall only observe that later in 1924, the London newspaper *The Sphere*, an imprint of *The Illustrated London News*, wanted to run a two-page illustrated article on the Everest expedition, and specifically on the question of whether Mallory and Irvine had climbed Everest. Their artist Douglas MacPherson was tasked with creating an impression of Odell's sighting; *The Sphere* asked for Odell's collaboration, and

Figure 9.9. Artist's impression of Odell's last sighting of Mallory and Irvine. (Douglas MacPherson / *The Sphere*, 25 October 1924, public domain)

Odell agreed. The article appeared in the issue of 25 October 1924, under the heading 'Has Everest been climbed? — a mystery which the death of Mallory and Irvine leaves unsolved', and with the subtitle 'Mr. Odell's story of how he witnessed the two climbers approaching 'the citadel' at the summit of Mount Everest before they were overwhelmed is now being told in London'.[29]

An extract from MacPherson's drawing is reproduced in Figure 9.9.

We can readily observe that MacPherson made some effort to create a perspective that corresponded to Odell's vantage point, in at least two respects:

- Odell had been at an altitude, by his own account, of at least 26,100 feet: about 4,000 feet higher than Noel (so that the true summit was visible to him, and not hidden as it was from Noel's 'Eagle's Nest').
- Odell had been about a mile to the southwest of Noel, and to the left of Noel's line of sight; therefore the summit snowfield appeared more face-on to him than it did to Noel.

Following Odell's narrative, MacPherson's drawing showed the climbers at two points, annotated in tiny letters 'first position' and 'second position'. We are entitled to read the drawing as a depiction of the two climbers below, and then above, what we now call the Third Step. The reader may judge.

Odell's first search

At the time of his sighting, Odell probably knew the contents of Mallory's note to Noel. He would later record that he had been 'surprised' to see them there (wherever 'there' was) as late as 12:50 pm, and he made a specific reference to the presumed lookout time of 8 am.[30]

At this stage, nothing in Odell's narrative conveys that he was alarmed. His account relates that after some time peering through the clouds, he continued his climb to Camp VI, and reached it at 2 pm. That interval alone tells us that the camp was not far above the point of his sighting; MacPherson's illustration in *The Sphere* made the camp appear not more than fifty feet above that point, and Odell did not correct it.

The remainder of Odell's first search may be briefly told. In the empty tent at Camp VI, he found 'a rather mixed assortment of spare clothes, scraps of food, their [he meant: Mallory's and Irvine's] two sleeping-bags, oxygen cylinders, and parts of apparatus; outside were more parts of the latter and of the duralumin carriers.'[31] He never recorded how many cylinders were there, and whether they were full or not; but none of this caused him concern. Recalling Mallory's instructions to evacuate Camp V, he left Camp VI at 4:30 pm, passed Camp V at 6:15 pm without stopping, and executed a 'fast standing glissade' in the snow down to Camp IV: literally, he slid down the mountain in a standing position. He reached Camp IV at 6:45 pm, sixteen minutes after sunset.

Had Mallory intended to bypass both Camp VI and Camp V, and return directly to Camp IV (as his note to Odell could be construed), and had he known how fast the descent from Camp VI to Camp IV could be (as perhaps he did), he might have permitted himself a turnaround time of 1:30 pm at the summit. But Odell's sighting of him and Irvine at 12:50 pm excludes that possibility; they could not have made the summit in less than two hours, say by 2:50 pm; that would make Camp VI the only safe destination for the return.

The tragedy

Of the further events of Mallory's and Irvine's climb, we know nothing, and without descending into speculation, we can say nothing. We can only return to Noel, to whom the task fell to record the disaster. In his eventual memoirs, he called it 'the culminating tragedy'; his phrase seems to imply that he had seen it coming. These are his words:

> '[8 June] *'8 a.m. went by, then 10 a.m., and clouds and mist then obscured the whole summit ridge.'*
>
> [8 June] *'They were going strong, as Odell described, when within 600 feet of [the summit].'*
>
> [9 June] *'There was no message even from the support party. ... The silence of the support party meant, we hoped, that they had gone out to search.'*
>
> [10 June] *'Two whole days and nights had now gone by, with hope fading at every hour. Norton, recovered sufficiently from snow-blindness, paced backwards and forwards in front of his tent, speaking little, visibly affected and, I think, already resigned to the worst.'*
>
> [10 June] *'... our watchers at the telescope called out that they saw figures on the crest of the Ice Cliff [Camp IV]! We riveted our eyes to the cliff-top. We saw through the telescope distinctly a line of men returning and entering the camp. ... It was Odell with his support party. ... I saw them place six blankets in the form of a cross. Then they went away.'*[32]

Postscript: out of the Couloir

As we observed above: we do not know whether Mallory and Irvine, on their way to the point where Odell saw them, entered the Norton Couloir; and if they did, how they climbed out of it. No-one alive has climbed a route from the Couloir to any rock step on the Northeast Ridge.

However, according to Elizabeth Hawley's Himalayan Database, six persons in history have climbed out of the Couloir to the summit. Their names, and the dates when they reached the summit, are as follows:

• Reinhold Messner	20 August 1980
• Timothy John Macartney-Snape	3 October 1984
• Gregory (Greg) Mortimer	3 October 1984
• Philip Michael (Phil) Ershler	20 October 1984
• Battista (Battistino) Bonali	17 May 1991
• Leopold Sulovsky	17 May 1991.

Two of these climbs – that of Messner, and that of Macartney-Snape and Mortimer – are sufficiently well documented that we could productively examine their routes, as models for where Mallory and Irvine might possibly have gone.

Messner

Reinhold Messner's climb on 20 August 1980 entered mountaineering legend as the first solo ascent of Mount Everest. The fact that he did it without oxygen made it doubly extraordinary. Previously, only he and Peter Habeler had reached the summit of Everest without oxygen (in 1978); and some climbers had disputed their achievement.

The story of the 1980 climb has been told brilliantly by Messner himself.[33] Here, we are interested solely in his route. In particular, we shall endeavour to learn how he succeeded where Norton in 1924, and Wager, Wyn Harris and Smythe in 1933, had all failed: namely, in climbing out of the Couloir.

We are indebted to Michael Tracy for his insight into Messner's strategy:

> *'In planning a climb without oxygen, you want to push as much difficult climbing as low down as possible. If you have a choice of traversing first and then climbing, or climbing first and then traversing, without oxygen you will always traverse first and then climb.'*[34]

This is what Messner did. He pitched his penultimate camp on the North Ridge, at 7,800m (25,591 feet). On 19 August 1980, on breaking camp, instead of continuing up the North Ridge towards the Northeast Ridge, as all the climbers of 1922 and 1924 had done, he immediately began a shallow traverse towards the Norton Couloir. In the first part of his traverse, he was following the example of the 1933 expedition, who had also set out westwards across the North face. But where the 1933 climbers turned southwards and upwards to the site of their eventual Camp VI, Messner continued low down and westwards. His traverse covered a horizontal distance of about 4,000 feet.

Figure 9.10. The approximate route of Messner on 19-20 August 1980 from his camp at 25,591 feet to the summit. (Base image © CNES / Airbus / Google Earth; contour lines by author from Contour Map Creator; graphics and legend by author; geolocations by author based on Reinhold Messner, *Der gläserne Horizont*)

When Messner pitched his high camp, near the eastern edge of the Couloir, his altimeter read 8,220m (26,969 feet). He had climbed a vertical distance of 420m (1,378 feet), and was below the altitude where Mallory and Irvine had made their Camp VI. Like Mallory and Irvine, he had around 2,000 vertical feet to climb; but he was only 2,500 feet horizontally from the summit. Like Mallory and Irvine, he was in uncharted territory, where no climber had set foot.

Messner, in his book *Der gläserne Horizont*, never delineated his route. His high camp can be geolocated by reference to the eastern rim of the Couloir and the 8200m contour. From then on, we are dependent on his account in *Der gläserne Horizont.* The following is this author's interpretaion of the original German text.

Messner recalled that an hour after he left his camp at about 27,000 feet, he came up against a cliff which he estimated at 100m (330 feet) in height, or possibly 200m (660 feet). At this point the Couloir formed 'a pear-shaped bay'. He climbed out of the Couloir to the west (climber's right), aiming for a 'blunt ridge' or 'blunt rib'; it is possible that his exit was via what modern climbers call 'the subsidiary couloir'. He subsequently continued along the ridge, avoiding snow slopes. After about an hour, he encountered 'a dark vertical rock wall', which he passed to the left. He traversed upwards for a further three hours, on what he described as a 'knife edge', moving always to the right. He reached the crest of the ridge, and continued westwards. Shortly afterwards, he arrived at the tripod that the Chinese expedition had installed in 1975. He was at the summit.

The cliff at the head of the Couloir, the 'pear-shaped bay', and the 'dark vertical wall' seem to be identifiable on Google Earth; the 'blunt ridge', 'blunt rib' and 'knife edge', to this author's eye, are not. Above the Couloir, Messner's route is necessarily conjecture. This author's approximation is presented in Figure 9.10. What matters for our reconstruction of Mallory's and Irvine's opportunities is as follows:

- There was a way out of the Couloir, but it was lower than Norton's high point.
- The exit was on the western rim of the Couloir; it led to a point on the final pyramid, approximately to the north of the summit.
- There were no difficulties in the climb, beyond route-finding and physical endurance.

Mallory and Irvine started on 8 June 1924 from their Camp VI which, by our calculations, was at 27,300 feet. In order for them to intersect with Messner's route, at some point they would have had to act counter-intuitively and stay on a horizontal contour; possibly even *descend.* If they had done this, they could have entered the Couloir somewhere near Messner's high camp, around 27,000 feet.

If they had found Messner's exit route; and if they had followed it as far as the final pyramid, they would then have had to traverse to the southeast, across the base of the pyramid to what is now called the Third Step, in order to be seen by Odell at 12:50 pm. Here we might observe that if at some point they had made the inspired decision to stay low on the North Face, it might explain why Odell saw them so late in the day.

In terms of time: Messner referred to one hour between his high camp and his exit from the Couloir; an hour along the 'blunt rib' to the dark wall; and then three hours on the 'knife edge'. Perhaps we can guess at six hours from his high camp at 26,969 feet to the summit at 29,032 feet: an average of something like 340 vertical feet per hour. Mallory and Irvine, when Odell saw them at 12:50 pm, had between 600 and 800 feet to go; and unlike Messner, they had oxygen. At Messner's climbing rate, they could have reached the summit by 3:30 pm. More than this, we cannot say.

Macartney-Snape and Mortimer

The other documented route to the summit from the Couloir is that of the Australian team Macartney-Snape and Mortimer, in 1984. We are fortunate to have an account of that route, in *White Limbo*, by Lincoln Hall who was a member of their party. Hall described their strategy and drew a map of their high camp and their ascent and descent routes. He wrote:

> *'... we would ... follow the Great Couloir to within eight hundred metres of the top [2,625 vertical feet, i.e. an altitude of 26,400 feet]. The last major obstacle was the steep rock section which ended the Couloir. The barrier of the Yellow Band, as the cliff was known, extended right around the summit pyramid.'*[35]

From Hall's map we observe the following similarities and differences between their climb and Messner's:

- Like Messner, the party made a strategic decision to approach the summit via the upper reaches of the Norton Couloir.
- Unlike Messner, rather than traversing the North Face, they chose to climb substantially the whole of the upper section of the Couloir.

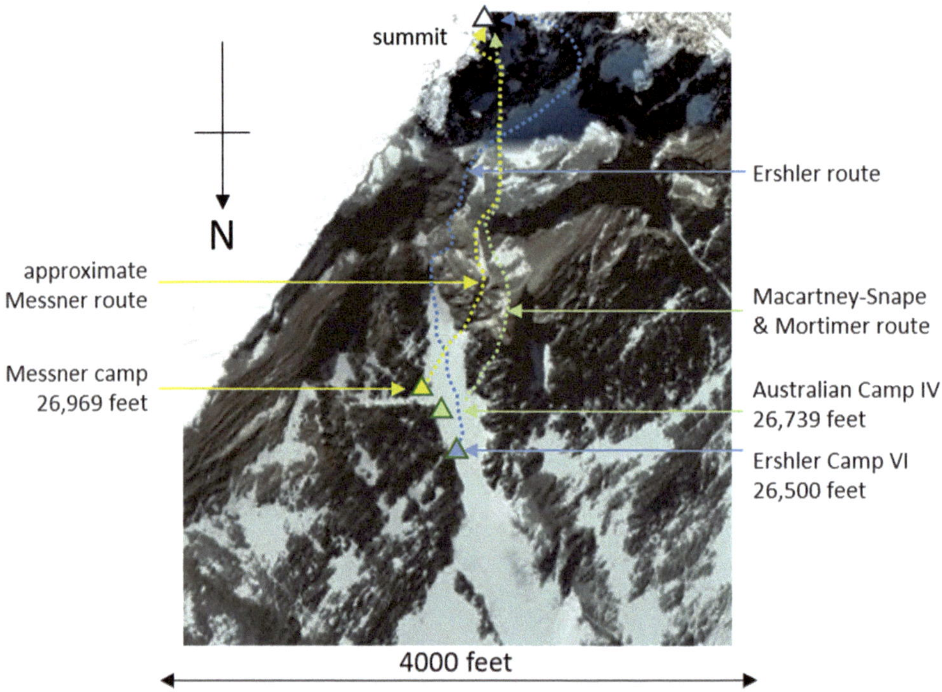

Figure 9.11. *Above*: Approximate ascent routes from the Couloir to the summit: Messner (1980), Macartney-Snape and Mortimer (1984), Ershler (1984). (Base image © CNES / Airbus / Google Earth; graphics and legend by author; routes by author based on Reinhold Messner, *Der gläserne Horizont*; Lincoln Hall, *White Limbo*; and Phil Ershler, personal correspondence)

Figure 9.12. Mallory and Irvine on the 1924 expedition. (Author, after a photograph by John Noel)

- Their Camp IV was also on the eastern rim of the Couloir. It was at 8,150m (26,739 feet), about 660 feet below the headwall and 230 feet below Messner's high camp.
- They also chose, rather than attempt the steep headwall of the Couloir, to climb out via the western rim. This was the most difficult part of the climb; Macartney-Snape described it as 'very, very steep for this altitude and very broken'.[36]
- They evidently reached Messner's 'dark vertical wall', and like him, they skirted it to the left.
- Subsequently, their route to the summit was broadly similar to Messner's, as far as we can tell from Messner's description; but possibly more to the east (climber's left).
- Apart from the exit from the Couloir, no part of the ascent was described as difficult or dangerous.

Macartney-Snape and Mortimer left their Camp IV at about 11:00 am. Climbing without oxygen, they reached the summit at about 8:15 pm. Hall wrote that they had been delayed by 'more involved climbing' on two rock strata on the western ridge.[37] Their ascent rate had been about 245 vertical feet per hour: somewhat slower than Messner's. They descended in darkness, guided by their headlamps, the lights from colleagues at Camp IV, and radio contact. Mallory and Irvine had had no such resources.

Shortly after Macartney-Snape's and Mortimer's ascent, Phil Ershler became the fourth person to climb successfully from the Couloir to the summit. He took a direct route through the Yellow Band, at the headwall of the Couloir. In the Yellow Band, he had the benefit of a fixed rope which the Australians had left in place; Mallory and Irvine would not have been so fortunate. Above the Couloir, the climb was hard work but not difficult.

In short, the climbs of 1984 provided a further demonstration that there were straightforward technical routes from the Couloir to the summit. If Mallory and Irvine had found any variation on those routes, or another route of their own devising, they would have reached the summit in daylight with several hours to spare. If so, disaster befell them on the descent; but in what form, we still do not know.

Chapter 10

Odell

To students of the mystery of Mallory and Irvine, the word 'Odell' defines the subject of discussion. The premise is simply stated: on 8 June 1924 at 12:50 pm, in a brief interval when the clouds parted, Noel Odell believed that he saw Mallory and Irvine climbing a rock step, high on the Northeast Ridge of Mount Everest.

Debate has raged to this day. Where was Odell when he made his famous sighting? Did he see anything, or was he deceived by an optical illusion? If he saw Mallory and Irvine, where were they? Was it the First Step, the Second Step, or the (then unrecognized) Third? If the Second (as Odell first affirmed, then qualified with doubts, and would finally insist), how could they have climbed an unclimbable wall? Were they irretrievably behind schedule … or not? Did they even have a schedule? Was Odell later pressured to change his story? On the position that one takes on these questions (for, on the available data, there are no answers), hinges the mystery as it is conventionally expressed: as to whether Mallory and Irvine were the first to stand at the highest point in the world.

In this chapter we shall set out the facts as known, and what we think are the physical limits of the possible. The opinions of contemporary and modern climbers, researchers and historians can be found elsewhere. An assessment of Mallory's and Irvine's climbing capabilities is outside our expertise. A reconstruction of the personalities, agenda and motivations, whether those of the climbers or of others who wished to define the narrative, is not part of our brief. All of these, we shall leave aside.

Odell

Noel Ewart Odell, at the time of the 1924 expedition, was thirty-three years old. He had graduated from the Royal School of Mines, where his specialization had been geology. His studies had been interrupted by the First World War, in which he had served and fought as an officer of the Royal Engineers. He had been a member of the Alpine Club since 1916 and had several respected climbing accomplishments to his credit.

After the 1924 expedition, Odell was a candidate to be a climbing member of the next expedition, which was scheduled for 1933. He withdrew for personal or business reasons.[1] He re-applied for the expedition of 1936 but was excluded, to his bitter regret.[2] However, he was accepted as a member of the 1938 expedition led by Bill Tilman. The reports of that expedition are imprecise as to Odell's role, but it appears that his highest point was Camp IV on the North Col,[3] probably around 23,000 feet, which was far below what he had achieved in 1924.

Figure 10.1. Noel Odell imagined at the moment of his sighting on June 8, 1924. (Author)

Later in life, he would earn his doctorate in geomorphology at Cambridge University, where he would make his career. In his long life, his greatest claim to fame was that he had been the last man to see Mallory and Irvine alive.

The facts of Odell's sighting are best presented through the contemporary accounts; and the closer the account to the event, the more confidence we may reasonably place in it. Here we shall draw especially on the 'Mount Everest Dispatches', as communicated by Colonel Edward Norton to *The Times* of London and to the Royal Geographical Society during the summer of 1924; *The Geographical Journal* of August 1924 and December 1924; and *The Fight For Everest 1924*, authored primarily by Norton and published in 1925.

Odell's climb to Camp VI

On 8 June 1924, Odell left Camp V at 8 am or a little after[4]. The camp was on the North Ridge, a little to the east (leeward) side of the crest, at an altitude of 25,300 feet.[5] By this time Odell had read, or at least had heard of, Mallory's ebullient note of 7 June addressed to the photographer John Noel. He therefore knew, or expected, that Mallory and Irvine had set off from their Camp VI and were somewhere on their ascent towards the summit.

As far as the record shows, Odell had only one specific mission in support of Mallory and Irvine: to deliver to their Camp VI, as per Mallory's request, the prismatic compass which Mallory had left at Camp V.

We do not know whether Mallory had told Odell, or indeed anyone, of his plan for a higher camp, well above Norton's site. Noel knew (as we learned in Chapter 9), because he had been following Mallory and Irvine by telescope; but Noel was in Camp III and Odell was in Camp V, which might as well have been on another planet.

Odell himself had been one of the two candidates to join Mallory on the final summit attempt, the other being Irvine; but Mallory had chosen Irvine. By any objective criterion, Odell was a far better climber than Irvine; but if he was dismayed by Mallory's decision, he never in his life said so. In any case, his agenda for 8 June 1924 had another dimension. Odell would write in his own words in the 'Mount Everest Dispatches' under the dateline 14 June 1924:

> *'At early morning of June 8 it was clear and not unduly cold at such an altitude. ... I especially wished to be free during an ascent I was to make*

for as wide a geological survey of the mountain face between Camps V. and VI. as possible.'[6]

In *The Geographical Journal* of December 1924, Odell elaborated a little on his plans for that fateful day. He would not follow the direct route from Camp V to Camp VI along the crest of the North Ridge, but would traverse initially towards the west, in the direction of the summit:

'After a breakfast ... I started my solitary climb to Camp VI., taking with me provisions for that camp in case of need. My plan was to make a rather circuitous route out on to the northern face, to examine the structure of the mountain.'[7]

Apart from the compass, Odell's writings give no indication that he was expected to deliver anything else, or do anything specific in support of Mallory and Irvine. The provisions that he mentioned seem to have been for himself. He never recorded what those provisions had been. His accounts imply that he had brought an altimeter; and as we shall see, he apparently carried binoculars. Since the weather was overcast, we can also surmise that Odell had no particular expectation of seeing Mallory and Irvine on the ascent:

'Soon after I had started on my task banks of cloud began to form ... Now and then there would be an accompaniment of sleet and light snow. I could see above me frequently during these squalls that there was a glow of light, indicating clearness at a higher altitude, ...'[8]

We know however that Odell had the intention to arrive at Camp VI. For a moment, let us fast-forward to his arrival.

'I continued my way up to Camp VI., and [arrived] there two o'clock.'[9]

But which Camp VI? Odell's accounts tell us that he found only one, and (as we shall see shortly) he found oxygen cylinders inside and pieces of oxygen apparatus outside, testifying that Mallory and Irvine had occupied it. As we calculated in Chapter 9, Mallory's Camp VI was probably just under the Northeast Shoulder, at 27,300 feet.

There is one piece of Odell's account that implies that he knew that Mallory's Camp VI was at 27,300 feet. Of his night at Camp V at 25,300 feet, on 7 June 1924, he wrote:

'I knew with what hopeful feelings and exultant cheer Mallory and Irvine would take their last look around before closing themselves in their tiny tent at [Camp] VI that night. ... I was 2,000 feet lower down the mountain-side than they ...'[10]

Odell did indeed arrive at Mallory's Camp VI; and in so doing, he made a vertical ascent of 2,000 feet in six hours or a little less. He therefore climbed at an average of 340 feet per hour, or more: a brisk pace for a climb with mainly geological objectives, but not extraordinary, and not difficult for a man of Odell's strength and fitness. This rate of ascent is significant because in a moment, it will help us delimit the location of Odell's sighting, to which we now return.

The break in the clouds

In contemporary reports, Odell related his sighting of Mallory and Irvine on at least four occasions: in 'The Mount Everest Dispatches', No. 9, dated 14 June 1924 and reprinted in *The Geographical Journal* of August 1924; in *The Alpine Journal* with the same dateline (and with almost identical wording); again in *The Geographical Journal* of December 1924, with additional recollections and a subtly different wording; and in a chapter of Norton's *The Fight For Everest 1924*, published in 1925, wherein Odell largely retained his wording of December 1924. This author's view is that what Odell wrote on 14 June 1924 is as authoritative a version as we shall ever see.

With that, we can find no better words than those of Odell:

> *'At 12.50, just after I had emerged in a state of jubilation at finding the first definite fossils on Everest, there was a sudden clearing of the atmosphere, and the entire summit ridge and final peak of Everest were unveiled. My eyes became fixed on one tiny black spot silhouetted on a small snowcrest beneath a rock-step in the ridge, and the black spot moved. Another black spot became apparent and moved up the snow to join the other on the crest. The first then approached the great rock-step and shortly emerged at the top; the second did likewise. Then the whole fascinating vision vanished, enveloped in cloud once more.'*[11]

Odell went on to describe what seemed a quite specific location for the climbers:

> *'... The place on the ridge mentioned is a prominent rock-step at a very short distance from the base of the final pyramid, ...'*[12]

However, by December 1924, Odell's narrative had acquired a certain hesitancy about the second climber, and a note of alarm:

> *'I noticed far away on a snow-slope leading up to the last step but one from the base of the final pyramid,* a tiny object moving and approaching the rock step. A second object followed, and then the first climbed to the top of the step. As I stood intently watching this dramatic appearance, the scene became enveloped in cloud, and I could not actually be certain that I saw the second figure join the first. I was surprised above all to see them so late as this, namely 12.50, at a point that according to Mallory's schedule should have been reached by 10 a.m. at latest.'*

Odell's reference to '10 am' is presumably an extrapolation from Mallory's mention of '8.0' [am]. There is no surviving document in which Mallory proposed to be anywhere at 10 am on 8 June.

Moreover, the references to a 'prominent rock step' and 'a very short distance' had disappeared; and Odell now took issue with a previous interpretation of his sighting. The asterisk in his report led to a footnote where he insisted:

> '* *Not the position indicated in illustration Geogr. Journ. [Geographical Journal] Vol.64 No.2 [August 1924], opposite p. 160, but the rock step to the left of this beyond the snow patch.*'[13]

Here we reproduce the relevant part of the illustration to which Odell objected. It was indeed in *The Geographical Journal* of August 1924, opposite page 160. The caption reads in part: 'Telephotograph of the summit of Mount Everest taken from the Base Camp in 1922'. In other words, the underlying photograph was more than two years old when it was published.

Odell had originally said that he had seen two tiny figures crossing a snowfield and then climbing a rock step; the last position (or at least that of one of them) had been at the crest of the step. He now identified that step as the Second Step. He was implying that there had been a snowfield *below* the Second Step. There is no such snowfield in the 1922 telephoto; but that does not exclude a snowfield there in 1924.

Had he wished, Odell could have added that *The Geographical Journal* had also mis-identified the high point reached by Norton and Somervell on 4 June 1924. Norton's high point was not on the Northeast Ridge, but in the Great Couloir, about 1,000 feet west of the point shown in the *Geographical Journal*.

Mallory and Irvine's last known position, as seen by Odell, was later assigned an altitude of 28,227 feet, on the basis of measurements with the theodolite, taken by Hazard from Base Camp.[14] This was consistent with later measurements of the altitude of the Second Step. The 1924 expedition did not calibrate the Second Step, but Michael Spender's map of 1936 placed the base of the Second Step at 28,140 feet. Since the Step

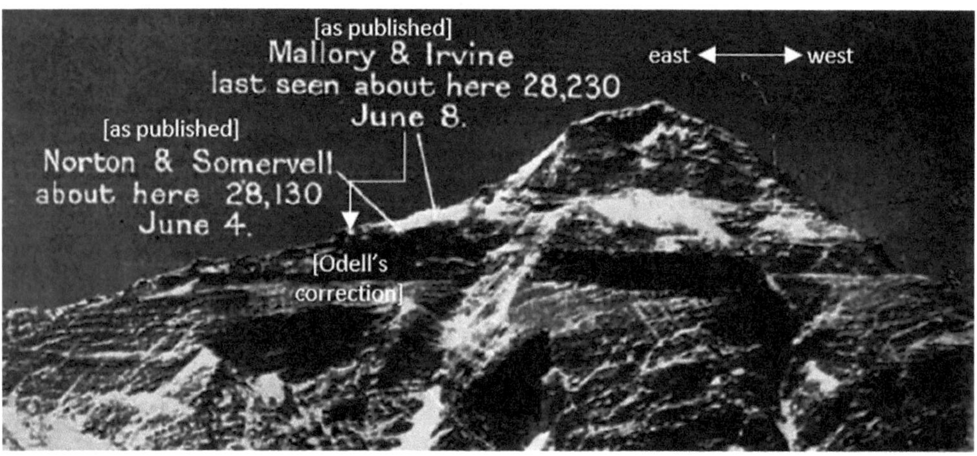

Figure 10.2. Mallory's and Irvine's last known location, as published by *The Geographical Journal*, Vol.64, No.2 (August 1924), and as corrected or disputed by Odell. (Base image and original annotations by (probably) John Noel; additional graphics by author)

is conventionally viewed as about 100 feet high (depending on where one defines the base), the crest would have been at about 28,240 feet by Spender's calibration.

In short, Odell's early narrations of his sighting placed the climbers squarely at the crest of the Second Step, though without ever naming the step. Then why the controversy?

Firstly, Odell's identification of the Second Step would open a debate as to what he meant by the distance from the base of the pyramid. The Second Step is about 1,620 feet horizontally from the summit[15]. Reasonable persons may differ on the location of the base of the pyramid; this author would use the Third Step as a reference and would locate the eastern base of the pyramid about 1,050 feet horizontally from the summit. In that case, the Second Step is about 570 feet horizontally from the base of the pyramid. Could that be considered 'a very short distance'?

Secondly, there began, and there remains, a more virulent debate about Mallory's climbing abilities. Many contemporary climbers believed, and many modern climbers believe, that Mallory could not have climbed the Second Step.

If Odell saw one of the climbers at the crest of the Second Step, it would follow that at least one of them must have climbed it. To diverge from that inference, we would have to disprove Odell's sighting; or to reinterpret it, or to relocate it.

The last step but one

Here, we come to our titular 'last step but one'.

Odell did not use this expression in his dispatch of 14 June 1924 when, as we may imagine, the events were fresh in his mind. He introduced it for the first time in his report 'The Last Climb of Mallory and Irvine', published in *The Geographical Journal* of December 1924. There, as we noted above, he referred to 'a snow-slope leading up to the last step but one from the base of the final pyramid'; and he was at pains to imply in the footnote that he meant the Second Step. We might nevertheless wonder why, if only for the avoidance of doubt, he did not name the step; the term 'Second Step' was certainly part of the 1924 climbers' vocabulary.

In *The Fight For Everest 1924*, to which Odell contributed Chapter 6, a further note of hesitancy appeared. Here he wrote of 'a snow slope leading up to *what seemed to me to be* the last step but one from the base of the final pyramid' (this author's italics). He went on to set the stage for what would become, in Everest legend, the scenario of Mallory's quixotic march to his doom:

> *'I was surprised above all to see them so late as this, namely 12.50, at a point which, if the 'second rock step,' they should have reached according to Mallory's schedule by 8 a.m. at latest, and if the 'first rock step' proportionately earlier.'*[16]

Odell here introduced the idea that possibly he had seen Mallory and Irvine, not at the Second Step about which he had been so emphatic in December 1924, but at the First Step. This location also was not calibrated in 1924, but in Spender's map of 1936, the base of the First Step was placed at 27,950 feet.

Odell could not know at what time Mallory and Irvine had left their Camp VI. Sunrise at Mount Everest on 8 June 1924 was at 4:41 am. by Darjeeling time (and we suppose, although it is nowhere stated, that the expedition members had kept their watches on that time).[17] He would be aware that there had been no moon before sunrise; so he might have assumed that the climbers had set off at about 5 am. An earlier time would have made no sense; the climbers would have had to make decisions on which route to adopt, and for that they would have needed light. A later departure would have eroded the margins of safety for a summit attempt: and Odell might wonder whether, in that situation, Mallory would have postponed the attempt until 9 June.

Odell evidently believed that Mallory intended to be at the final pyramid at 8 am.

> *'Before ... he left Camp VI Mallory had sent a note to Noel at Camp III saying he hoped to reach the foot of the final pyramid (about 28,300 feet odd) by 8 a.m.'*

But as we argued in Chapter 9, Mallory's note had not necessarily referred to the final pyramid; this was an assumption on the part of Odell; and the note had made no reference to any altitude.

Odell was a geologist and we may credit him with a mathematical mind. It may be productive to reconstruct his mental calculations in the aftermath of his sighting:

- He may have known, or had reason to believe, that Mallory's Camp VI was at 27,300 feet.
- He could reasonably have estimated Mallory's and Irvine's start time at 5 am.
- He believed that he had seen the climbers at between 28,200 and 28,400 feet at 12:50 pm.
- Therefore they had apparently climbed 900 to 1,100 vertical feet in seven hours and fifty minutes; an average ascent rate of 115 to 140 feet per hour. Such speeds were well below the slowest achieved on the expedition's previous climbs (although much faster than the last hour of Norton's high climb).

In this light, it is logical that Odell should be surprised to see the climbers where he saw them. Yet there is no sign that he was concerned for their safety. Perhaps there was nothing that he could do; he had no means of communication either with the climbers or with Camp IV. Perhaps he assumed that they would turn around at a logical moment.

What is more difficult to understand is why Odell should later introduce the Second Step and the First Step into the narrative. In all the records of the 1924 expedition, there is no discussion about the two Steps. We would surely surmise that there was no serious consideration of climbing them; they were obstacles to be avoided at all costs. Norton said as much:

> *'... a feature on the skyline ridge which we called the second step ... looked so formidable an obstacle where it crossed the ridge that we had chosen the lower route rather than try and surmount it at its highest point.'*[18]

For Odell to suggest that he had seen Mallory and Irvine at the Second Step was to imply, firstly, that they were taking a route that had no precedent and had not even been contemplated, much less debated, by other climbers; and secondly, that their ascent rate was even slower than if they had reached the base of the final pyramid. Suggesting the First Step would further amplify the mystery.

The narrative of the Steps would inevitably open a debate wherein others would perform similar calculations, and would extrapolate them. Those who favoured a sighting at the Second Step would conclude that Mallory and Irvine had been at about 28,140 feet[19]; at their average climb rate, they would need six and three quarter hours to reach the summit. That would place them at the top at 7:35 pm. It would be dark; sunset on 8 June 1924 would have been at 6.29 pm[20]. Those who favoured the First Step would posit a climb from 27,950 feet, requiring eight and a quarter hours, and implying an arrival at the summit at 9:05 pm. In both cases, the return to Camp VI (or to any other camp) would have to be by moonlight. On that day on Mount Everest, the moon would have risen at 9:25 am and would set at 11:47 pm.[21]

However, three crucial elements of data were missing: the time of Mallory's and Irvine's departure from their Camp VI; Odell's location when he made his sighting; and an unequivocal identification of the rock step which the climbers had surmounted. Absent these data, the debate could only become a contest of preconceived narratives. In that state, it has remained to this day.

The snowfield

Odell's narratives of June 1924 and December 1924 both left an anomaly unexplained. In both narratives, he spoke of the two tiny figures crossing a snowfield (he used the terms 'snow crest' and 'snow slope' respectively) before reaching the rock step. They were moving from east to west (from left to right from Odell's viewpoint, and in the illustration in *The Geographical Journal*). Therefore, the snowfield should have been to the east of the rock step (on the left in the illustration). But in that illustration, there is no snowfield to the east of the Second Step. There is however a prominent snowfield to the west of, and above, the Second Step, and this is where the designers of the illustration had placed Mallory and Irvine, to Odell's evident consternation.

Snowfields on Mount Everest are stable; they persist from year to year. John Noel, in 1922, took a telephoto of the North Face from Base Camp. In 1924, he annotated the photograph with his estimate of where Odell had seen Mallory and Irvine. That point looks like the crest of the Second Step, as Odell had said. He published the photograph, with his annotations, in his 1927 book *Through Tibet to Everest*, on page 285; we reproduce an extract in Figure 10.3. The snowfield from 1922 is above the Second Step and below what we now call the Third Step (a formation which, in 1924, had no name).

If therefore we treat the snowfield as the central element in Odell's observation, we are compelled to conclude that the rock step that he saw was not the Second Step, but (in modern terminology) the Third Step. His narrative then makes sense: the climbers cross the snowfield below the Third Step, and then they approach the crest of the Third Step.

If we wanted to run with that ball, it would be a new ball game. The Third Step is no obstacle for climbers; it is an easy scramble. No modern climber would doubt that Mallory and Irvine could have surmounted it. But if at the same time we were

Figure 10.3. Telephoto of the North Face of Mount Everest (probably from 1922), with John Noel's superimposed graphic of Mallory's and Irvine's last known position, on the basis of Odell's sighting on 8 June 1924. (John Noel: additional graphics by author)

to insist that they did not climb, or could not have climbed, the Second Step, that we would be compelled into another inference: that they reached the Third Step by another route.

The Third Step: A, B and C

In the context of our consideration of the Third Step, we are indebted to Michael Tracy for a concept that we have seen expressed only on his YouTube channel and nowhere else: the idea that what we call the Third Step is not one step but three.

In Tracy's video 'Odell's view of Mallory & Irvine at 12:50', the narration includes the following:

> *'[18m48s] ... the [Third Step] is broken down into three parts, there's sort of an Alpha, a Bravo and a Charlie.*
>
> *[22m00s] ... and here you can clearly, more clearly see the Alpha, the Bravo and the Charlie. ... there's essentially three little mini steps in here; and he's [Odell is] just referring to them as ridge rock steps. That means a rock step that's on the ridge. And there are, ..., the Charlie's kind of small, but Alpha sticks out, Bravo sticks out.'*[22]

Below is Tracy's image of the Third Step formations, taken from approximately due north. The implication of Tracy's narration are as follows:

- that the last step before the final pyramid is not the whole of the Third Step but part of it, probably 'Bravo' since 'Charlie' is indistinct;

Figure 10.4. The Second Step and Third Step, viewed from approximately due north, showing the components of the Third Step formation. (Michael Tracy: graphics and legend by author)

- and that Odell's 'last step but one' was not the Second Step, but the distinctive 'Alpha' section of the Third Step.

Tracy's interpretation is consonant with Odell's reports in the following respects:

- It places Mallory and Irvine on a 'prominent' rock step.
- The step may be perceived as 'the last step but one' from the final pyramid.
- The step is certainly 'a very short distance' from the base of the final pyramid (probably a few tens of yards, depending on one's view of where the base begins).

This interpretation completely removes the Second Step from the equation, and thereby eschews all debate about whether Mallory and Irvine could have climbed the Second Step.

Where was Odell?

In the *Mount Everest Dispatches*, as published in July and August 1924, Odell gave no specific location for his own position at the moment of the sighting. From his contemporary reports, we can only infer that it was on or near the North Ridge, between Camp V and Mallory's Camp VI in terms of altitude, and that, given his 'circuitous route' onto the North Face, it might not be on the crest of the North Ridge, but some way to the west (to climber's right). It was not until six months later, in December 1924, that he gave a clue to the altitude for the sighting:

> *'At about 26,000 feet I climbed a little crag, ... There was perhaps 100 feet of it.'*[23]

In Norton's *The Fight For Everest 1924*, published in 1925, Odell contributed a chapter in which he used an almost identical wording, except that the 'little crag' was scaled down to 'scarcely 100 feet of it'.[24]

These reports have entered the conventional wisdom. In all the literature that this author has seen, the assumption has been that Odell saw (or did not see) Mallory and Irvine from a vantage point at 26,000 feet (or possibly 26,100 feet including the height of the 'little crag').

Yet these altitudes cannot be even approximately correct.

Odell certainly had a timepiece. We can reasonably assume that his timing of the day's events – 8 am at Camp V, 12:50 pm at the sighting location and 2 pm at Mallory's Camp VI – was essentially correct. We can allow five minutes for the sighting, and five minutes to descend the crag, and assume that he departed the sighting location at about 1 pm.

Here's the rub.

By Noel's and Odell's accounts, Mallory's and Irvine's tent was at 27,300 feet. If the location of Odell's sighting had been as low as 26,100 feet, his climb to the tent would have involved a vertical ascent of 1,200 feet in one hour.

This author has found only one other instance of a comparable vertical speed at a comparable altitude: in 1922 Finch, Bruce and Tejbir climbed from 25,500 feet to 26,500 feet in an hour and ten minutes, averaging 857 vertical feet per hour

Figure 10.5. A detail from the illustration in *The Sphere* of 25 October 1924, depicting Mallory's and Irvine's Camp VI in relation to the location of Odell's sighting of the two climbers. (Douglas MacPherson / *The Sphere*, public domain)

with oxygen.[25] Otherwise, the ascent rates on the 1922 and 1924 expeditions had been typically in the range 200 to 300 vertical feet per hour. As an example: on 4 June 1924, Norton had climbed from Camp VI to his high point of 28,126 feet in six hours and twenty minutes, averaging 209 vertical feet per hour.

Here we must quote an intriguing statement by Hugh Ruttledge, leader of the 1933 British expedition:

> *'It was somewhere in the neighbourhood of Camp VI that Odell thought he saw Mallory and Irvine. The distance from this point to the second step is about one mile ... '*[26]

Norton's final estimate for the altitude of his and Somervell's Camp VI had been 26,800 feet, and Ruttledge repeated that estimate. Ruttledge was probably not aware that Mallory's and Irvine's Camp VI had been higher than Norton's and Somervell's Camp VI. And what did he mean by the 'neighbourhood' of Camp VI? This author would hazard a guess that Ruttledge placed the location of Odell's sighting at around 26,800 feet.

On 25 October 1924, the London illustrated newspaper *The Sphere* published a drawing of Odell's sighting, prepared by their artist Douglas MacPherson. Odell himself had collaborated with MacPherson, at the request of *The Sphere*. The drawing does not show Odell on a 'little crag' or anything resembling one. However, it does show Camp VI (presumably Mallory's and Irvine's), to Odell's left, and uphill from his position. It does not seem to be in a cleft in the rocks, as Norton had described his own Camp VI. It looks more like it is at the base of a cliff.

MacPherson's drawing gives the altitude of this Camp VI as 26,700 feet, which had been the initial estimate for Norton's and Somervell's Camp VI. This suggests to us that MacPherson was unaware that Mallory's Camp VI had been higher. Odell should have known, but perhaps he was not consulted on this specific point.

The pointed gendarme and the little crag

We recall from Chapter 9 that in 2001, Jake Norton rediscovered Colonel Norton's and Somervell's Camp VI near a 'pointed gendarme' of rock, on the crest of the North Ridge. Norton's kmz file for the camp is, on Google Earth, at 26,621 feet. We could conjecture that the 'gendarme' is one and the same as Odell's 'little crag'. This is a hypothesis that we can test.

The specifications of the 'little crag' are as follows:

- It is either on the crest of the North Ridge (if Odell had regained the crest after his 'circuitous route' in search of fossils) or it is to the west (on the North Face).
- It is less than 100 feet high from base to crest (though there may be uncertainty as to where the base is).
- It is probably an isolated formation rather than part of a cliff or slab.
- It is above 26,000 feet.
- It has to be within one hour's climb to Mallory's camp at 27,300 feet (and here we have to consider Odell's climbing rate at this altitude, without oxygen).

Thanks to Contour Map Creator[27], we can add contour lines to Google Earth. Thereby, we can select a geographical area on the North Face, to the west and north of Mallory's

Camp VI, and draw the contour lines at 200-foot intervals from the camp down to 26,000 feet. The results are shown in Figure 10.6.

We can see on Google Earth four possible candidates which match the specifications of Odell's 'little crag':

- Crag A: latitude 28.00043 north, longitude 86.9334 east, altitude 26,850 feet (450 feet below and 699 feet horizontally from Mallory's Camp VI); an isolated pointed rock, at the head of a major snow-filled gully known as the Zakharov Couloir
- Crag B: latitude 28.0008 north, longitude 86.9321 east, altitude 26,630 feet (670 feet below and 1,027 feet horizontally from Mallory's Camp VI); less well-defined, accessible via a north-south gully
- Crag C: latitude 28.0012 north, longitude 86.9314 east, altitude 26,370 feet (930 feet below and 1,325 feet horizontally from Mallory's camp); relatively well-defined, easily accessible from a snowfield to the north.
- Crag G (Jake Norton's "pointed gendarme" of 2001): at 26,560 feet on the crest of the North Ridge.

In judging the probabilities that one of these formations was Odell's 'little crag', we surely have to give weight to the rate of climb needed to reach Mallory's camp in one hour. This criterion greatly favours Crag A.

The main argument against Crag A is that it overlooks the spot where, as we asserted in Chapter 9, Colonel Norton pitched his Camp VI. In 2001 at that site, Jake Norton found the following:

Figure 10.6. The area of the North Face of Everest to the north and west of Mallory's and Irvine's Camp VI, with 200-foot contour lines and three candidates for Odell's 'little crag'. (Base image © CNES / Airbus / Google Earth; contour lines by author from Contour Map Creator; graphics and legend by author)

'Along with the tent pole, we found 6 wooden matches and solid meta-fuel from the stove, shredded remnants of the tent and its guylines, leather strapping likely from an oxygen system, a woollen mitten, an Acid Drops candy can full of loose-leaf tea, and a single tattered sock with a tiny laundry label stitched on the side.'[28]

As we recall, the tiny label bore the name 'Norton'. What Jake Norton did not find was any of the items reported by Odell when, on the afternoon of 8 June, he first looked into Mallory's and Irvine's tent, and when on 10 June, he abandoned hope for them:

(8 June) *'Within were ... oxygen cylinders, and parts of apparatus; outside were more parts of the latter and of the duralumin carriers ...'*[29]

(10 June) *'[I] took from within Mallory's compass ... That and the oxygen set of Irvine's design alone seemed worth while to retrieve.'*[30]

The items that Jake Norton found, and those he did not find, tell us that he had rediscovered Colonel Norton's tent, but not that of Mallory and Irvine. Therefore we may surmise that Mallory did not take Colonel Norton's tent, but simply asked his porters to collect the bedding and provisions, and to carry them uphill to his own Camp VI. There he pitched his own tent, and stored the oxygen sets which Odell would find the following day. Thus we may understand Noel's later reference to 'two light tents' at the Northeast Shoulder.

In that case, Odell was likely to be able to see Norton's tent about 270 vertical feet below and 550 feet horizontally from his 'little crag'. Perhaps he saw no reason to mention it; and after his sighting of the two climbers, he continued up the mountain, to where he knew Mallory's camp to be.

In any event, the three candidates for the 'little crag' are not far apart. We may now develop a hypothesis of what Odell could have seen.

Intervening terrain

Several modern climbers have observed that at various locations on the North Ridge, especially at altitudes around 26,000 feet, the view of the Northeast Ridge is partially blocked by intervening terrain. Below, for example, is a screenshot from Michael Tracy's video 'Odell's view of Mallory & Irvine at 12:50'. Tracy apparently intended to suggest that the top of the cliff on the left of the frame could have been the location of Odell's sighting.

Tracy's narration prior to this frame was as follows:

'The ridge is always going to be somewhat, this stuff will always block off something; nobody down this far, 26,000 feet, can see the entire Northeast Ridge, it's impossible from any position at that altitude. So, the question is how much of it was blocked? And so, I have two different samples from just about, ..., 100 feet apart. This one that has the First Step not blocked; [8m13s] there's this one here which is below some terrain, and obviously the First Step is blocked. [8m15s]'[31]

Figure 10.7. Part of the Northeast Ridge of Everest, seen from about 26,000 feet on the North Ridge. (Michael Tracy)

Figure 10.8. Part of the Northeast Ridge of Everest in 2003, seen from about 26,900 feet on the North Ridge. (Jake Norton)

As noted above, any point at 26,000 feet is too low to be a possible location of Odell's sighting. Figure 10.8 (above) is a photograph taken by Jake Norton in 2003, also on the North Ridge but at about 26,900 feet: which is about the right altitude for Odell's position.

Visual angles

In his official reports, Odell never said whether he had seen Mallory and Irvine with his naked eye. But the expedition's chief photographer John Noel would later recall that Odell had carried an optical instrument. In *Through Tibet to Everest*, published in 1927, Noel related from memory what Odell had told him in 1924:

> [Odell said] '... *I saw another speck move up to join the first. It was no other than Mallory and Irvine within 600 feet of the summit. They seemed to be going strong. I dropped my geologizing, took out my glasses and riveted my attention on the spot.* '[32]

Here the word 'glasses' would mean field-glasses, or binoculars.

However, in the telephoto which Noel reproduced on page 285 of the same book (and which we reproduced in Figure 10.2 above), the annotation said that Odell's optical aid had been a telescope:

> *'Odell through his telescope sees the two men within 600 feet of summit.* '[33]

Noel's book included Donald MacPherson's drawing of Odell's sighting. It does indeed show Odell with some kind of instrument, probably binoculars, in his right hand. We reproduced a detail from that drawing in Figure 10.5.

In *the Alpine Journal* and *The Geographical Journal*, Odell had placed Mallory and Irvine above the Second Step, and had quoted Hazard as measuring this altitude as 28,230 feet. Noel presumably retained the figure of 600 feet from a conversation with Odell; and since the summit was at that time calibrated at 29,002 feet, this is probably the origin of Noel's belief that Odell had seen Mallory and Irvine at 28,400 feet.

If he did, we may make an assessment of what objects he could resolve with an optical instrument. Let us assume that, at the moment of his sighting, he was on or near 'Crag A'. In that case, he was about 4,300 feet horizontally, and about 1,500 feet vertically, from the crest of the Third Step. By Pythagoras' Law, his slant distance to the crest of the Third Step was about 4,500 feet.

Figure 10.9. Climbers at a distance of 4,500 feet. (left) and full moon with naked eye. (right) x5 magnification, and full moon with naked eye. (NicePNG.com; design by author)

We can now calculate the size of the tiny dots that Odell saw. At a distance of 4,500 feet, a six-foot man would subtend a visual angle of four arc-minutes.[34] By comparison, the full moon subtends about 31 arc-minutes. If the Third Step is where Mallory and Irvine were when Odell saw them, and if he saw them with the naked eye, they would have appeared about as large as in the image at left in Figure 10.9. However, if Odell had been using binoculars with a magnification of five (a typical power for instruments of the era), the climbers would have appeared about as large as in the image at right in Figure 10.9. In both images, for comparison, the full moon is shown as seen with the naked eye.

If Odell had had an optical instrument, he would have been certain that he was seeing Mallory and Irvine, and not rocks or birds. Later, he would tell colleagues that he had been able to distinguish Mallory from Irvine by their respective body language. Why his sighting was disputed for so many years is another aspect of the mystery.

The shape of the mountain

With the data that we have assembled so far, we are now in a position to make several working assumptions about Odell's sighting, as follows:

- that his timings of the climb from Camp V to Mallory's Camp VI were accurate to within a few minutes
- that at the moment of his sighting, he was on or near 'Crag A' on the North Ridge, at about 26,900 feet by the modern calibration
- that he did indeed see Mallory and Irvine and not an optical illusion
- that he had an optical instrument and was able to distinguish Irvine from Mallory
- that he saw the two climbers moving from east to west (from left to right in his field of vision), first crossing a snowfield, and then at least one of them surmounting a rock step
- that his sighting lasted a matter of minutes.

We may now consider what Odell could and could not have seen, from his vantage point on the mountain.

As we observed earlier, there are places on the North Ridge where the view of the Northeast Ridge is partially blocked by intervening terrain. We have some modern climbers' photographs of the Northeast Ridge, taken from various points on the North Ridge. We have no photograph taken from a point that can be confidently identified as the 'little crag'.

However, the shape of Mount Everest has not changed between 1924 and today. Google Earth has recorded the shape of the mountain; it is our aid in modelling the geometry of Odell's field of vision.

Firstly, we should acknowledge that the three Steps are large and irregular formations; and it is not straightforward to establish where each Step begins and ends. Perhaps for this reason, the locations of the Steps have never been authoritatively defined. Michael Spender's classic map, which appeared in *The Geographical Journal* of October 1936, showed the base of the First Step, and that of the Second. As late as 1936, what we now call the Third Step was not recognized. No-one alive had climbed it; the British expedition of 1933 did not try.

In any case, to assess Odell's sighting we need the altitudes of the crests, rather than the bases. The Steps are visible on Google Earth, and the shadows that they cast give a sense of where they are highest. This author has identified the approximate locations and altitudes of the crests as follows:

- First Step (crest): latitude 27.99322 north, longitude 86.93004 east, altitude 27,987 feet
- Second Step (crest): latitude 27.99139, longitude 86.92850 east, altitude 28,084 feet
- Third Step (crest): latitude 27.98998 north, longitude 86.92730 east, altitude 28,371 feet.

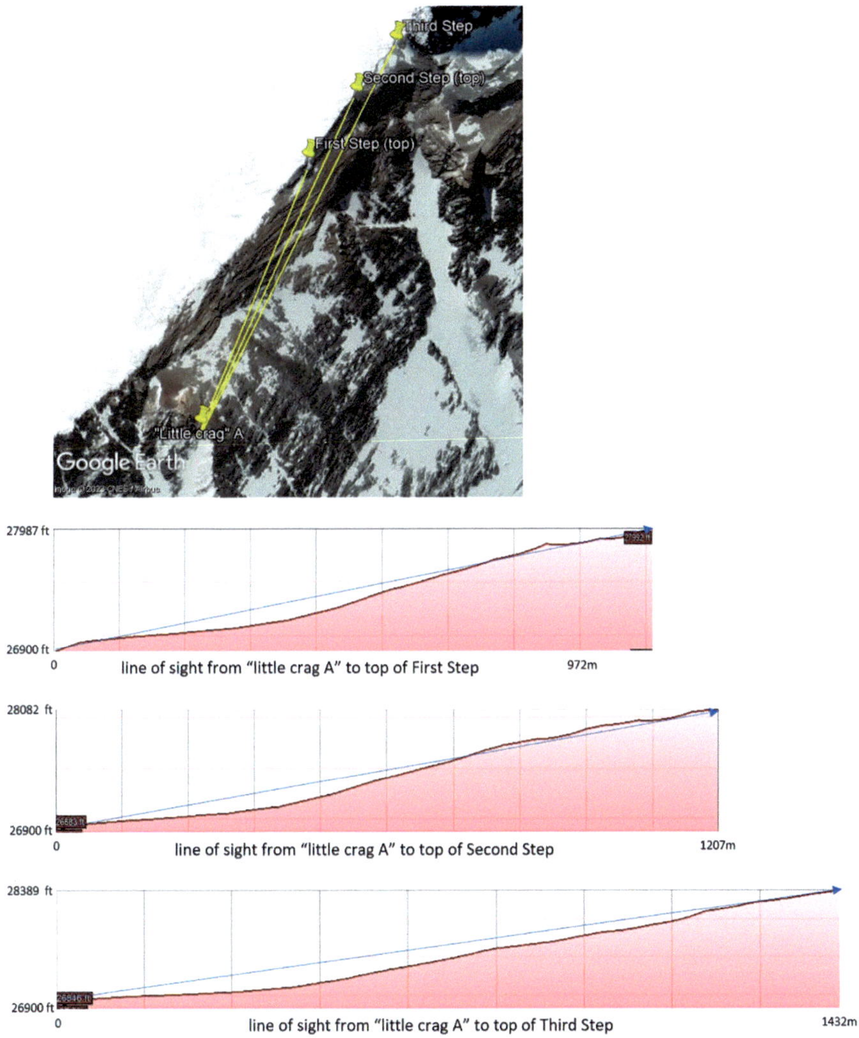

Figure 10.10. Author's reconstruction of the sight line from Odell's presumed vantage point ('Crag A') to the crests of the First, Second and Third Steps. (Base image © CNES / Airbus / Google Earth; graphics and legend by author)

On these assumptions, we can construct Odell's sight lines from 'Crag A' to the First, Second and Third Steps. The geometry of his sight lines is illustrated in Figure 10.10. From this graphic, we may reasonably conclude that Odell could (just about) see the crest of the Third Step. However, he could not see the crests of the First or Second Steps; they were blocked by intervening terrain.

We now have fourfold support for the hypothesis that Odell saw Mallory and Irvine on the Third Step, as follows:

- there was a snowfield to the east (to the left from Odell's viewpoint); in contemporary photographs, there is a snowfield to the east of the Third Step;
- at least one of the climbers scaled the step with alacrity (as does every modern climber who is fit and acclimatized);
- some element of the Third Step formation could be viewed as 'the last step but one' (with acknowledgement to Michael Tracy's insight)
- and this is the only one of the three Steps that can be seen from the vantage point that we have called 'Crag A'.

We can thereby defend the hypothesis that Mallory and Irvine climbed the Third Step, where Odell briefly saw them; that they reached that point without previously climbing the Second Step; and that there was another route to the Third Step, and it was not the Northeast Ridge as the conventional wisdom has held for almost a century.

Third Step to the summit

If we accept that Odell saw Mallory and Irvine on the Third Step, we are now in a position to restate the calculation that Odell might have made, but did not express.

As Odell must have surmised, their ascent rate would have been slow in comparison to the earlier high climbs; but no-one else had been that high, and no-one else knew the route. We have, and Odell had, no way of knowing how much time Mallory and Irvine spent on finding the route, even on false trails and backtracks.

However, from that point to the summit, there was no technical obstacle. If Mallory and Irvine had been able to climb the undemanding last 600 feet at between 200 and 300 feet per hour, and if no stroke of fate or physiology had intervened, they would have reached the summit between two and three hours after Odell saw them. This interpretation of Odell's sighting permits us to imagine that on 8 June 1924 between about 3 pm and about 4 pm, Mallory and Irvine were the first humans to stand at the highest point on the earth.

In later chapters, we shall examine the claimed sightings of the climbers' remains; what we might learn from the discovery of Mallory's body; and the traces that remain of Mallory's and Irvine's journey, from which, as the world knows, they never returned.

Part III

AFTERMATH

Chapter 11

Traces

After the disastrous expedition of 1924, nine years would pass before the British returned to Everest. On the 1933 expedition, they found the first traces of Mallory's and Irvine's last climb. It was Percy Wyn Harris who made the discovery.

Harris (later to be Sir Percy Wyn-Harris), like most British members of the early Everest expeditions, was from an affluent family and was a product of an elite English public school and the University of Cambridge. At the time of the expedition he was a colonial civil servant, working in Kenya. He was also a fine mountaineer. In the summer of 1933, he was twenty-nine years old.

The leader of the 1933 expedition was Hugh Ruttledge. Having learned from the experiences of 1924, he knew that they would need a significantly higher camp than before. Accordingly, they pitched their Camp VI at 27,400 feet. Ruttledge later wrote that the location of their Camp VI was well defined, because it was about 300 feet below the two prominent rock towers on the North Ridge, northeast of the First Step. These two towers, which modern climbers know colloquially as 'the Warts', are easily identified today on Google Earth, by the shadows that they cast. Below and to the north of the towers, we can clearly see the ledge on which Ruttledge's team installed their high camp.

Ruttledge wrote that his expedition's Camp VI was 600 feet higher than the Camp VI of 1924, by which he can only have meant Norton's and Somervell's

Figure 11.1. Percy Wyn Harris at Camp V on the 1933 Everest expedition. (Author, after a frame from *The Fourth Everest Expedition*, filmed mainly by Wyn Harris)

Camp VI; we infer that he was unaware that Mallory and Irvine's last camp had been higher, at 27,300 feet.

In terms of horizontal distance, Ruttledge described his high camp as about 400 yards east (meaning northeast) of the First Step[1]; on Google Earth, it looks more like 425 yards.

The ice axe

In the end, no-one from the 1933 team reached the summit. Lawrence Wager, Percy Wyn Harris and Frank Smythe came close, all three arriving at approximately the point in the Couloir that Norton had reached in 1924, and there turning around. It fell to Ruttledge to report the results of the expedition. On 6 November 1933, he read a paper to the Alpine Club in London; in the course of his speech, he recounted that the first climbing team had consisted of Wager and Wyn Harris. They had set off on their summit attempt on 30 May 1933. Ruttledge described what Wyn Harris had found:

> *'... at a point about 200 yards east of the first step and 60 feet below the crest of the north-east arete, they found lying upon gently inclined but smooth slabs an ice-axe. It looked perfectly new, the axe-head of bright polished steel. This axe can only have belonged to Mallory or Irvine ...*
>
> *On the way back ... Wyn Harris retrieved the ice-axe, leaving his own in its place ...'*[2]

In the book of the expedition, published in 1934, Ruttledge gave a further outline of the story:

> *'... the moment the sun appeared, nearly an hour after they had left Camp VI, Wager sat down to remove his boots and rub his feet. Soon after this, about 60 feet below the crest of the ridge and 250 yards east of the first step, Wyn Harris, who was leading, found the ice axe about which there has been so much controversy. It was lying free on smooth, brown 'boiler-plate' slabs, inclined at an easy angle but steepening considerably just below. It was in perfect condition, looking quite new.'*[3]

Here we observe that Ruttledge, offering no explanation, had moved the location of the ice-axe by fifty yards to the north-east, away from the First Step and correspondingly closer to Camp VI.

Evidently this discovery unleashed a storm of debate and speculation, at least among mountaineers and, one may assume, the members of the Alpine Club and the Royal Geographical Society. That the ice axe had been carried by Mallory or Irvine, there could be no doubt. No-one else had been that high on the mountain, prior to the 1933 expedition. How it had come to be there was another matter. An early proposal was that the ice axe had been dropped, and that it marked the scene of an accident. Who had dropped it – whether Mallory or Irvine – was the issue.

However, Wyn Harris corresponded with Odell on this issue, and showed the axe to Odell, who subsequently wrote to the Alpine Club as follows:

> '*[The axe] was on a gently inclined slab about 200 yards east of the First Step and about 60 ft. below the crest of the N.E. arete. ... what struck me at once was its entirely undamaged condition. It cannot, therefore, have fallen far, if at all. ... it is unlikely that the position of the axe marks the scene of an accident, at any rate on the ascent. ... It seems to me very possible that one of them - and more plausibly Irvine, who was less used to carrying an axe on a rock-climb than Mallory - may have decided to leave his axe on the ridge during the ascent, to be picked up on the descent, in view of the climbing being almost entirely on rock under the conditions prevailing at that time.*'[4]

Forty-four years would pass before Wyn Harris would tell his version of the discovery. In 1978 at the age of seventy-four, Sir Percy (as by then he was) wrote his memoirs for his grandchildren. These memoirs have never been published; we reproduce extracts from them by the kind permission of his grandson Steve Wyn-Harris. Therein, Sir Percy wrote:

Figure 11.2a. Wager and Wyn Harris, imagined at a point some tens of yards southwest of where Wyn Harris found the ice axe. First Step at centre of image; summit at centre right. (Author, after a frame from *The Fourth Everest Expedition*, filmed mainly by Wyn Harris)

Figure 11.2b. A view of the Yellow Band from the First Step, including the approximate location where Wyn Harris found the ice axe. (The Airborne Rangers Club of Finland)

> *'Before we reached the first step and 250 yards short of it and 60 feet below the crest of the [Northeast] ridge, I practically stumbled on an ice axe. The thing that particularly astonished me was that the steel of the axe was all absolutely bright and the wood was as if it had been cleaned with sand paper.'*[5]

200 or 250 yards

Before we construct any scenario or hypothesis relating to the ice axe, we have to make some attempt to pin down its location. We have four accounts from three men – Ruttledge, Wyn Harris and Odell. Ruttledge's first account, therefore the closest in time, placed the ice axe 200 yards from the First Step; in 1934 Odell (who could have had his information either from Ruttledge or from Wyn Harris) also placed it at 200 yards. Wyn Harris's memoirs in 1978, the most removed in time, placed it at 250 yards. The difference may be significant.

The second uncertainty relates to the location of the First Step. This is a substantial rock formation, some tens of yards long in the northeast-to-southwest axis. The crest is clearly defined, but the base is not; the formation merges chaotically into the Northeast

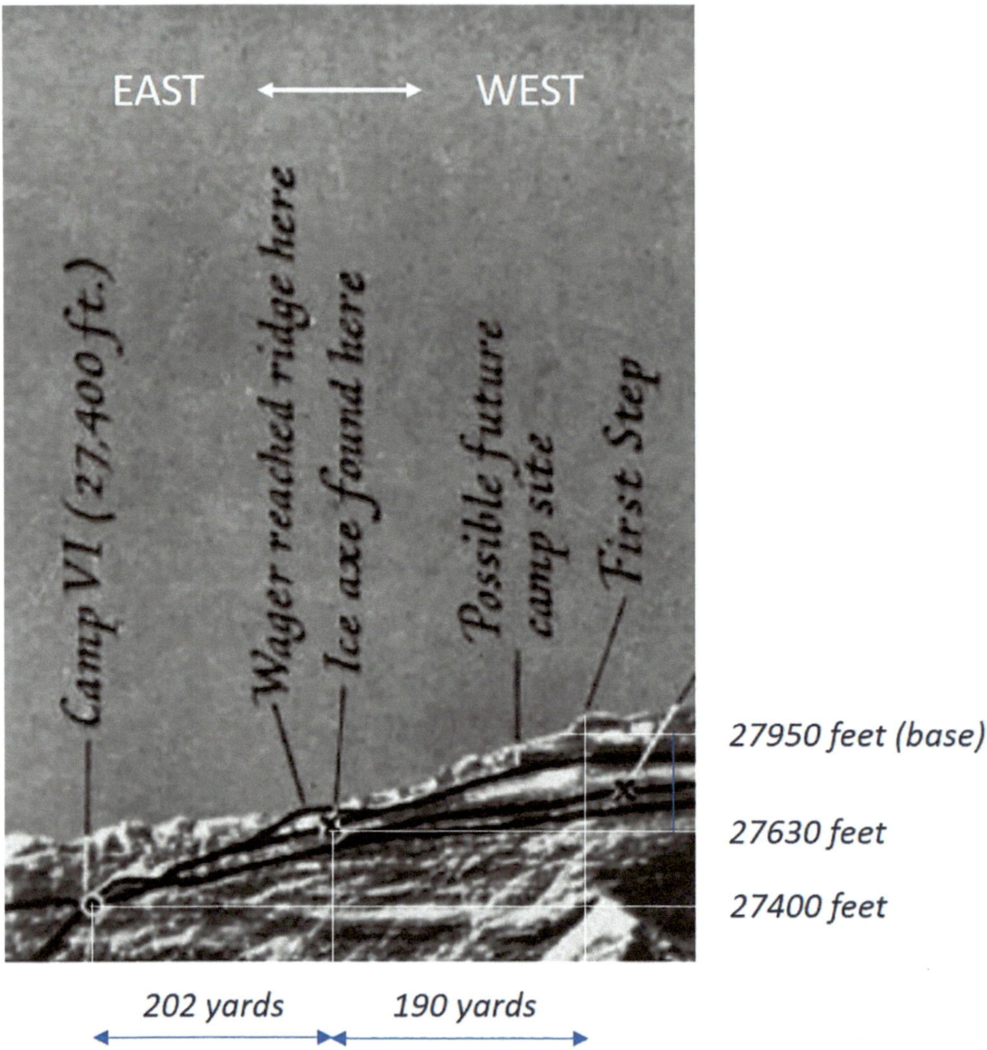

Figure 11.3. The ice axe location: a detail from the annotated photograph in *Everest 1933*, p.156. Altitude of base of First Step from Spender (1936). (Image and original graphics: Hugh Ruttledge; horizontal and vertical distances are author's calculations; additional graphics and legend by author)

Figure 11.4. The ice axe location: a detail from the annotated photograph in *The Geographical Journal*, January 1934, following p.9. (Image and original graphics: Lawrence Wager; additional graphics, legend and perspective correction by author)

Ridge. In any case, Ruttledge and Wyn Harris did not clarify whether they had been measuring from the base of the Step or from the crest.

There is no record that either Wager or Wyn Harris took a photograph of the ice axe *in situ*; nor that they recorded the altitude where Wyn Harris found the axe.

However, there are three pieces of evidence that favour the 200-yard mark.

Firstly the book of the expedition, *Everest 1933,* included a hand-drawn map of the climbers' routes, superimposed on a photograph of the North Face of Everest. It shows that the climbers never attempted to scale the First Step, but passed below it at distances that look like 100 feet (Wager and Wyn Harris) to 300 feet (Smythe); so the crest would be a logical landmark. Certainly the map defined the First Step by its crest, not by its base. The location of the ice axe was marked at a point almost exactly midway (horizontally) between Camp VI and the First Step: that is, 200 yards from the First Step.

Secondly Ruttledge, writing in *The Geographical Journal* of January 1934, included Wager's photograph of the North Face with hand-drawn annotations, including the location of the ice axe. Again, that location looks like the 200-yard mark horizontally from the crest of the First Step.

Thirdly, by reference to Wager's and Wyn Harris's timing, we can exercise some judgement as to where they were at the time of the discovery.

Ruttledge reported that the climbers had set off at 5:40 am from their Camp VI at 27,400 feet; and that after nearly an hour's climbing, followed by a short stop, Wyn Harris found the ice axe. That places the discovery at 6:40 am or a little after. After finding the axe, they proceeded to 'the foot of the first step'.

Later, Frank Smythe would confirm a large part of Ruttledge's account. He would write that Wager and Wyn Harris had left their tent 'shortly after 5:30 a.m.'; that an hour later they had stopped briefly; and that 'not far beyond' the halt, Wyn Harris had found the ice axe.[6]

Ruttledge recorded that the two climbers had reached the foot of the First Step at 7 am.[7] If we are to believe this account, Wager and Wyn Harris had climbed 450 vertical feet in 80 to 90 minutes, averaging between 300 and 338 feet per hour. These are good rates of ascent at such an altitude, without oxygen; and it gives us an idea of Mallory's and Irvine's ascent rates from their Camp VI to the ice axe location (when they were probably using oxygen as sparingly as possible).

Ruttledge's account implies that at the ice axe location, the climbers were closer to the First Step than to Camp VI. This gives further weight to the 200-yard mark.

Google Earth

In any event, we can plot both variants on Google Earth.

The crest of the First Step (recognisable by the shadow that it casts on the North Face in the Google Earth image) is at 27.9932° north, 86.9300° east. When Ruttledge wrote 'east', he meant approximately north-east (along the crest of the ridge); the heading of the crest is 36 degrees from true north. On Google Earth, one can identify the two points to which Ruttledge and Wyn-Harris referred. The respective locations of the ice axe are as follows:

- 200-yard mark at 27.9947° north, 86.9309° east, altitude 27,700 feet (27,670 feet by the 1924 calibration)
- 250-yard mark at 27.9950° north, 96.9311° east, altitude 27,650 feet (27,620 feet in 1924).

These locations are shown in Figure 11.5.

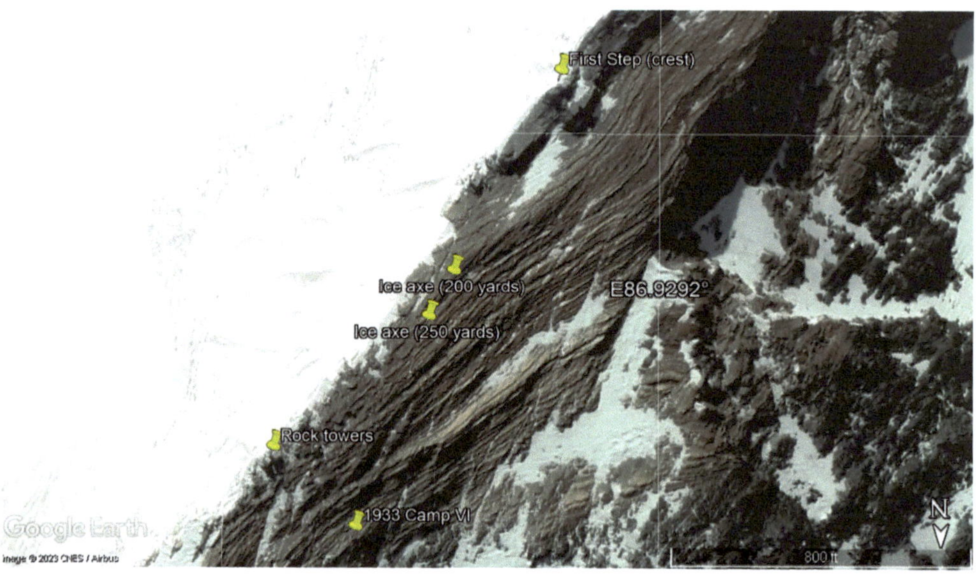

Figure 11.5. Two alternative locations for the 1924 ice axe, based on Ruttledge's accounts in 1933 and 1934, and Wyn Harris's account in 1978. (Base image © CNES / Airbus / Google Earth; graphics by author)

Somervell?

Back in 1924, Norton had recounted an incident from his climb with Somervell on 4 June 1924. He had written:

> *'Soon after we started down, at about 2 p.m., Somervell's axe slipped from his numb fingers and went cart-wheeling down the slopes below. This must have been somewhere about the point where an hour or two before he had taken his highest photograph. ... [it] disappeared from our view still going strong.'*[8]

It appears that at some point in 1933, someone suggested that the axe could have been Somervell's. Ruttledge was quick to dismiss this idea:

> *'Norton and Somervell traversed by a lower line ... Some have suggested that this was the axe dropped by Somervell soon after he and Norton turned to descend. But they were much farther to the west when this happened, and Somervell's axe fell straight down the mountain-side ...'*[9]

Indeed, Somervell's famous photograph, from about 28,000 feet, was taken several hundred yards to the west of the ice axe location, in the direction of the summit; and Norton's account leaves no possibility that the ice axe could have been Somervell's.

Mallory or Irvine?

The ice axe that Wyn Harris found now resides in the Alpine Club in London. How it got there is explained by Wyn Harris in his memoirs:

> *'... I left my own axe at Camp VI as I could not carry two. My own axe is still there at Camp VI*[10] *and I used the one, now in the Alpine Club, for the journey home.*
>
> *I offered the axe to the Alpine Club and got the unrewarding reply from the official to whom I offered it that they had plenty of axes in the roof of the Club and did not want any more. As I had considerable difficulty in bringing the axe home and had abandoned my old friend [his own axe] at Camp VI, I offered it to Charterhouse School where Mallory had been a [school] master. I took no further action about the axe until the Alpine Club had second thoughts on the matter and claimed it.'*[11]

The Alpine Club, to this day, takes the position that the ice axe probably belonged to Andrew Irvine. In its *Everest Centenary* exhibition in 2021, the Club assembled a collection of photographs, paintings and artifacts from the early Everest expeditions. The description of the exhibition, on its website, includes the following statement:

> *'Items on display include ... Sandy [Andrew] Irvine's ice axe, lost on Everest during his fateful summit attempt with Mallory in 1924, and discovered in 1933.'*[12]

This author has viewed the ice axe at the Alpine Club (but photographs were not permitted). The Club confirms that it is 95cm (37.4 inches) long; and that the blade is about 27cm (10.6 inches) from tip to tip. On the stock, there are three rough notches, about eight inches from the blade; and a crude 'X' or cross, about 0.4 inch wide and about twenty inches from the blade. About fifteen inches from the blade, the stock bears a brass plaque which states 'A. C. Irvine (probably) or G. L. Mallory'. On the blade is the maker's stamp, which reads 'Jos. [Josef] Willisch, Bergfuhrer, Taesch – Zermatt'.[13]

The legend that the ice axe was Irvine's property arose from the notches, which were thought to be characteristic of the way that Irvine marked his belongings. Specifically, it was said that Irvine had owned a 'swagger stick', a term which until the 1920s referred to a short stick carried by off-duty military officers; and that he had made three similar parallel notches on this stick. However, Irvine never served in any branch of the armed forces. Michael Tracy writes:

> '*The stick was found in 1962 among the belongings of Andrew Irvine's father Willie when he passed away. The other four sons did not remember having such a swagger stick, so it was assumed to belong to Sandy Irvine, and passed on to Noel Odell.*'[14]

Wyn Harris, however, had another story. He clearly had known from the start that the axe had historical significance and needed to be identifiable. In a letter to Odell in 1934, he described and interpreted the marks as follows:

> '*The triple III was on the axe when I picked it up. At least I noticed them when I got to camp 3 but the X was not there. The X was put on by 'Pugla' my servant, who had an unfortunate habit of marking everything he looked after. ... I imagine he put them on to identify my property.*
>
> *... I think it almost certain ... that the triple III was a porter's mark – either to mark his own axe or to mark his master's.*'[15]

In his memoirs of 1978, he doubled down on the attribution of the marks to porters:

> '*... the axe which is in the Alpine Club bears a plate which says that the axe belonged to Irvine. This [plate] I believe was inserted on the axe because there is a mark on the axe which was assumed to be Irvine's. Any marks which are now on the axe were put on by my own porter Kusang Pugla who was threatened with dire penalties if he mixed up the axe on the journey home.*'[16]

Wyn Harris's recollections are not entirely consistent, but he was there, and he believed that there was no mark on the axe which linked it with any climber. In any case, whether Irvine had the habit of marking his gear, or not, does not matter for our purposes. The axe was carried either by Mallory or by Irvine; it may or may not have been the personal property of either man; and there is no evidence one way or the other.

Figure 11.6. An ice axe which belonged to Andrew Irvine, now on display at Shrewsbury School, England; not the ice axe discovered by Wyn Harris in 1933, which is six inches shorter. (Andrew Parkinson)

Shrewsbury School

As noted above, the ice axe at the Alpine Club is 37.4 inches long. At Shrewsbury School in England, where Irvine studied from 1916 to 1921, the Irvine Room is named after him. On display in this room is an ice axe; the school has advised this author that it was one of several owned by Andrew Irvine, and that it is not the one that Wyn Harris found on Everest[17]. It is 110cm (43.3 inches) long. We might ponder whether Irvine, who stood six feet two inches, would have carried sometimes an axe of 43.3 inches and sometimes another, six inches shorter.

Accident or intention?

To this day, there is no specific evidence of an accident at the location of the ice axe. If there was an accident at the site, it was one in which the ice axe was lost, and nothing else. The 'accident' school of thought arose not from evidence, but primarily as the only imaginable alternative to an intentional placement of the axe. It was expressed thus by Ruttledge:

> *'... no mountaineer climbing the north face of Mount Everest regards his axe as an encumbrance. It is his best friend and greatest safeguard. ... neither climber would be likely to abandon it deliberately on the slabs ...'*[18]

Smythe had much the same point of view:

> *'No mountaineer of Mallory's calibre would have deliberately discarded so vital an aid to success.'*[19]

Wyn Harris, writing in his memoirs, would echo this thought:

> *'To me the axe had only one explanation. It marked the scene of a fall by a climber either from the ridge 60 feet above or from the place where the axe was lying. No climber could possibly have left the axe deliberately at the place where I found it.'*[20]

Ruttledge, Smythe and Wyn Harris were expressing the 'argument from personal incredulity' – a concept made popular much later by Richard Dawkins[21] – that an unexplained phenomenon must necessarily conform to their personal beliefs. The history of Everest is replete with such arguments. This view became the conventional wisdom regarding the last climb of Mallory and Irvine.

However, nothing is lost if we consider alternatives.

Frank Smythe, who had equalled or surpassed Norton's high point, set down an account of the ice axe that was more detailed than those of Ruttledge and Wyn Harris:

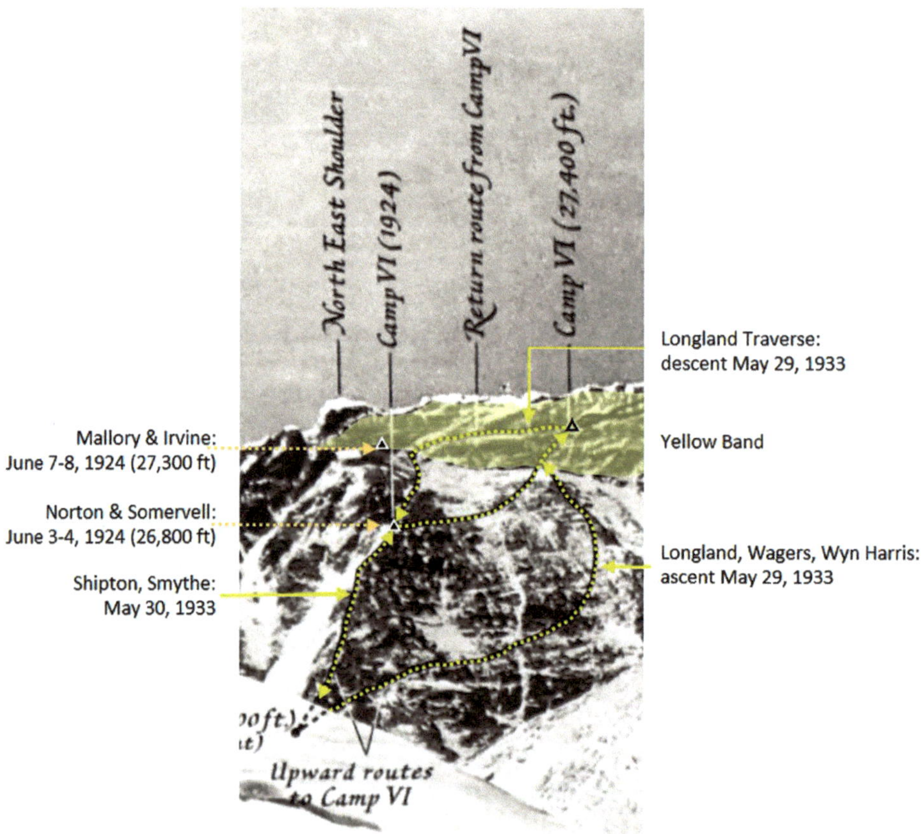

Figure 11.7. The ascent and descent routes of the 1933 British expedition, and the locations of the two Camps VI of 1924. (Hugh Ruttledge, public domain; additional graphics and legend by author)

> *'The first thing Wyn [Harris] did [on his return] was to fling down an ice axe at the entrance of the tent. "Found this," he said. "Must have belonged to Mallory or Irvine." ... Wyn discovered the ice axe which can only have belonged to Mallory or Irvine ... lying on the slabs, which are hereabouts inclined at an angle of 35°-40°, unsupported by crack or ledge, and dependent on friction alone for its lodgment.'*[22]

The proponents of the 'accident' scenario therefore had to believe that the ice axe had fallen from a climber's grasp and had stopped in the same spot, where no protrusion or indentation could arrest it. An object that falls even three feet is moving at 13 feet per second. Yet according to the 'accident' hypothesis, this falling smooth object had stopped on a smooth slab inclined at an angle of thirty-five to forty degrees.

In short, the 'accident' scenario defies the laws of physics. More than this, with available data, we cannot say.

The Tibetan museum

For due diligence we must record that in Lhasa, Tibet, there is a tourist attraction named the Tsering Chey Nga Snow Mountain Museum. At the time of writing, it is closed, apparently abandoned. In 2020 it was the subject of a documentary on the Chinese Global Television Network. The cameraman briefly recorded a section of the museum devoted to objects from the 1924 Everest expedition. One of them was an ice axe. How it got there, and whose it had been, is another mystery.

Figure 11.8. An ice axe attributed to the 1924 British Everest expedition, on display at the Tsering Chey Nga Snow Mountain Museum in 2020. (China Global Television Network)

Oxygen bottle #9

In 1991 Eric Simonson, in the course of an expedition on the North Face of Everest, at a location which he would later remember as 'just below the First Step', noticed an oxygen cylinder. He recognized it as old. He took no photographs, nor made a note of the location. Jochen Hemmleb would later paraphrase Simonson's recollection as follows:

> *'Simonson had a mental image of at least one oxygen bottle tucked beneath a boulder somewhere below the First Step.'*[23]

Eight years later, both Hemmleb and Simonson were on the expedition that set out to find the mortal remains of Mallory and Irvine. As the world knows, the expedition found the remains of George Mallory, thus making the greatest discovery in the history and mystery of the 1924 expedition. That story has been told; in a later chapter, we shall attempt to glean from it such insights as we can. Here, our interest is in their discovery of an oxygen cylinder near the First Step; either the one that Simonson remembered, or one much like it.

On 17 May 1999, climber Tapley Richards found the cylinder. He was accompanied at the time by Jake Norton. Simonson had told Norton and Richards that there was a cylinder somewhere near the First Step, under a boulder. There were hundreds of boulders near the First Step; so Richards did not expect to find anything. However:

> *'... not three minutes later, Jake [Norton] and I were standing at a big brown boulder with an oxygen bottle wedged beneath it.'*[24]

Richards and Norton did not take a photograph of the cylinder *in situ*, nor did they record its GPS co-ordinates. It was Hemmleb who made the identification of the cylinder as from the 1924 expedition; not only that, but it appeared to have an identification number:

> *'Hemmleb recognized it immediately by its distinctive shape and dimensions as a 1924 cylinder. On the bottle, in faded paint, was the number 9 ...'*[25]
>
> *'The unique valve assembly, shape, and size as well as a stamp E.O.C. (Everest Oxygen Cylinder) conclusively identified the bottle as stemming from the 1924 British Everest Expedition and therefore from Mallory and Irvine, the only climbing party [in 1924] that used oxygen.'*[26]

The number nine would prove to be an additional key to the association of the cylinder with Mallory and Irvine. In Mallory's pockets, the climbers had discovered a letter from someone whose signature looked like 'Stella'. On the envelope, there were two columns of numbers, in handwriting which resembled Mallory's. The left-hand column contained numbers, each one either 100 or 110; the right-hand column was headed 'No.' followed by ditto marks. The fifth row read: '110 [ditto] 9'.

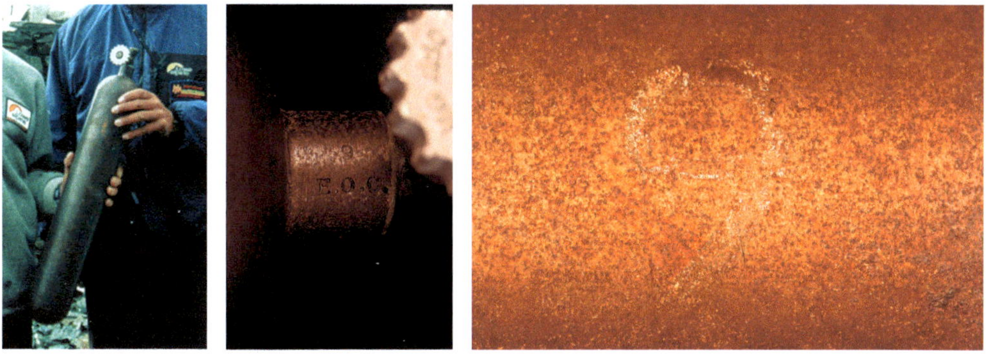

Figure 11.9. (left) The oxygen cylinder found by Tapley Richards on 17 May 1999. (© Jochen Hemmleb)

(centre) The serial number 9 and the acronym "E.O.C." (probably "Everest Oxygen Cylinder") stamped on the oxygen bottle found on 17 May 1999. (© Rich Reanier/Jochen Hemmleb, 1999 Mallory & Irvine Research Expedition)

(right) The serial number 9 painted on the oxygen cylinder found on 17 May 1999. (© Rick Reanier/Jochen Hemmleb, 1999 Mallory & Irvine Research Expedition)

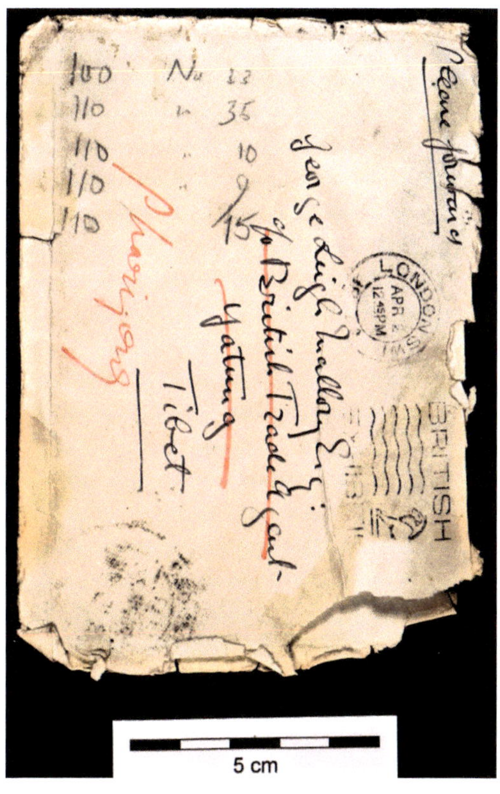

Figure 11.10. The two columns of numbers on the envelope of the letter from 'Stella'. The presumed cylinder #9 is in the fifth row. (Rick Reanier/ Archiv Jochen Hemmleb)

The expedition members concluded that the numbers in the right-hand column were codes for oxygen cylinders, and those on the left were pressures in atmospheres; therefore, that cylinder #9 had contained (at some point) 110 atmospheres, as compared to a full charge of 120 atmospheres. This would correspond to 490 litres of oxygen at normal pressure[27]. The cylinder found by Richards was presumed to be that which Mallory had listed on the envelope. If so, we may reasonably suppose that either Mallory or Irvine discarded or cached it where Richards found it in 1999.

As usual in the story of Mallory and Irvine, there are several, somewhat diverging, accounts of the location of the oxygen cylinder. This author is indebted to Jochen Hemmleb for the following authoritative estimates:

> *'I recently revised the location of the bottle with Eric Simonson, who first saw the bottle(s) in 1991. If the top of the First Step is taken as a reference point, the horizontal distance is 170 m (c. 560 ft.).'*
>
> *'The altitude is 8465-8470 m (27,774-27,790 ft.).'*
>
> *'Your estimation* [of about 60 feet below the Northeast Ridge] *is about correct. The bottle was located above the ramp ascended by Wager & Wyn-Harris in 1933 (who found the axe) but below the modern-day approach to the First Step ...'*[28]

We may observe that this location does not self-evidently correspond to what Simonson remembered as 'somewhere below the First Step'; raising the possibility that there may be another cylinder from 1924, near the First Step.

The location specified by Hemmleb can be identified on Google Earth Pro. It is at 27.9945° north, 86.9310° east. That location is shown in Figure 11.11. Google Earth gives the location a slightly lower altitude than Hemmleb: 27,715 feet by the modern calibration.

Figure 11.11. The location of oxygen cylinder #9 as found on 17 May 1999, based on data kindly provided by Jochen Hemmleb. (Base image © CNES / Airbus / Google Earth; graphics by author)

The location of cylinder #9 is revealing. By our calculations, it is within 20-30 yards of Ruttledge's first reported location of the ice axe, namely 200 yards from the First Step. However, as per our data from Hemmleb, it is on a higher slab; one which a climber would not necessarily wish to climb up or down.

As we noted earlier, the 200-yard mark has more evidence for it than the 250-yard mark.

If the 200-yard mark for the ice axe is correct, this tells us that Mallory and Irvine parted company with the ice axe and with the oxygen cylinder on different journeys:

- If they dropped or placed the ice axe on the ascent, then they continued westwards, towards the summit, passing below the place where, on the return journey, they would discard the cylinder.
- If they discarded or cached the cylinder on the ascent, they were above the place where, on the return journey, they would drop (improbably) or put down (more probably) the ice axe.
- Or (here's a ball out of left field) they cached the ice axe and the cylinder on different days: conceivably, the cylinder on June 7 and the ice axe on June 8. We have reason to believe that caching oxygen was part of Mallory's plan. On June 7, after pitching their Camp VI, they had several hours of daylight: enough time to climb up and cache one or two cylinders for the following day.

Are we permitted to conjecture that, in some way, the ice axe was a marker for the cylinder? This would only make sense if, firstly, the cylinder was full and needed to be recovered on the way down; and secondly, if our data is less accurate than we imagine, and the ice axe and the cylinder were on the same slab. All the parties concerned are long gone, and we have no way to know.

If, as seems less probable, the 250-yard mark for the ice axe is correct, then the two events could have occurred on the same journey. There is an easy path between the 250-yard mark and the cylinder; and then there is no necessary link between the stories of the axe and the cylinder.

A second cylinder?

We should record a possible observation, although reported at second hand, of another oxygen cylinder near the First Step:

> *'[An expedition member] appeared to recall seeing an old oxygen bottle sticking out of the snow below the exit from the Yellow Band during the ascent. A sherpa had picked up this bottle and later cached it higher up the ridge.'*[29]

This author has corresponded with that climber, who did not recall such a discovery[30]. In any event, the account does not make much sense. We might ask why a Sherpa (unnamed, as per Everest tradition) should retrieve and move an old oxygen bottle, and on whose instructions. We again have the sense that a reference to the Sherpa was good for any unexplained event. One wonders if any of the team had read *The Right Stuff*; replace 'Sherpa' with 'the hatch on the Mercury capsule', and you have Gus Grissom's get-out-of-jail card: 'I didn't do anything. It just blew'.

In any case, there remains the possibility that Richards' improbable discovery was not serendipity; that he did not discover the specific cylinder that Simonson remembered seeing eight years earlier; and that there were at least two old cylinders to the east of the First Step, and maybe more.

Full or empty?

To draw any substantive inference about the significance of the cylinder, we should first wish to know if it contained any oxygen, or not. For due diligence, we should report a statement on Jake Norton's YouTube blog, dated sometime in 2022. Replying to a comment on a Chinese cylinder from 1960, which he had found in 2004, and which had some residual pressure, he wrote:

> *'So did the 1924 one we recovered in 1999.'*[31]

However, a photograph of the cylinder, of which an extract is reproduced in Figure 11.9 above, shows a climber holding the cylinder lightly in his left hand. A full cylinder would weigh about sixteen pounds and could hardly be held with so little effort. So our assumption is that the cylinder, when found, was empty or nearly so.

There are at least two possible inferences:

- that the cylinder was discarded in 1924 when empty or nearly empty
- that the cylinder was discarded or cached in 1924 when full or nearly full, and lost pressure slowly over the following seventy-five years.

The fact that the cylinder was 'wedged' beneath a boulder seems a possible argument against being discarded when empty. Other than this, we have no way of knowing which inference is correct. But possibly we can test both inferences, and see where they lead.

Ascent or descent?

The location and condition of cylinder #9 *per se* tell us nothing about whether it is a marker of the ascent or the descent; nor even whether it was a marker of the summit day.

Here we must recall that cylinder #9 was not accompanied by any part of the carrying frame; if it had been the final cylinder discarded on the descent, we might expect the frame to be present. Certainly, Odell's famous photograph of Mallory and Irvine departing Camp IV, on 6 June 1924, shows a frame on Irvine's back and possibly on Mallory's (though Mallory was facing the camera). On 8 June, Odell found what seemed to be parts of a frame or frames at Camp VI. There is no evidence, and there is no necessity, that Mallory or Irvine used the frames on their last climb.

Let us assume that the original contents of cylinder #9 were 490 litres. The maximum flow rate was 2.5 litres per minute; therefore, the minimum time to consume the contents was 3.27 hours. If the cylinder was set down on the summit day, we have two scenarios to consider:

- If Mallory and Irvine set down cylinder #9 on the ascent, it was when they had climbed between 474 and 490 vertical feet (using our estimate for their Camp VI, and Hemmleb's for the cylinder). If they had used it at maximum flow, 3.27 hours had elapsed since their departure. That implies an ascent rate of 145 to 150 feet per hour: which is improbably slow, for this relatively easy terrain. We are encouraged to think that they did not use oxygen in this part of the climb, and cached cylinder #9 with its full contents. At that point, they would have 1,242 to 1,258 vertical feet between them and the summit: if Mallory's assumption was an ascent rate of 300 feet per hour, they would expect to need four hours, equivalent to another cylinder each, at slightly below full flow.
- If the climbers consumed and set down cylinder #9 on the descent, then barring accidents or other misfortunes, we can estimate their vertical speed as at least 600 feet per hour. The vertical distance of about 1,200 feet from the summit to the cylinder location would have taken at most two hours. A descending climber would not have needed the full contents of cylinder #9. In this scenario, one climber discarded cylinder #9 with some oxygen remaining; and possibly, the other climber discarded another cylinder nearby.

The third scenario is that the climbers cached cylinder #9 on 7 June: the day before their summit attempt. It was about 440 to 460 vertical feet above their Camp VI; a climb of about an hour and a half, plus a half hour for the return to the high camp. On summit day the climbers either returned to that location and did not need the cylinder; or they did not return to the location. In any event, there cylinder #9 would remain, for seventy-five years.

We have no real way to assign probabilities to any of these scenarios. Cylinder #9 could have been full, part full or empty; it could have been cached or discarded; if discarded, it could have been on the ascent or the descent, or the previous day. For the moment, we have to leave it there.

The mitten

Again as a matter of due diligence, we have to mention the mitten.

On 29 April 2001, Jake Norton was on the North Face of Everest as part of the 2001 Mallory and Irvine Research Expedition. Later, he recalled:

> *'On April 29th, Brent [Okita] and I fixed fresh line through the Yellow Band and up to the Northeast Ridge. ... Knowing that the top of these gullies can be difficult to find at times, I began looking around for something with which to mark the route. A bit of brown cloth protruded from a snowy hole at my feet; looking closer, I pulled an old, felt mitten from the slope.'*[32]

Jochen Hemmleb, who was on the same expedition, confirmed to this author that the mitten was found on the crest of the ridge, just west of the Warts. Hemmleb evaluated the mitten as follows:

> *'A woollen mitten of unknown provenance, but very probably from Mallory and Irvine, was recovered in 2001 from 27,700 feet (8,440 m) on the Northeast Ridge.'*[33]

This altitude would be about 300 feet above the 1933 Camp VI, and about 280 feet below the base of the First Step, therefore near the point which Wager and Wyn-Harris had passed in 1933. Absent any geolocation of the mitten, it seems possible to attribute it to a member of the 1933 expedition; at least it does not seem self-evident that it had belonged to Mallory or Irvine.

Camp VI

After Odell's hopeless searches of Mallory's and Irvine's Camp VI on 8 and 10 June, 1924, at least three parties are known to have visited the remains of a high camp from 1924. Two were in 1933, and the third was in 2001.

The members of the British Everest expedition of 1933 knew of only one Camp VI from 1924; as their map shows (and as illustrated in Figure 11.11), it was Norton's and Somervell's Camp VI at 26,800 feet on the North Ridge. As Ruttledge would write (probably incorrectly):

> *'... Norton's Camp VI of 1924 [was] where Mallory and Irvine spent their last night of life ... '*[34]

Ruttledge and his colleagues had no knowledge of a Camp VI at 27,300 feet. Possibly only John Noel believed or knew that Mallory had pitched a camp at that altitude; he had written his account of Mallory and Irvine's climb in 1927, but Ruttledge presumably had not read it.

The first climber to find Norton's tent was Jack Longland. On May 29, 1933, he set out with Wager, Wyn Harris and eight porters to establish their own Camp VI. To save time after a late start, they traversed out to the west and diagonally across the North Face. After pitching Camp VI with a single tent for the first summit attempt, it was Longland's task to escort the porters back to Camp V. It was on this descent that he took what later became famous as the 'Longland traverse'; that story has been told by Ruttledge and others.

What matters for our story is that on his traverse, Longland must have passed within a hundred yards of Mallory's and Irvine's high camp. But he never knew it; instead, he found the remains of Norton's and Somervell's Camp VI; he identified it as 'the 1924 Camp 6' (since he was aware of only one).

Longland paused among the ruins, and took a moment to retrieve some artifacts. He brought them down to Camp V, joining Shipton and Smythe who were waiting for their turn to ascend. Smythe would recall what Longland had found:

> *'[Longland] flung a flat object on to the floor— a folding lantern in a leather case. They had come across the remains of the 1924 [Norton and Somervell] Camp 6 and it was lying amid the debris. Also an electric torch ... an old-fashioned mechanical dynamo-driven affair. I picked it up and pressed the lever. Instantly the dynamo hummed and the bulb lit up. It had lain there for nine years and not a speck of rust adhered to it.'*[35]

Shipton and Smythe, on their climb from Camp V to Camp VI on May 30, 1933, also passed by Norton's camp, but evidently did not stop to investigate. As Smythe later wrote:

> *'Some two and a half hours above Camp V we passed the remains of the 1924 Camp VI. The tent had long since been blown to ribbons, and its green fabric lay forlornly among its weather bleached poles.'*[36]

Mallory and Irvine, on 7 June 1924, would have had the opportunity to collect the lantern and the torch from Norton's camp on the way to their own high camp; but they did not. Possibly they had lighting equipment of their own; we have no way to know.

As far as the record shows, sixty-eight years would pass before anyone attempted to rediscover Mallory's and Irvine's last lodgings. On 30 April 2001, Jake Norton and Brent Okita searched on the North Ridge for a Camp VI from 1924. As we related in Chapter 10, Jake Norton found the remains of a tent, and among the debris, an old sock with the label 'Norton'; clearly the sock had once been owned by Edward Norton, who with Somervell had occupied the tent on the night of 3-4 June 1924. But it was not Mallory's and Irvine's Camp VI.

The camera?

It is a matter of record that neither the 1933 nor the 2001 expedition found any trace of a camera or film at the site of Norton's and Somervell's Camp VI; that no camera was found on George Mallory's body in 1999; and that no-one has found a 1924 camera anywhere on Mount Everest. In the decades following Mallory's and Irvine's disappearance, no official account or private memoir ever suggested that either of them had carried a camera on their last climb; and yet a legend exists, of unknown provenance, that one or both of them did.

Let us examine the evidence, for and against.

On the 1924 expedition, John Noel was the official photographer, as he had been in 1922. He had a personal contingent of porters reporting to him, as well as animals for the transport of his equipment, and a tent reserved for his dark-room and his photographic supplies. Noel's principal objective was cinematography, as well it might be, as he had offered £8,000 to the Mount Everest Committee for the photographic rights of the expedition. He took the last image of Mallory and Irvine alive, as specks on a short film clip, somewhere on the North Ridge.

It fell to Bentley Beetham to maintain a record of the expedition in still images. As Norton wrote later:

> *'[Beetham] contributed the majority of the still photographs this year ... The name of Noel is as familiar to most of you as his work. This year he specialized on the cinema [cinematography], leaving most of the still photography to Beetham.'*[37]

As to what the climbers had in the way of photographic equipment, Beetham summed it up:

> *'Concerning the rest of us, ... our photographic outfit was most essentially of the tourist description - a battery of nine hand-cameras amongst ten men! These ranged in size from a spacious post-card down*

to the vanishing point in the V.P.K.'s [Vest Pocket Kodaks]. These latter are probably ideal for photography high up on the mountains, where every ounce of weight and every mechanical detail, bother, or intricacy, are of importance ...'[38]

There were thus nine still cameras available for carrying on climbs. An unknown number of these were Vest Pocket Kodaks: probably the only model of camera that could in practice be operated on a high climb. Somervell carried one such camera on his climb with Norton on 3-4 June 1924. He used it to take his famous photograph of Norton at about 28,000 feet, at a spot that, at the time, was billed as the highest point at which any photograph had ever been taken.

There was apparently at least one portable cine-camera available to climbers; and on June 4, 1924 Irvine had access to it:

'Have brought Noel's pocket cinema [camera] up but not used it yet.'[39]

However, Irvine did not take it with him on his last climb. As the camp diaries testify, it was retrieved from Camp IV on 10 June:

'15.15 hrs. [3:15 pm] Nima and Mingma leave [Camp IV] for Camp III with Mallory and Irvine's kit, Noel's cine camera and a note for Norton.'[40]

Irvine certainly had taken some photographs during the trek across to Tibet, mainly of people and scenery. There is no certainty as to what camera he used. At one point he surreptitiously took a 70-second exposure in a temple; but this could be done with either a plate camera or a Vest Pocket Kodak. If he took any photographs on Mount Everest itself, none has survived. As to whether he carried any other camera on 8 June 1924, the record is mute.

As for Mallory: he had taken a few photographs on the 1921 expedition. In 1922, he seemed to have no interest in photography, and sometimes wrote as if it were a job for others:

'Down at the Base Camp we would often sit on, those of us who were not expert photographers ...'[41]

[on the high climb of 20 May 1922] 'Two of us, Norton and I, as Somervell's photograph proves, appeared positively dainty ...'[42]

'Somervell's photographs will convey more to the trained eye of a mountaineer than any words of mine ...'[43]

His comments suggest to us, like much of his writing, that he saw himself as a wordsmith, a poet, a man of letters; not as a cameraman.

In the course of the 1924 attempt, Mallory's thoughts were preserved only in his letters to his wife, and to a few friends. Some of these letters were published in *The Fight For Everest 1924*. In thirty-nine pages, there is only one reference to photography, when Mallory alluded to 'some attempts at photographing the remarkable houses' in Sikkim. If he took any photographs on Mount Everest on the expedition, he never wrote of it.

However, there was one camera that belonged to Mallory. Irvine, in his diaries on Everest in 1924, referred to a long afternoon that he spent repairing 'Mallory's camera'.[44] Whether it was a plate camera or a Vest Pocket Kodak, and whether the repair was successful, he did not say.

On 7 June 1924, prior to his last climb, Mallory sent his brief and famous note to Noel. It read *inter alia*: '… it won't be too early to start looking out for us … at 8.0 p.m. [am]'[45] Mallory knew that Noel would have a telephoto lens trained on the summit; and Noel had assured Mallory that, given visibility, he could record climbers at a distance of three miles. We are entitled to believe that, if Mallory needed proof of his ultimate success (and surely he did), Noel would be the man to furnish it; not Mallory himself.

Somervell's camera

Finally, for due diligence, we must quote from Graham Hoyland, a cousin of Howard Somervell. In 2013, Hoyland related a story that Somervell had told him around 1971, when Hoyland was thirteen years old and Somervell was eighty-one:

> *''We met Mallory at the North Col on his way up. He said to me that he had forgotten his camera, and I lent him mine. So, if my camera was ever found … you could prove that Mallory got to the top.''*[46]

We recall that on 4 June 1924, when Somervell started his descent from his high point, he had had a near-death experience; he had, in his own words, 'sat down in the snow to die'. He lived to tell the tale; and Norton recorded that 'Odell and Mallory met us well above the North Col, and by 9:30 p.m. escorted us into No. IV. Camp …'[47]

There is one typewritten note in the Camp IV diary for 4 June 1924, which confirms Norton's and Somervell's return, with the name Mallory handwritten alongside. It reads:

> *'After sunset and just before dark two men (considerably separated) were observed coming down the snow ridge. Odell and Mallory at once set out … after going some way up the ridge this party met Norton and Somervell who were lighting themselves down with a torch. All reached [Camp] IV at 9.30 pm.'*[48]

Odell, who shared with Mallory the task of escorting Norton and Somervell, never recorded a handover of a camera. The same night, Norton shared a tent with Mallory; Norton, likewise, never referred to Mallory's borrowing a camera. Apart from the note in the Camp IV diary, Mallory left no record.

Indeed, Somervell had had his Vest Pocket Kodak on his high climb with Norton. In *After Everest*, which includes by far the most detailed account of the climb, he devoted a whole paragraph to his struggles with the camera:

> *'I tried several times to take a photograph of the wonderful early-morning view, but could only expose my bare hand to the wind for a second or two at a time. The first time the gloves were off I got the camera opened but could not press the shutter-release. Gloves on again;*

> *hands warmed up, and another shot at it—no good; hands won't work. The third attempt was successful ...* '[49]

It is a matter of record that Somervell did get to grips with his camera and the wind. Later, the film was developed, and it yielded at least two celebrated images of Norton: one in which he was climbing onwards and upwards alone, at around 28,000 feet; and one on the descent, sitting on a rock and drinking tea.

In order for Somervell to lend his camera to Mallory, he had to do it on the North Col, in darkness, in a state of physical collapse; or he had to come to Mallory's and Norton's tent after 9:30 pm and hand it over. Furthermore, in order for his photographs of Norton to be preserved (as they certainly were), he had to rewind and remove the film and replace it with a fresh roll; and arguably he would explain to Mallory the operation of the device and the struggle with the cold. No record of this exists.

Instead, in *After Everest*, Somervell told the story of his exhausted return to Camp IV, after which he went straight to bed:

> '*... we entered the camp [IV] soon after nine, and within an hour were warmed and fed and asleep.*'[50]

May we be forgiven for filing the story of Somervell's camera next to *The Beale Papers*.[51]

Traces of traces

In summary: Mallory or Irvine left an ice axe 200 or 250 yards to the northeast of the First Step: probably intentionally, but we do not know. They left oxygen bottle #9, and maybe another bottle, somewhere closer to the First Step; whether they left it on the ascent or the descent, we do not know. Did they cache the cylinder on June 7 and leave the ice axe as a marker on June 8? We do not know. They may have left or lost a mitten somewhere near the Northeast Ridge, or it may be someone else's; we do not know. Over the years, climbers found a torch, a lantern and other items at Norton's and Somervell's Camp VI; they may have no significance. Mallory and Irvine may or may not have carried a camera; we do not know. Those, today, are the physical traces of their passage. The most momentous discovery, as inconclusive as all the others, would be the mortal remains of George Mallory himself.

Chapter 12

'Old English Dead'

Elizabeth Hawley's *Himalayan Database* recorded that as of the spring of 2021, in a period of almost 100 years since the last journey of Mallory and Irvine, there had been 8,505 individual journeys to the north face of Mount Everest[1]. Of these, 998 climbs had been by citizens of China.[2] It may come as no surprise that Chinese climbers have accounted for nearly all of the putative sightings of Mallory or Irvine.

Probably the most celebrated sighting was that of Wang Fu-zhou, a member of the Chinese 1960 expedition and one of the three who reached the summit. He reported his sighting for the first (and apparently only) time in 1965, in what is now Saint-Petersburg, Russia. In 2002, his remarks were quoted by the Alpine Club of Saint-Petersburg as follows:

> *'At an altitude of about 8,600 meters [28,215 feet], we found the corpse of a European.'...*
> *'Why do you think it was a European'?*
> *'He was wearing braces.'*[3]

This was the first of a series of reports of sightings by Chinese climbers, continuing into 2022. But when reading the accounts that circulated on the internet, this author has

Figure 12.1. Wang Fu-zhou, member of the summit team on the Chinese 1960 expedition, (left) in 1960, (right) on Chinese state television in the 2000s. (Xinhua, CCTV)

had the impression that they were at best second- or third-hand and that the reader was invited to engage in a game of Chinese whispers (no pun intended).

This author was impelled to initiate a correspondence with Dr Cheng Li-lan, a modern Chinese climber who had summited Mount Everest in 2016 and had produced an engaging video documentary of his experiences.[4]

> [this author] '*... there have been many references in Western media to sightings by Chinese climbers of the bodies of pre-1950s English climbers. In particular, these sightings include those of Xu Jing (1960), Wang Fu-zhou (1960) and Wang Hong-Bao (1975). I would like to locate the original source documents in which these sightings were first disclosed. I presume that they might be among the archives of the Chinese Mountaineering Association or the China Tibet Mountaineering Association.*'

On the Chinese archives, Dr Cheng said:

> '*... from what I have read so far, the problem of the reported sightings by Chinese climbers of the bodies or tents of the early English climbers is that there's no written record of exactly what was said, and definitely no follow-up investigation right after the claimed sightings. ... I don't know where, if any, an official report is kept.*'[5]

Dr Cheng's comments raised the question of whether, and if so where and how, serious researchers might locate the source documents relating to the Chinese sightings.

What follows in this chapter is an attempt to enumerate all the claimed sightings of deceased pre-war European climbers, in the chronological order in which they were reported in Western media.

1. Charles Warren and others, 1935 (reported 1935)

In August 1935, a British expedition discovered the body of Maurice Wilson, who had disappeared on Everest the previous year. Wilson's diary, found on his body, established his identity. Charles Warren, one of the party that found Wilson, wrote in his own diary:

> '*The body was lying on its left side with the knees drawn up, in an attitude of flexion. ... The torn remains of a tent were pulled out of the snow ... No sleeping bag was to be found. ... we wrapped him in his tent ...*'[6]

Eric Shipton and Edwin Kempson wrote the official account for the benefit of the Indian government authorities:

> Shipton: '*You will probably have heard that we found Wilson's body about 300 yards above our old camp III ...*'[7]

> Kempson: *'On our way up, only 200 yards short of [Camp] 3x, we came across a sad sight, sequel of a tale that happened 13 months ago. ... A man named Maurice Wilson had left Darjeeling disguised as a Tibetan ... We found his body by his tent just 200 yards from the [food] dump ... We burried [sic] him in a crevasse ...'*[8]

Since the 'old Camp III' was the 1933 Camp III, which had been at about 21,000 feet, we may infer that Wilson's body was at about 22,000 feet. Subsequent sightings at this approximate altitude can only refer to Wilson.

2. Xu Jing and others, 1960 (reported 1960)

The earliest reference to Chinese sightings that this author found was dated just three weeks after the Chinese summit on 25 May 1960 (but was not a reference to the 'European in braces'). In *Sovietski Sport* of 15 June 1960, Xinhua correspondent Guo Chao-Zhen wrote as follows:

> *'... the climbers reached a point at an altitude of 5900 meters [19,357 feet] above sea level, where camp number 2 was set up. ... At the bottom of one rock they found a corpse in a faded green suit made of English cloth. This, obviously, was the remains of an English climber who, 20 years ago, tried to climb to the top of Chomolungma [Everest] from the north. Despite fatigue and a snowstorm, the Chinese athletes dug a grave in the snow with the help of ice axes and buried the tragically deceased English climber. ... At the appointed time, the Chinese climbers reached the place where it was planned to set up camp number 3, at an altitude of 6400 meters [20,997 feet].'*[9]

The exact date of this discovery was published in 1993:

> *'March 26 [1960] reached the 5,900m [19,357 feet] camp. March 27 [1960] found a mummified unrecognizable body in English made green down suit. Buried it.'*[10]

Xu Jing, deputy leader of the 1960 expedition, was one of the climbers who saw the body. He gave an interview to the US online journal *EverestNews*, probably on 15 December 2004. Xu was quoted as follows:

> *'100 meters [328 feet] below this second site [6,500m / 21,325 feet] we saw a body said to be a British climber who had tried to climb Everest by himself but had run out of food and oxygen. When we saw him we covered him with snow. He was lying on his side on the ground, with his arms up around his face. His clothes were old and his sleeping bag disintegrated when you touched it. Half of him was lying in the bag, his upper half was exposed to the air, the corpse was very thin, black, mummified and you could see some white bones. His head was pointing north.'*[11]

Figure 12.2. Xu Jing, deputy leader of the 1960 Chinese expedition, in 1964. (Xinhua, CCTV)

There cannot be any doubt that all three of these reports by Chinese climbers describe the remains of Maurice Wilson. What Xu thought was a sleeping bag was probably the remains of the tent in which the 1935 British team had wrapped Wilson's body.

3. Wang Fu-zhou (and others?), 1960 (reported 1965)

The next, and arguably the most famous, reference was that of Wang Fu-zhou, a member of the 1960 Chinese summit party, which we cited above. Here we may insert the context of his remarks, as recalled in 2002 by Dr Yevgeniy Konstantinovich Yordanishvili of the Saint-Petersburg Alpine Club:

> *'8,600 meters [28,215 feet], Mallory and Irvine were last seen here 36 years ago. And ... here climbers stumble upon a mummified corpse. ... Five years later [i.e. in 1965], in the overcrowded assembly hall of the Geographical Society of the USSR, in Leningrad, Wang Fu-zhou, talking about the ascent, said a sensational phrase.'* [12]

And here followed Wang's story of the 'European in braces'.

Perhaps six observations may be permitted.

Firstly, this could not be a spontaneous comment on Wang's part. It was certainly approved by the Chinese authorities at some level. It had a political intent: surely to demonstrate that Chinese had succeeded where Europeans had failed. Perhaps paradoxically, this reinforces the credibility of Wang's sighting; it would have had much more political impact if Wang had seen two deceased Europeans, not just one.

Secondly, Wang said 'we'. It is implicit that at least three members of the summit party (Gombu, Qu Xin-hua, and Wang) saw the body; probably so did the fourth, Liu Lian-man, who fell behind after the Second Step. However, this author could find no record that Gombu, Liu or Qu ever spoke about the sighting.

Thirdly, Wang said 'European', not 'English'. Could he have been allowing his Soviet audience to ponder the fate of the reported 1952 Soviet expedition, which was erased from history?

Fourthly, the word 'mummified' was not attributed to Wang. There is no record that Wang described the condition of the body. It might have been an invention of Dr Yordanishvili, or a conflation with the body of Maurice Wilson.

Fifth, the 1960 climbers followed the Northeast Ridge, which is the modern route from the north. Allowing for Wang to have rounded his number to the nearest 100m, the body could have been between 8,550m [28,051 feet] and 8,650m [28,379 feet]. The lower altitude would have been near the crest of the Second Step; the upper altitude would have been well above the Second Step. Could the body have escaped the attention of hundreds of subsequent climbers on the Northeast Ridge?

Finally, does any evidence exist that on 8 June 1924, either Mallory or Irvine was wearing braces? These devices, with their canvas straps and metal buckles, should survive longer than other clothing accessories. The 1999 expedition made no report of finding braces on Mallory's body. But on April 23 or 24, 1924, at Shekar Dzong on the way to Everest, Noel Odell took one photograph of Irvine outside his tent. Irvine was wearing braces.

4. Wang Hong-bao and others, 1975 (reported 1979)

Wang Hong-bao, a member of the 1975 Chinese expedition, was subsequently a member of the Sino-Japanese expedition of 1979. During that climb, he recounted his sighting to Ryoten Hasegawa, a fellow climber. Wang was said to have told Hasegawa that in 1975 he had seen 'English' at 8,100m [26,575 feet]. Wang has become associated with the phrase 'old English dead' (for which this author has found no source document). The day after his conversation with Hasegawa, Wang perished in an accident.

It is undisputed that Wang Hong-Bao's sighting of 'old English dead', interpreted and elaborated by Jochen Hemmleb's research, led to the discovery in 1999 of Mallory's body.

This author felt that it would be productive to search for the source document which most closely represented Wang's original account. In the *American Alpine Journal*, there is this report:

> *'Bodies on Mount Everest. The accident occurred on October 12 [1979]. Three Chinese died. Among them was Wang Hong Bao, who had climbed five times to the North Col and had reached over 8000 meters [26,247 feet]. The day before the accident, Mr. Wang told our Japanese member R. [Ryoten] Hasegawa that he had seen two corpses when he was a member of the 1975 Chinese Everest expedition. One was near the lateral moraine below Camp III on the East Rongbuk Glacier. This might have been [Maurice] Wilson. The other was at 8100 meters (26,576 feet) on the northeast ridge.*
>
> *Mr. Wang could not speak English, but he repeated the word 'English! English!' to Mr. Hasegawa. When he had touched the clothing, it had broken to bits and was blown off by the wind. Then he had put snow on the body and buried it. (This may well have been the body of either Mallory or Irvine. — Editor.) Hiroyuki Suzuki, Japanese Alpine Club'.*[13]

Large parts of this story raise questions for which there is no ready answer.

Firstly, the only points on the northeast ridge with an altitude of 8,100m (26,575 feet) are in the neighbourhood of the Three Pinnacles. To the best of this author's knowledge, the 1975 Chinese expedition was never in that area.

Secondly, we are told that Wang spoke no English (except the word 'English'); implicitly, English was the only language in which Wang and Hasegawa might have hoped to communicate. Therefore, we infer that Wang spoke no Japanese and Hasegawa spoke no dialect of Chinese. One wonders therefore how the famous phrase 'old English dead' arose. In Mandarin, it would be pronounced 古英死 (*gu ying si*), but if this is what Wang said, Hasegawa could not have understood.

Thirdly, one wonders how, without a common language, Wang could have conveyed his elaborate story. We can imagine him miming the concepts 'two', 'dead', 'touching', 'blowing' and 'burying'. But how would he imply 'old'? How would he explain the altitudes? How would he mime burying with snow? If, for example, he made a scooping motion with his hands, how would Hasegawa know that he meant snow and not gravel?

Fourthly, we might ask why, four years after the event, Wang was keen, indeed insistent, to tell his story to a foreigner. By Tom Holzel's account, in 1975 Wang had already told the story to several Chinese colleagues including his tent-mate Zhang Jun-yan. On the basis of an interview in 1986, Holzel quoted Zhang as follows: 'He [Wang] mentioned it to me and to several of our climbing companions on the way down.'[14] Indeed, from Mark Synnott's claim of a 1975 sighting by Phanthog and others (of which, more below), we might surmise that Wang had shared the story with the whole 1975 expedition. Even in 1979, there were five other Chinese members of the expedition, with whom Wang would have been able to communicate in Mandarin if not in his own dialect.

Finally, Suzuki's article makes no reference to the condition or position of the body, nor to any specific injury; nor is there any implication that Wang moved the body or removed anything from the body. This author has read Western narratives that seem to have embellished Suzuki's story in these respects.

Notwithstanding all of these imponderables, this article was apparently the source for all subsequent Western accounts of Wang's sighting. But it is a third-hand account: Suzuki quoting Hasegawa quoting Wang. The question that we should try to address is: does there exist an anterior, or more primary, source document?

It may be assumed that there exists no first-hand account by Wang Hong-bao. But in principle, second-hand accounts might exist in one or more of the following forms:

- an official account of the 1979 expedition by the Japanese Alpine Club (probably in Japanese)
- an account authored by Ryoten Hasegawa (probably in Japanese)
- an account authored by Zhang Jun-Yan or other members of the 1975 expedition.

5. Chhiring Dorje, 1995

The next report of a sighting is that of Chhiring Dorje, a member of the 1995 Nihon University expedition. Pete Poston wrote that '[on] his way to high camp, he [Chhiring] saw an old body at 8,400m [27,559 feet] in 'army-colored' clothing.'[15]

Figure 12.3. Chhiring Dorje.
(Chris Klinke)

The official report of the expedition[16] confirmed that the last camp, Camp 7, was above 8,500m [27,887 feet], but made no reference to Chhiring's sighting. This author did not find any source document that quoted Chhiring directly. His report seemed to place the body close to the Northeast Shoulder. By 1995, at least 130 persons had died on Everest; we need to hear a first-person account from Chhiring to understand why he believed the body was old.[17]

6. Xu Jing (and others?), 1960 (reported 2001-2008)

The next disclosure was again that of Xu Jing, who in at least four interviews between 2001 and 2008, claimed that he and/or other members of the 1960 expedition had seen a second body, in addition to that we presume to have been Maurice Wilson. The first of these interviews was with Jochen Hemmleb and Eric Simonsen in August 2001, via an interpreter who spoke with Xu in Chinese; they quoted Xu as follows:

> *'There is a body, 8,200 meters [26,903 feet] high, one body ... in a sleeping bag. That person is frozen there. ... He thinks, maybe it is at 8,200 meters [26,903 feet] or 8,300 meters [27,231 feet], between that area.'*[18]

Xu gave another interview to *The Sunday Times* of London, published 27 April 2003:

> *'He had found the body during the descent from Camp VII, on the day his colleagues attempted the summit [24 May 1960]. It was face-up in a narrow gully at 27,300 ft. The body was intact, but its skin was blackened.'*[19]

The reference to a sleeping bag looked like a conflation with the discovery of Wilson. In subsequent interviews, Xu did not mention the sleeping bag.

In his 2004 interview with *EverestNews*, Xu repeated his reference to a second body and implied that his colleagues (presumably Gombu, Liu, Qu and Wang) had also seen it:

> *'I saw another body, although I didn't see very much. It was very dark, it was 24 [May 1960] ... They found the body between First and Second Step. ... I saw the body on the side ... a good bit along from First Step, on Ridge. ... we were definitely past First Step.'*[20]

'Another body' could only mean 'other than the one at 6,400 meters', to which Xu had previously referred in the same interview, and which was undoubtedly that of Maurice Wilson.

In 2008, Xu gave another interview to Jochen Hemmleb. Xu told Hemmleb of a body in a '*Hoehle*' (this could translate as 'cavity', 'hollow' or even 'gully') on the Northeast Ridge. In one version Xu placed it between the First and Second Step; in another version, it was near the Pinnacles.

There are at least six anomalies in the four accounts which are attributed to Xu.

Firstly, according to what appears to be an official account, Xu Jing was not a member of the summit party at all. Shih Chan-chun, the leader of the 1960 expedition, in his article 'The Conquest of Mount Everest by the Chinese Mountaineering Team', stated:

> *'At 09.30 hours Peking [Beijing] time, May 24 [1960], Wang Fu-chou, Chu Yin-hua, Konbu [Gombu] and Liu Lien-man left the assault camp at 8,500 m. [27,887 feet] and embarked on the last 340 m. [1,115 feet, vertical distance] of their march to the summit.'*[21]

Wang Fu-zhou, writing in *China Reconstructs*, confirmed the composition of the party, and the time of departure:

> *'By noon of May 23 [1960] we had reached the assault camp at 8,500 metres. [27,887 feet] ... It was decided that Liu Lien-man the Harbin fireman, Chu Yin-hua the Szechuan lumberjack, Gonpa the Tibetan armyman and I should be the ones to make the final 382-metre [1,253 feet, vertical] assault. ... At 9.30 a.m. [Beijing time], after finishing final preparations, we strapped on 10 kilogramme loads, which included ice axes and oxygen equipment. After a two-hour climb [i.e. at 11:30 am Beijing time] we began to work our way up the Second Step.'*[22]

The story of the Chinese ascent has been told elsewhere. Here, our interest is that neither Shih nor Wang made any mention of Xu as a member of the summit team. It seems implicit that Xu did not ascend above the assault camp, and therefore did not reach the First Step, nor the Second Step. This is confirmed by Dr Yordanishvili's article, which states that Xu was part of the assault party until possibly 22 May, but did not leave (or was not authorized to leave) the assault camp:

> *'On May 17 [1960], the five go on the assault. ... Overnight stay on May 22 in the pre-summit part of the Everest massif, at an altitude of 8.100 m [26,575 feet]. The next day [23 May 1960] is already 'pre-assault'. ... The head of the assault squad, Xu Jing, remains in the camp to provide communications and in case of unforeseen circumstances ...'*[23]

Secondly, if Xu was referring to a sighting by the summit party (as the phrases 'they found' and 'we saw' suggest), they were not in darkness between the First and Second Step. Wang Fu-zhou wrote that the summit party reached the Second Step at 11:30 am Beijing time. That would have been broad daylight on Mount Everest.

Thirdly, Xu's reference in 2004 to a location between the First and Second Steps is inconsistent with the altitude of 8,200-8,300m [26,903-27,231 feet] of which he had spoken in 2001, and 27,300 feet in 2003. There is no point on the ridge between the First and Second Steps which matches either of those altitudes.

Fourth: if Xu's reference in 2004 meant the 'European in braces', he was at odds with Wang Fu-zhou who had placed that sighting at 8,600m (28,215 feet): that is, between the Second and Third Steps.

Fifth: as far as is known in the public domain, the 1960 Chinese expedition at no point traversed what we now call the 'Pinnacles'.

Sixth: Xu's statements in 2001 and 2003 appear to refer to a sighting that he personally made, on a descent from the high camp (implying that he started his descent without waiting for the summit party to return). His statement in 2004 reads as if he is referring to a sighting by the summit party on their ascent ('past the First Step'), and somehow implies that he was a member of that party (which he was not).

The interviews with Xu were presumably in Mandarin, translated to English by an interpreter. The Mandarin for 'I' is 我('wo'), for 'we', 我們 ('women'), and for 'they', 他們 ('tamen'). In this author's experience, it is not unusual for Mandarin speakers, especially when speaking to foreigners, to use 我們 for 'I', as a way of diffusing individual identity, or of aligning the speaker with an official narrative. It is entirely possible that the interpreter used 'I' when the original concept was 'we'; it is not necessary that Xu himself was part of the 'we'. This author is tempted to think that Xu might have been using a collective 'we', and that he might have been referring to an event that he did not personally experience.

In order to read Xu's story to the effect that he personally saw a body on 24 May 1960, we have to assume that he departed the high camp alone, for reasons on which official accounts are silent. Shih's and Wang's accounts give no indication of when, if ever, the summit party re-joined Xu; only that they and 'all members of the climbing party' arrived at Base Camp on 30 May 1960. After the summit date, Xu disappears from the official narrative.

7. Pan Duo (Phanthog) and others, 1975 (reported 2008?)

Mark Synnott published an article in *Salon* on 8 April 2022, in which he referred to a sighting by Pan Duo (Phanthog) and other members of the 1975 Chinese expedition. Synnott quoted Wayne Wilcox, a retired US Marines officer, who had arranged for an interview with Pan Duo around 2008.

Wilcox later described this interview as follows:

> *'I had a friend who worked for The Economist in Beijing and he, I told him the story, and he said, well, I can loan you one of my reporters to go interview her. So he sent one of his Chinese language staff reporters to interview Pan Duo with a list of questions about the camera.'*[24]

The interview, as quoted by Synnott, reads in part as follows:

> *'Economist: Roughly where on Everest did you discover the body?*
>
> *Pan Duo: Probably at around 8,200 meters. [26,903 feet] ... It was a foreigner, and he had a yellow zhangfeng [tent] with nothing else inside. The things had probably already been carried away. ... He probably*

Figure 12.4. Phanthog (Pan Duo), probably in 1975. (Chengdu 2021)

> *froze to death. ... We buried him under a pile of stones: it wasn't bad. We stood there freezing. The body lay on the floor, when we went to pull him, maybe spleen or whatever, all would have been damaged. We considered it and then put small stones on his body, to show our grief/ mark the grave.'*[25]

Pan Duo is a Sinicized version of the Tibetan name Phanthog, and refers to the Tibetan-Chinese climber who participated in the 1975 Chinese expedition and reached the summit.

To assess the authenticity of the report, we need first to understand the language in which the interview was conducted. Wilcox's friend sent a Chinese-speaking interviewer; Phanthog spoke Mandarin fluently. We may suppose that the questions were written in English; the interviewer and Phanthog spoke Mandarin; and the interpreter made a transcript in English for Wilcox. However, the Chinese words for 'grief' 悲傷 (*beishang*) and 'grave' (墓 *mu*) do not sound even approximately the same; the use of both English words in the transcript seems to imply that the interviewer used a similar-sounding word, which was never resolved.

In Chinese, the word 'yellow' 黃(*huang*) could refer to any mid-range colour between bright yellow and light brown.

The Chinese word for 'tent' is 帐篷 (*zhangpeng*). The word transliterated as '*zhangfeng*' in the interview may have been 帐缝 which could mean something like 'tent seam'. If the word '*zhangfeng*' really meant a tent, the word 'yellow' excludes a tent from the 1924 expedition, in which the tents were universally described as green:

> (Mallory) *'[we] ... set to work pitching our ample green marquee. ... the floor, a large sheet of green canvas ...'*[26]

> (Smythe) *'... the remains of the 1924 Camp VI. ... its green fabric lay forlornly among its weather bleached poles.'*[27]

If the word '*zhangfeng*' meant a garment of some kind, then the word 'yellow' seems at least to exclude Mallory. Descriptions of the clothing found on his remains make no mention of a yellow item. In recent years, monochrome photographs from the early expeditions have been colourized, but we do not know what colours the climbers really wore.

Figure 12.5. The approximate location of Mallory's body, and the 8200m (26,903-foot) contour. (Base image © CNES / Airbus / Google Earth; graphics and legend by author; geolocation and contour line calculated by author by reference to data kindly provided by Jake Norton, and Contour Map Creator)

Phanthog's reported comment that the climber 'probably froze to death' also seems to exclude Mallory, whose injuries would have been as apparent to her as they were to the climbers who found his body in 1999.

Likewise, if Phanthog and her colleague buried the body under a pile of stones, it could not be Mallory, whose body was found largely above ground.

As for the altitude: 8,200m (26,903 feet) is very close to that at which Mallory's body was found (26,864 feet), as shown in Figure 12.5; and also was the altitude of one of at least two sites of the 1975 Camp VI.[28] Phanthog did not say where the body was in relation to any landmark, or to any Chinese camp; in any case, the locations of the camps were never published. Nor did she make any reference to Wang Hong-bao, her late colleague from the 1975 expedition, who had famously reported seeing 'old English dead'.

The body was not that of the English eccentric Maurice Wilson. The 1935 British expedition indeed wrapped Wilson's body in the remains of his tent and buried him, where the Chinese climbers in 1960 would rediscover the body. Wilson never reached the altitude that Phanthog recalled.

This author wrote to *The Economist* to ask if they could help locate the original interview; the enquiry was closed with no reply. A second letter, this time to the Editor, produced the automated reply: '*The Economist* thanks you for your letter, which has been passed to the author of the article.' A third, to the current China correspondent of *The Economist*, awaits a response.

Finally, twenty-two years before her interview for Wayne Wilcox, Phanthog was saying that her memory of the ascent had faded. In the *Beijing Review* of 11 August

1986, Zhao Zonglu wrote an article about Phanthog and her climb of Chomolongma (Mount Everest). He quoted her as telling reporters, in fluent Mandarin with a Beijing accent, that 'though she could still feel the after-effects of reaching the peak, she could no longer remember the details of the climb …'[29]

We are compelled to file the story of Phanthog and the yellow tent, like others of its nature, next to *The Beale Papers*.

The European in braces

Most of the climbers who reported these sightings have passed away: Wang Hong-bao in 1979, Xu Jing in 2011, Phanthog in 2013, Wang Fu-zhou in 2015, Liu Lian-man in 2016, Qu Yin-Hua in 2016. If Gombu is still alive, he is about ninety years old.

In summary, apart from Wilson's and Mallory's remains, we have six reports of an unidentified and presumed European body on the North Face, at altitudes variously recalled as 26,903 feet (Pan Duo), 26,903-27,231 feet (Xu Jing), 27,300 feet (Xu Jing), 27,559 feet (Chhiring Dorje), 27,887 feet (Xu Jing) and 28,215 feet (Wang Fu-zhou).

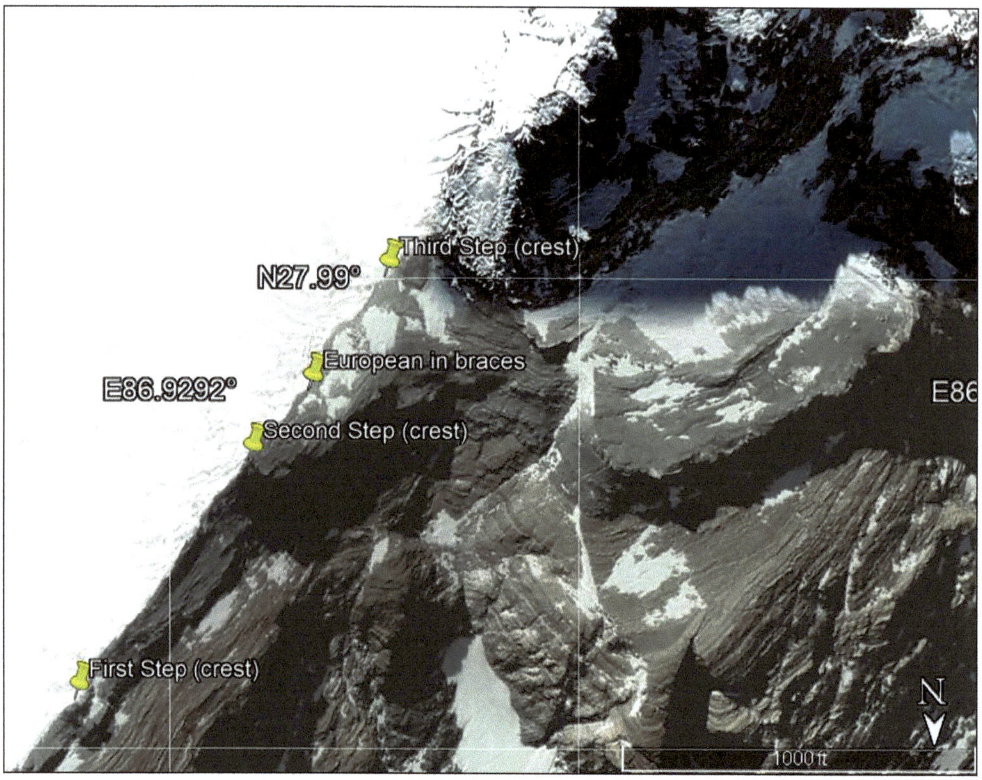

Figure 12.6. The possible location of Wang Fu-zhou's sighting of the 'European in braces' in 1960. (Base image © CNES / Airbus / Google Earth; geolocation by author)

Of these reports, that of Wang Fu-zhou was surely the most authoritative, the closest in time to the event described, and the least investigated. Unequivocally, it was not a sighting of the body of George Mallory nor that of Maurice Wilson. Therefore, it could only be that of Andrew Irvine.

Wang's status as a representative of the People's Republic of China, the proximity in time to the events, and the nature and quality of his audience, to this author's mind endowed his remarks with more credibility than those of the others.

At the moment of his sighting, Wang had left the high camp and was accompanied by Qu Yin-hua, Gombu, and Liu Lian-man. All four climbers must have seen the body: although to the best of this author's knowledge, Gombu, Liu and Qu never spoke of it in public. Xu Jing, who did not ascend from the high camp, cannot have seen the body (notwithstanding his later claims), but certainly his colleagues must have told him of it.

In Figure 12.6, we have attempted to geolocate Wang's sighting on Google Earth. The questions that demand further research are as follows. Does there exist a map, sketch or orthophoto that delineates the most probable route of the Chinese party on 24-25 May 1960, from their high camp to the summit? And if so, can we estimate the maximum possible lateral diversions from the route? Has there ever been a systematic search of the terrain between the Second and Third Steps? If so, we could construct a polygon wherein we could place Wang's sighting; and at least we might develop an informed view of the extent to which the body could have been concealed or moved by natural causes.

Figure 12.7. Irvine at Shekar Dzong on 23 or 24 April 1924. He is working on the oxygen apparatus, and wearing braces. (Author, after a photograph by Noel Odell)

Chapter 13

Finding Mallory

In the spring of 1999, the Mallory and Irvine Research Expedition set out on Mount Everest, to find traces of the two men who had disappeared on 8 June 1924. Eric Simonson led the expedition; Jochen Hemmleb advised and directed the climbers. Hemmleb had worked primarily from the accounts of the 1975 Chinese expedition: in particular the account of Wang Hong-bao, who had reported a sighting of 'old English dead' on the North Face at about 8,200m (26,903 feet). On this basis, Hemmleb had defined a possible search area. It is fair to say that Hemmleb's original research was crucial to the success of the expedition.

As the mountaineering world knows, on 1 May 1999 the climbing members of the team found the mortal remains of George Mallory. The first person to sight Mallory was Conrad Anker; he was joined by Dave Hahn, Jake Norton, Andy Politz, and Tapley Richards. It was clear that Mallory had died after a fall. The climbers removed artifacts from his body and his pockets, took samples of his clothing and his skin, and covered his body with stones.

The story of the expedition, the discovery and subsequent events has been told: notably by Anker and David Roberts[1], and by Hemmleb[2]. This author cannot add to that narrative. Here, our interest is to focus on the location and condition of Mallory's body, and the nature of the artifacts found on him; and thereby perhaps to gain insight into the events of his and Irvine's last climb.

First, the location. The expedition never publicly released the altitude, latitude or longitude of the site where Mallory was found. That was understandable, given that precise co-ordinates in the public domain could lead to more, and not necessarily respectful, visits to Mallory's grave. This author is indebted to Jake Norton for advising, through his Undefined Community forum, that the altitude was '26,864 feet, give or take a bit'[3], and that the location was within an ellipse approximately centred on latitude 27.9983 north, longitude 86.9301 east.

The altitude of Mallory's body was approximately the same as that of Colonel Norton's and Somervell's Camp VI, which was most recently calibrated (also by Jake Norton) at 26,900 feet or possibly higher. But he was about 1,600 feet to the west of that camp. Had he been alive at that point, he would have had what looks like (on Google Earth) a relatively easy traverse, almost horizontal, to safety.

Mallory's body was about 1,000 feet below the crest of the Northeast Ridge, and about 900 feet below where the ice axe and oxygen bottle #9 had been found. He was in a place where no modern climber treads. On the North Face, whenever the Chinese government permits climbing, all modern climbers follow more or less the crest of the Northeast Ridge.

If for any reason, rather than returning to his unoccupied and unsupported Camp VI, Mallory had been attempting to reach Camp V, it was about 1,500 feet below him

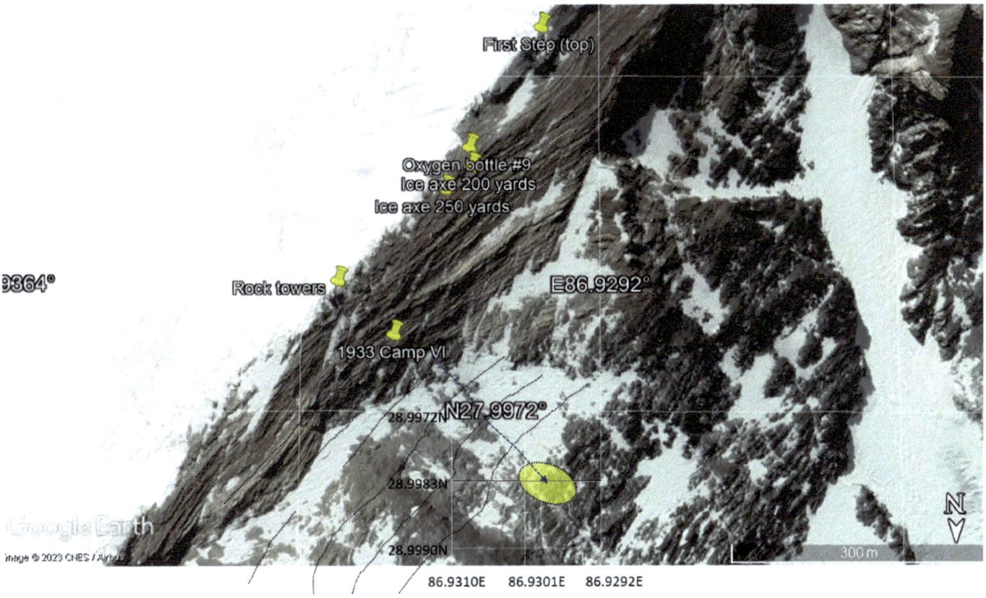

Figure 13.1. The approximate location of Mallory's body, and other relevant points on the North Face of Mount Everest. (Base image © CNES / Airbus / Google Earth; contour lines by author from Contour Map Creator; graphics and legend by author)

on a diagonal traverse. For a climber in good physical condition, even without oxygen, it would be a descent of about two and a half hours, maybe less. Again, on such a route he would be on unknown terrain.

One inference seems indisputable: Mallory could not have fallen from the location of the ice axe. A falling body should follow a trajectory approximately perpendicular to the contour lines. On the Google Earth image in Figure 13.2, we have superimposed some of the relevant contour lines. Mallory's fall line was in approximately a north-westerly direction: about 42 degrees from true north.

Whether Mallory had fallen from within or below the Yellow Band, his fall line was at least 300 feet to the east of the closest possible location of the ice axe. To this author's mind, a body that falls even as much as 900 feet cannot travel 300 feet horizontally.

The fall line

If Mallory fell from the higher slabs of the Yellow Band, his fall would have taken him within a few yards of the site where, nine years later, the 1933 expedition would pitch their Camp VI. That site was at 27,430 feet by the modern calibration. Mallory's body was found about 565 feet below that site.

We can identify the site of the 1933 Camp VI on Somervell's famous photograph of Edward Norton, resting on the descent from his high climb on 4 June 1924. We do not know the location or altitude at which Somervell took the photograph. But in the background of the image there is a massive buttress, facing northwest, composed

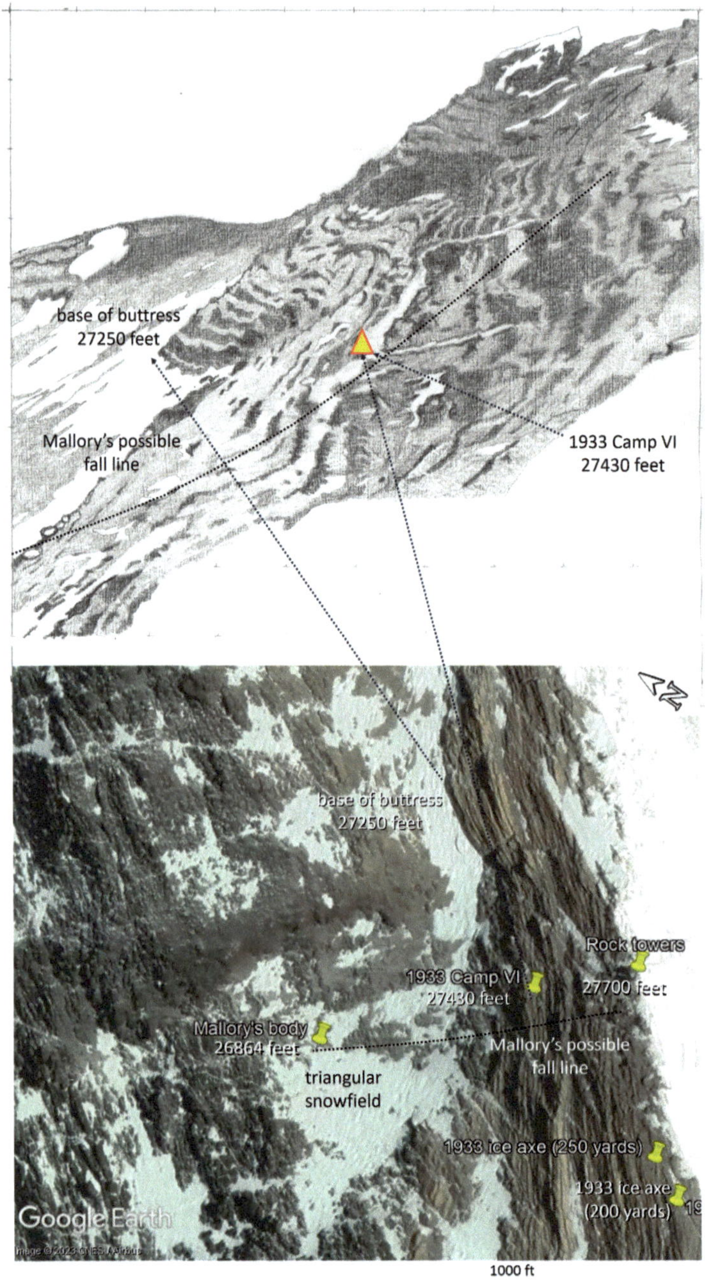

Figure 13.2. Mallory's possible fall line (if from high in the Yellow Band). (above) The view from Colonel Norton's rest spot on 4 June 1924. (Author, after a photograph by T. Howard Somervell) (below) Base image © CNES / Airbus / Google Earth. Graphics and legend by author.

of approximately horizontal slabs. It has a curved base; above the base there is a pronounced upturned ledge. There is nothing like it elsewhere on the North Face. We can see that buttress on Google Earth. That enables us to insert the approximate position of the 1933 Camp VI, as shown in Figure 13.2.

This in turn enables us to sketch Mallory's possible fall line in relation to Somervell's photograph. If Mallory fell from high in the Yellow Band, he fell past the place where Norton had been sitting on 4 June: maybe no more than tens of yards to the northeast.

The slope

In images on Google Earth, at the base of the Yellow Band and above the location of Mallory's body there is a triangular snowfield, about 600 feet wide in the northeast-southwest axis. During the expedition of 1999, there was very little snow; the triangular snowfield may have been entirely absent. Photographs of Mallory's remains, taken presumably on 1 or 16 May 1999, show bare rock for at least tens of yards in all directions.

We do not know for sure whether the snowfield was present in 1924. It was outside the frame of the photograph that Somervell took on 4 June 1924; but the narrower snowfield to the south, which is within Somervell's frame, matches what we see on Google Earth today. That gives us reason to think that the triangular snowfield was there on 8 June 1924, when Mallory and Irvine were on their last climb.

Figure 13.3. The site where Mallory's body was found on 1 May 1999. Mallory's body is below the foot of the image. (© Jake Norton)

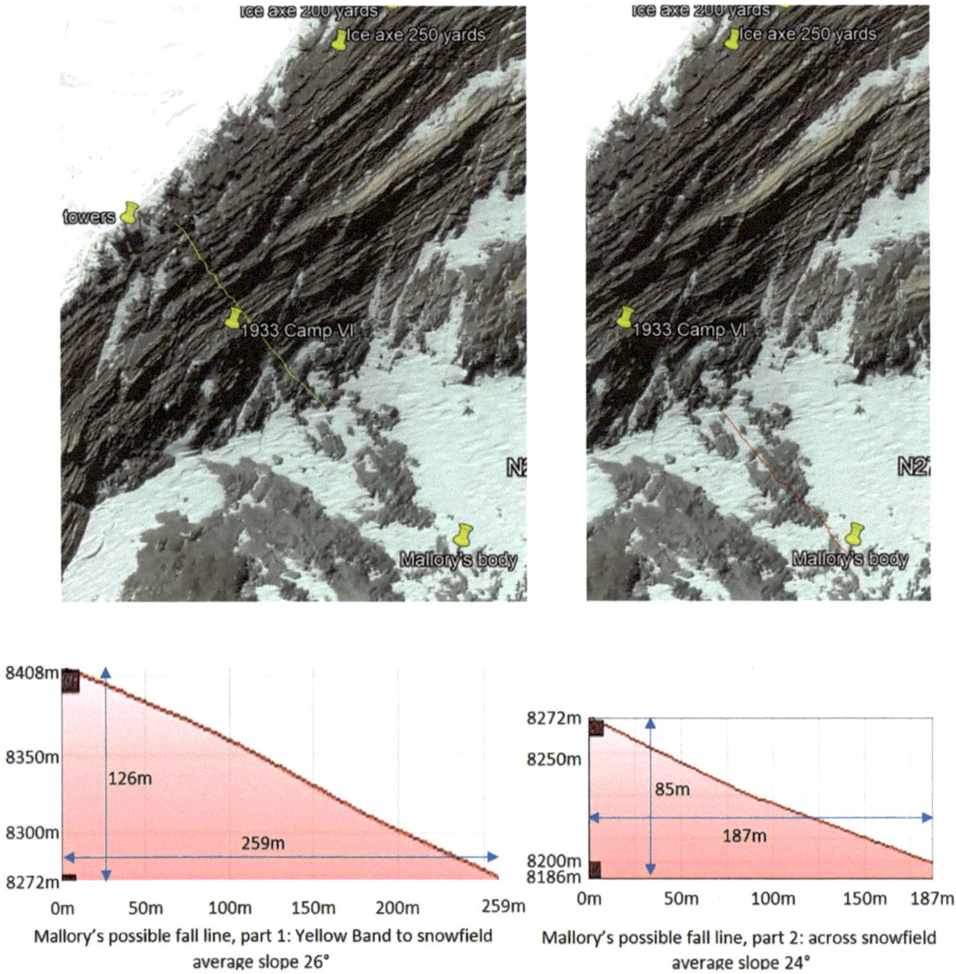

Figure 13.4. Two possible components of Mallory's fall line. (left) from high in the Yellow Band to the triangular snowfield. (right) across the triangular snowfield. (Base image © CNES / Airbus / Google Earth. Graphics and legend by author)

If so, to reach the position where his body was found, Mallory had to tumble, slide or roll through some part of the triangular snowfield. If he fell from the Yellow Band, then he fell through the whole of the snowfield. We can use the snowfield to mark a boundary between two possible components of his fall.

If Mallory fell from the slabs of the Yellow Band, at the same level as the ice axe (that is, from about 27,600 feet, near the upper slabs), and reached the top of the snowfield, then his body had to travel about 850 feet horizontally and about 415 feet vertically. The average slope of that triangle is 26 degrees[4].

If Mallory fell from below the Yellow Band, he would have been on slightly flatter terrain. If he fell at the top of the snowfield, his body covered about 615 feet horizontally and about 280 feet vertically. That slope averages 24 degrees.

Neither of these slopes is very steep. At a ski resort, they would not be considered dangerous; maybe above beginners' level, but not much more.

The point where Mallory came to rest can be seen in a famous photograph taken by Jake Norton. The terrain at that point appears to have a slope of about 33 degrees.

Orientation

The 1999 expedition members never disclosed the orientation of Mallory's body as they found it. We know that they excavated the body twice; we do not know whether they changed the orientation when they buried and reburied it. This author is grateful to Jake Norton for his recall of the approximate orientation of the body. He remembered that Mallory's head was pointing roughly in the direction of the 'Warts'.[5] The feet were downhill on a heading of about 300 degrees from true north; the head was uphill on a heading of about 120 degrees.[6]

We have estimated that Mallory's fall line was approximately in a north-westerly direction: on a bearing of about 318 degrees. If he maintained approximately a constant body orientation as he fell, then he fell feet first, and with his body at about 18 degrees to his fall line. That divergence gives us cause to wonder if he was rolling as he fell.

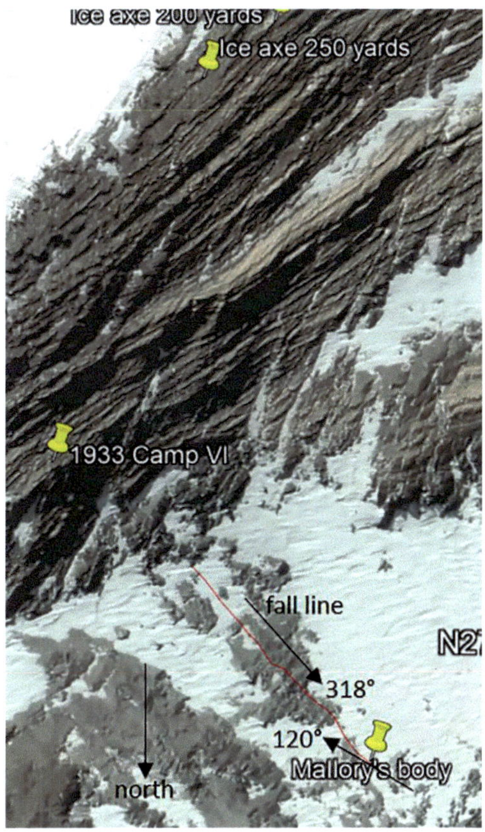

Figure 13.5. The orientation of Mallory's body relative to his presumed line of fall. (Base image © CNES / Airbus / Google Earth. Graphics and legend by author)

Injuries

As far as is known in the public domain, no medical or paramedical professional has ever expressed a view on the sequence of Mallory's injuries or the cause of his death. However, this author is indebted to Jake Norton for the following medical comment based on a description of Mallory's final position:

> *'... when Jochen [Hemmleb] and I were with the King County Coroner in the autumn of 1999 ... Despite the [Mallory's] head injury, the coroner was adamant that his positioning was not that of someone who died before they came to rest there, but died after.'*[7]

Essentially, what we know about the condition of Mallory's body is based on the statements of members of the 1999 expedition.

When the climbers found Mallory's body on 1 May 1999, it was face down and partly covered by frozen scree. Most of his clothes were gone. His back, torso, legs and upper arms were clear of the ground. His arms were outstretched above his head. His head was almost completely buried. His hands were partly buried, but it could be seen that they were bare. On a first inspection, they could see that his major observable injury was a broken right leg:

> (Anker and Roberts) *'His right leg was badly broken, both tibia and fibula. With the boot still on, the leg lay at a grotesque angle. They weren't compound fractures — the bones hadn't broken the skin — but they were very bad breaks. ... The right elbow looked as if it was dislocated or broken. ... The right scapula was a little disfigured. And above his waist on a right rib, I could see the blue contusion ...'*[8]

> (Hemmleb) *'The tibia and fibula of his right leg were broken above the top of his boot, and his right elbow was either broken or dislocated. There were a number of still-visible cuts, abrasions, and bruises along his right side as well, and the climbing rope in which he was tangled had compressed his rib cage and tugged at his skin.'*[9]

The climbers observed that the unbroken left leg was crossed, at mid-calf, over the broken right leg.

Other than the injuries that appeared directly attributable to Mallory's fall, it was clear that predators had attacked the body:

> (Anker and Roberts) *'Goraks — the big black ravens that haunt the high Himalaya— had pecked away at the right buttock and ... had eaten out most of the internal organs ...'*[10]

> (Hemmleb) *'Though the body was remarkably intact, Everest's goraks*[11] *had pecked at it and damaged one leg, his buttocks, and the abdominal cavity.'*

On the second disinterment of the body, on 16 May 1999, Politz and Pollard made a more complete excavation of Mallory's head. They found that he was wearing a leather helmet. Pollard found an injury which had not previously been detected.

> (Pollard) *'The face was in perfect condition ... It was ever so slightly distorted — pancaked, in effect — by the years of bearing the weight of snow. His eyes were closed. I could still see whiskers on his chin. ... Over his left eye, there was a hole. There was dried blood, and two pieces of skull sticking out.'*[12]

Finally, Anker and Roberts referred to the 'absence of frostbite on Mallory's mummified body'.[13] However, a photograph has circulated on the internet, attributed to 'Andy Politz/ Mallory & Irvine' and watermarked 'Getty Images', showing Mallory's lower left arm and left hand[14]. The image appears to have been taken after the second excavation, on 16 May 1999, as the back and head are partially covered with rocks. This author is indebted to Michael Tracy[15] for confirming with Pollard that the photograph is authentic.

In this image, Mallory's left arm is bare. When he was found on 1 May 1999, his left sleeves of his jacket and shirts had been largely intact; the climbers must have removed them. His left thumb and three fingers are visible; all are black, as far as the first or second joint. To this author, who claims no medical knowledge, this is evidence of frostbite. These injuries can only have occurred prior to Mallory's death.

This author's interpretation of the condition of Mallory's body, as found and as reported, is as follows:

- Before he fell, Mallory had been descending without gloves, for a period long enough for both hands to suffer frostbite.
- Mallory fell an indeterminate distance, between about 300 and about 700 feet vertically.
- Given the single puncture wound to his forehead, and no other damage to his face, Mallory did not slide face-down.
- Given the final orientation of his body and his crossed legs, Mallory's fall had some element of rolling motion in additional to his movement downwards. His outstretched arms may be a consequence of a rolling fall rather than a voluntary positioning.

The rope

The climbers found, entangled around Mallory's body, a rope:

> Anker: *'... a white, braided cotton rope [was] tied to his waist, about three eighths of an inch in diameter. The rope was tangled around his left shoulder. About ten feet from his waist, I could see the frayed end where the rope had broken ...'*[16]

This naturally raised the question of whether, at the moment of his fall, Mallory had been roped to Irvine. If so, Mallory should have had rope injuries; and Irvine, if he had perished in the same event, should be on or near the same fall line. Absent any pathology report, the evidence and the climbers' recollections led to no conclusion:

> *EverestNews*: *'We asked some of the climbers who found Mallory. They told us they saw no rope injuries (except that the rope was frozen into and around his body).'*[17]

Pollard: '... *George Mallory did NOT have rope burns, or other clear indications that the rope pulled into his body, when he fell.* '[18] [upper case in original]

Simonson: '*The Mallory rope was cut by the 1999 team with a knife to get it off his body (it was tightly wrapped and frozen around it). Later, we tried to compare the cut ends which had been cut by knife with the ends from 1924...to see if there was a difference. It was inconclusive .... we couldn't really tell one way or the other, if, for example if the 1924 end had been cut or broken in a fall.* '[19]

To this author, as a non-climber, the simplest interpretation is that Mallory was equipped for roping up with Irvine if necessary; the rope does not tell us that the two were roped together when Mallory fell.

Artifacts

Mallory's right boot was still on his foot. His left boot had disintegrated; all that was found of it was part of the leather upper. The climbers removed the right boot and what remained of the left; these were eventually donated to the Royal Geographical Society, which periodically has placed them on public display in London and at Chester Cathedral in England.

The climbers took samples of what remained of Mallory's clothing. These samples, in themselves, have never led to any meaningful research on Mallory and Irvine's climb or on the manner of Mallory's death. The samples did provide a basis for the manufacture of a replica of Mallory's climbing outfit (excluding his boots), on which we reported in chapter 4.

Among the artifacts that the climbers removed, the following might have had some forensic significance:

- the envelope of the letter from 'Stella', on which we reported in chapter 11, and which appeared to bear Mallory's notes of five oxygen cylinders and their respective pressures
- '… a pair of goggles. The frames were bent, but the green glass was unbroken.'[20]
- '… adjustable webbing straps attached to a metal spring clip (to hold an oxygen mask to the flying helmet) …'[21]
- 'a single fingerless glove'[22]
- '… a smashed altimeter … with a range from 20,000 feet to 30,000 feet … Inscribed on the back, in fine script, was 'M.E.E. II'[23] … The hand was missing from the dial …'[24]
- and finally, a discovery by Politz on 16 May 1999: '… a wristwatch. The glass was gone from its face, and the minute and second hands were broken off, but the short hour hand pointed to between one and two, a little closer to two. (Later, the hour hand was accidentally broken off as they carried the watch down to Base Camp.)'[25]

Hemmleb would later recall that no-one had reported finding the glass from the watch or the altimeter, or fragments of the glass, in Mallory's pockets. Therefore, there could

Figure 13.6. The watch found in Mallory's trouser pocket; a photograph taken before the hour hand was lost. (Thom Dharma Pollard)

be an inference that the glass of both items had been broken before Mallory put them in his pocket.

Here we should record that the watch was found to be in working order. The spring had run down, and when it was re-wound, the watch started working again.

This author's interpretation of the artifacts, from the perspective of a non-climber, is as follows:

- Mallory and Irvine had at least five cylinders of oxygen, all full or nearly full, available at Camp V on 6 June 1924, or at their Camp VI on 7 June. How many they carried on the last climb, we cannot say.
- The goggles carried in a pocket, tell us that, as Politz was the first to observe, Mallory fell at a time of day when goggles were not needed; either in the residual daylight after sunset, or in darkness.
- The straps for the oxygen mask tell us that Mallory fell when he was not using oxygen.
- The single inner glove, in a pocket, tells us that Mallory had lost one inner glove, a pair of outer gloves, and possibly also a pair of mittens.
- The altimeter and the watch tell us nothing about Mallory's and Irvine's last climb.

Here we may recall the injunction of Sherlock Holmes about the dog that did not bark in the night. The following items were not found on or near Mallory's body, or in any radius of the body that was searched in 1999 or on subsequent expeditions:

- an oxygen cylinder, a carrying frame, an oxygen regulator, a breathing tube or fitting, an oxygen mask, or any part of any of these
- an ice axe or any part or fragment of one

- a compass
- a torch or lantern
- a camera, film or any part thereof (nor, as we observed in chapter 11, would we expect it).

Finally, in Mallory's pockets, the climbers found an assortment of personal items, none of which could shed light on the nature of his climb; and no rocks of any kind.

From the condition of Mallory's body, from all the objects known to have been found, and from those not found or never reported, we can reasonably conclude that Mallory fell after sunset, and had not been prepared to be in the open at that time of day. He was on a descent; he was not carrying oxygen cylinders; his hands were frostbitten but his face and feet were not. We do not know whether he fell on 8 June 1924 or later (though it could hardly be later than 9 June). We do not know whether he was with Irvine, or alone.

Pollard and Politz

For a climber's perspective on Mallory's fall, and one which seems to have no preconceived narrative, this author acknowledges the generosity of Pollard and Politz. On 11 August 2022, Pollard published this conversation with Politz, about the events of 1 May 1999, when the team discovered Mallory's body:

> Pollard: *'[you] went down to the Mallory site, by going way out west from Camp Six, not that far, and zigzagging down ...'*
>
> Politz: *'... my goal was to go up there, are we sure the camera hadn't just fallen out? Yeah, so the idea with the metal detector was to sweep the area, sweep up high, down ... and I walked straight down to George Mallory. I don't know if I deviated more than fifty feet. And so I walked down his fall line ... and I'm pretty sure he fell out of this gully I was going up into.'*
>
> Pollard: *'So, 27,000 feet approximately, would you say?'*
>
> Politz: *'... below the Yellow Band, yeah, steep gully, it's real slabby rock, would have been very difficult to down-climb ... but how Mallory fell, that's a whole 'nother discussion.'*[26]

Figure 13.7 includes this author's approximation of the down-climb that Politz made on 1 May 1999, from the steep gully in the Yellow Band, to Mallory's body. The high point of that track, in the gully, is at about 27,300 feet.

In short, Politz believes that Mallory did not fall from high in the Yellow Band, but from near the base, in the gully. If that was so: what Mallory was doing there, and where he was going, or trying to go, is indeed another discussion.

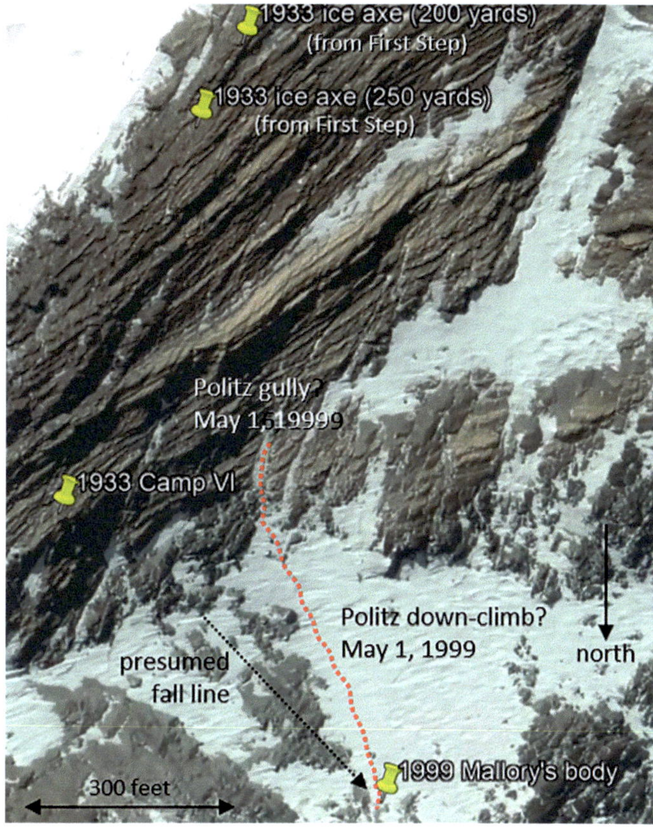

Figure 13.7. An approximation of the down-climb by Andy Politz on 1 May 1999. (Base image © CNES / Airbus / Google Earth. Climb track adapted from map of 1999 search areas and findings, by courtesy of Jake Norton. Legend and graphics by author)

2001 and beyond: an odyssey

With Mallory discovered, and the mystery of his last climb unresolved, attention turned to Irvine. Among believers in a camera, there was still the possibility that Irvine had carried one; and if so, that it might still be on or near his body; and if so, that the film might still be developed.

After 1999, at least eight expeditions made some attempt to search for further traces of Mallory, or for the remains of Irvine: in 2001, 2004 (at least two separate parties), 2010, 2011, 2012 and 2019 (two parties). Of these expeditions, only that of 2001 conducted what we might call a systematic area search; the others appear to have made linear searches, along narrow trajectories. Probably the totality of the searches does not exceed a few per cent of the area of the North Face.

In April 2001, six members of the 1999 team returned to Everest: Simonson as leader, Hahn, Norton, Politz and Richards as climbers, and Hemmleb as historian and researcher. The team was completed by four new Western members and twenty-three Sherpa from Nepal. This author is indebted to Jake Norton for sharing an unpublished map which shows that the team searched the North Ridge; an expanse of the North Face to the northeast of Mallory's body; and parts of the Yellow Band and the Northeast Ridge above the body.[27]

As we recorded in chapter 11, it was on this expedition that Norton and Okita rediscovered Colonel Norton's and Somervell's Camp VI; and Norton found a woollen mitten near the top of the Yellow Band. Norton and Okita recovered several artifacts, but none that was positively linked to Mallory or Irvine. The 2001 expedition found many traces of British expeditions from the 1920s and 1930s, and some from the Chinese climbs of 1960 and 1975; but with regard to Mallory and Irvine, nothing was found that could advance our understanding of their last climb.

In April and May 2004, Hahn and Norton made another search on the North Face[28]. Their main search areas were on the North Ridge above the 1924 Camp VI, and in the Yellow Band, mainly between the 1933 Camp VI and the First Step.[29]

Norton later wrote on his blog:

> *'In 2004, while Dave Hahn and I were searching, EverestNews also conducted a search with two Sherpa doing the work: Chhiring Dorje ... and Nawang Jimba ... '*[30]

As we reported in chapter 12, an account exists that Chhiring Dorje was a member of the 1995 Nihon University expedition to Everest, led by Kiyoshi Furuno[31]; and that during this climb, Chhiring saw a body somewhere near the Northeast Ridge. This has been not confirmed publicly by Chhiring himself, and his presence on Everest that year is not listed in the Himalayan Database. Between 1998 and 2018, Chhiring climbed Everest at least fourteen times[32]. In May and June 2004, he was a member of the SummitClimb Everest Expedition 2004, led by Daniel Mazur[33]. If in fact he was searching on behalf of *EverestNews*, no results of this search exist in the public domain.

Regarding the searches in 2010, 2011 and 2012, this author is grateful to Jake Norton for confirming the following:

- On 26 May 2010, Guenther Goeberl and Sepp Bachmaier[34] searched in the Yellow Band near the two rock towers, above the 1933 Camp VI. Jake Norton's report: '[They] searched into the area of the Warts [the two rock towers] as part of Jochen Hemmleb's 2010 expedition. They found nothing.'[35]
- On 22 May 2011, Phurba Ongel[36] down-climbed the Yellow Band to the northeast of the two towers.
- On 27 May 2011, Stefan Fritsche, Pasang Gelu and Phurba Ongel[37] made a search on the North Face. Jake Norton reported that they searched the 'area through the Yellow Band to the Longland Traverse, up to the Northeast Ridge and out northeast along the Ridge toward the Pinnacles, and finally back again beneath the Warts to the traditional [modern] climbing route. Nothing of note was discovered.'[38]
- On 27 May 2012 Jamie McGuinness[39] made a brief search of a ledge about halfway up the Yellow Band: '... I only explored one long ledge similar or identical to your [Jake Norton's] 19 May 2004 search ... The most sheltered

'alcove' was entirely snow-free and I looked very carefully to spot old fabric etc – nothing'[40].

At the time of writing, the most recent climbs in search of Irvine were those of 2019, by Norton, Sid Pattison and Ken Sauls[41], and by an expedition sponsored by *National Geographic*[42]. Norton's climb was virtually on the crest of the Northeast Ridge, about 300 feet above the 1933 Camp VI. Norton later wrote as follows:

> *'On May 24, 2019, Sid Pattison and I, along with cameraman Ken Sauls, searched again the area of the Warts. ... Sid and I were able to push through the Warts and into the terrain beyond [to the northeast], but found nothing ... '*[43]

Finally, Mark Synnott, of the *National Geographic* expedition of 2019, recounted his descent from the approved climbing route, to the 'slot' where, on the basis of film from a drone camera, he had been instructed to find the body of Irvine:

> *'There was nothing there. '*[44]

and in an interview with Pollard on 18 April 2022, he said with disarming frankness:

> *'... I think I can say with a fair amount of certainty that we were on a complete wild goose chase. '*[45]

Figure 13.8. Mallory imagined, at peace, 16 May 1999. (Author, after a photograph by John Noel; after a detail from our cover painting by Balázs Petheő; after the description on p.199 by Thom Dharma Pollard)

Epilogue

However Improbable

The American poet John Godfrey Saxe, in the year 1872, published a poem titled 'The Blind Men and the Elephant'. The first verse was as follows:

> *'It was six men of Indostan / To learning much inclined / Who went to see the elephant / (Though all of them were blind) / That each by observation / Might satisfy his mind.'*[1]

Saxe's poem was based on an ancient parable, said to have originated in India and possibly to have been told by the Buddha. It concerned six blind men who attempted, by touching an elephant, to determine what kind of object it might be. (We can see where this is going.) One blind man, groping the vast side of the elephant, proclaimed it to be a wall. Another, grasping the trunk, took it to be a snake. A third, seizing the tail, was sure that the elephant was a rope. And so on … None of them could grasp that the elephant might be all of these things.

So it is with Mallory. Placing our hands on the mystery of Mallory and Irvine, we are at risk of making Mallory the elephant, and ourselves the blind men. That is, we can construct a Mallory who is smart or stupid; meticulous or scatter-brained; careful or foolhardy; gay or straight; clumsy or graceful; a tweedy Englishman or a big hard hero. Then we might fight among ourselves, as in one version of the parable the blind men did, over whether Mallory was this or that.

We are not entitled to invent a Mallory of our own devising, and then to demand that his actions on any given day conform to our invention.

Sherlock Holmes liked to say to his friend Dr Watson that when one had eliminated the impossible, what remained, however improbable, must be the truth. Our mission in this book has not been as ambitious as that of Holmes; that is, we have not tried to eliminate the impossible, but merely to eliminate the more improbable. Thereby we may remain with the less improbable. The elephant is an improbable creature; so was Mallory. The events of 8 June 1924, *a priori*, were improbable.

In the foregoing chapters we have endeavoured to adhere to the facts of that day, and of the preceding days and years, as related by those who were there. We have attempted to avoid opinions, speculation, and preconceived narrative.

Some of these facts permit the following statements of improbability:

- It is improbable that Mallory and Irvine departed their Camp VI before dawn.
- It is improbable that Mallory and Irvine attempted to climb either the First Step or the Second Step, or took any prolonged route on the crest of the Northeast Ridge.
- It is improbable that Mallory fell on the ascent.

- It is improbable that Mallory fell from the location where the ice axe was found.
- It is improbable that Mallory fell during the hours of daylight.

In the mystery of Mallory and Irvine, one observation is central: Odell's sighting of them at 12:50 pm. If we do not believe that sighting at all, then all bets are off. If we do believe it, then we have to conclude that Odell saw the climbers at the base of the summit pyramid: that is, on or near the formation that modern climbers call the Third Step. If we believe that, then there was no obstacle of any consequence between them and the summit: and it would follow that sometime between 3 pm and 4 pm on 8 June 1924, they were the first human beings to stand at the highest point in the world.

What happened thereafter remains, for now, a mystery. It may be resolved or elucidated if any climber or drone operator should discover the mortal remains of Andrew Irvine; or if anyone should climb any of the routes that we called the "Norton variations", and find any artifact thereon.

As to Irvine's final resting place: among all the reported sightings of "old English dead", there is one which was made on the highest authority, has never been challenged or repudiated, and is not a sighting of Mallory. It is that of Wang Fu-zhou, a member of the 1960 Chinese summit team, who in 1965, in his speech to the Geographical Society of the Soviet Union, said that he had seen the body of a "European in braces"[2].

Wang's reference to the altitude implied that the unfortunate climber had probably been between the Second Step and the Third Step. The modern climbing route threads a narrow and well-defined line between those steps, and hundreds of people have taken that route, but Wang's story has never been the subject of a serious investigation.

If we accept Wang's narrative, it is impossible that the body was that of Mallory; whatever remains, however improbable, is Irvine. Then Irvine died at the place where Wang (and probably Wang's three companions) saw his body. We know that Mallory died elsewhere. We are compelled to believe that Mallory and Irvine were separated at some point, and that Mallory made his descent alone, to the place where he met his end.

If the China Mountaineering Association or the Russian Geographical Society should ever verify Wang's story, or adduce additional evidence, there would be a new mystery. We would be compelled to ask how Irvine could have perished on or near the Northeast Ridge of Everest, while Mallory met his end hundreds of yards to the northeast, and a thousand feet or more below. That would be another story.

Appendix 1

Key locations on Mount Everest

location	latitude	longitude	elevation (1920s calibration)		elevation (modern calibration)		notes
	decimal	decimal	meters	feet	meters	feet	
summit	27.98836	86.92520	8,840	29,002	8,849	29,032	from Google Earth
Third Step (top)	27.98998	86.92730	8,638	28,341	8,647	28,371	from Google Earth
Second Step (top)	27.99139	86.92850	8,550	28,052	8,559	28,082	from Google Earth
First Step (top)	27.99322	86.93004	8,487	27,845	8,496	27,875	from Google Earth
1922 Camp IV	28.01516	86.92441	7,010	23,000	7,020	23,030	all climbers
1922 Camp Va	28.00670	86.92970	7,620	25,000	7,629	25,030	Mallory, Norton, Somervell
1922 Camp Vb	28.00484	86.93120	7,772	25,500	7,782	25,530	Geoffrey Bruce, Finch
1924 Camp IV	28.01827	86.92327	6,919	22,700	6,928	22,730	all climbers
1924 Camp V	28.00568	86.93080	7,711	25,300	7,721	25,330	all climbers
1924 Camp VI	28.00119	86.93262	8,169	26,800	8,178	26,830 (a), 26,621 (b)	Norton, Somervell
1933 Camp VI	27.99652	86.93172	8,352	27,400	8,361	27,430	Shipton, Smythe, Wager, Wyn Harris
ice axe 1933 (a)	27.99467	86.93092	8,435	27,674	8,444	27,704	about 200 yards east of First Step; 60 feet below crest
ice axe 1933 (b)	27.99500	86.93112	8,423	27,635	8,432	27,665	about 250 yards east of First Step; 60 feet below crest
oxygen bottle #9	27.99451	86.93098	8,456	27,742	8,465	27,772	170m horizontally from top of First Step, 15m? below ridge
			8,461	27,759	8,470	27,789	
Mallory's body	27.99765	86.93028	8,179	26,834	8,188	26,864	approximate

Latitudes and longitudes are author's estimates: summit and Steps derived from Google Earth; camps and ice axe from contemporary accounts; 1924 Camp VI by courtesy of Jake Norton; oxygen bottle #9 from correspondence with Jochen Hemmleb; Mallory's body (approximate) from correspondence with Jake Norton.

Altitudes: summit and Steps based on author's estimates derived from Google Earth; 1922 camps from Mallory, George and Norton, Lieutenant Colonel Edward F., in *The Assault on Everest 1922*, p.59, 169, 256; 1924 camps from Norton, Lieutenant Colonel Edward F. The Problem of Everest, *The Alpine Journal*, Vol. 37, No. 230, p.2; 1924 Camp VI (a) from Edward Norton (b) as found by Jake Norton in 2001; oxygen bottle #9 from correspondence with Jochen Hemmleb; Mallory's body from correspondence with Jake Norton.

Appendix 2

British Mount Everest expedition 1924: recorded ascent and descent speeds

low point		high point		distance	height difference	direction	no. of times recorded	average time	fastest time	average speed
camp	feet	camp	feet	miles	feet			hh:mm	hh:mm	ft/hr
Base	16,800	I	17,800	3.75	1,000	up	4	02:35	01:55	387
I	17,800	II	19,250	3.25	1,450	up	7	02:40	01:55	545
II	19,250	III	21,200	4.00	1,950	up	2	03:10	02:20	615
III	21,200	IV	22,700	1.50	1,500	up	6	03:40	03:00	410
III	21,200	IV	22,700	1.50	1,500	up	1 (a)	02:40	02:40	563
IV	22,700	V	25,300	1.33	2,600	up	3	05:10	03:15	503
V	25,300	VI	26,800	0.50	1,500	up	2	04:50	04:50	310
VI	26,800	Couloir	28,100	0.75	1,300	up	1 (a)	06:20	06:20	205
Base	16,800	I	17,800	3.75	1,000	down	1	01:30	01:30	752
I	17,800	II	19,250	3.25	1,450	down	3	01:20	00:55	1190
II	19,250	III	21,200	4.00	1,950	down	1	01:45	01:45	1114
III	21,200	IV	22,700	1.50	1,500	down	3	02:40	01:30	564
IV	22,700	V	25,300	1.33	2,600	down	2	01:35	00:30	1646
V	25,300	VI	26,800	0.50	1,500	down	2	*02:00*	*01:00*	750
VI	26,800	Couloir	28,100	0.75	1,300	down	1 (b)	*02:30*	*02:30*	520

Source: Norton, Lieutenant Colonel Edward F. 'The Problem of Everest'. In *The Alpine Journal*, Vol. 37, No. 230 (May 1925), p.2

Note: (a) with oxygen; all others without. (b) Norton and Somervell; both recorded as "very weak party".

Abbreviations and Conventions

' "	feet, inches
&	and
[ ]	author's note or translation
[sic]	quoted exactly as in original
° ' "	degrees, minutes, seconds (of latitude or longitude)
°F	degrees Fahrenheit
...	omission from quotation
a.m.	*ante meridiem* (morning)
Capt.	Captain
Col.	Colonel
Dr	Doctor
E	east
F.	Fahrenheit
FRS	Fellow of the Royal Society
hrs.	hours
ft	feet
I	1
II	2
III	3
IV	4
Lt.Col.	Lieutenant Colonel
M.E.E.	Mount Everest Expedition
m	meters
min.	minimum
Mt.	Mount
N	north
NE	northeast
NW	northwest
p.m.	*post meridiem* (afternoon)
S	south
temp.	temperature
ther.	thermometer
V.P.K.	Vest Pocket Kodak
V	5
VI	6
VII	7
Vol.	Volume
W	west
XV	15

Acknowledgements

This author would like to acknowledge the indebtedness of this work to the initiatives of the following persons and organizations:

- The Alpine Club, for digitizing most of the historical issues of *The Alpine Journal*
- The Internet Archive, for making many books and documents from the 1920s and 1930s accessible to the modern reader
- Google Earth, for their extraordinary work in mapping our planet
- Jake Norton, for his Undefined Community forum
- JSTOR, for making many academic journals accessible online
- Magdalen College, University of Cambridge, for preserving and digitizing George Mallory's letters
- Merton College, University of Oxford, for preserving and digitizing Andrew Irvine's letters and diaries
- Michael Spender, for his topographic map of the North Face of Mount Everest, published in 1936
- Michael Tracy, for his iconoclastic YouTube channel
- The Mountain Heritage Trust, for creating a replica of the clothing that George Mallory wore on his last climb
- The Royal Geographical Society, for preserving and granting public access to George Mallory's boots
- Wolfgang Schroeder, for his Perspective Image Correction software
- The University of Durham, for preserving and digitizing Bentley Beetham's historic photographs from the 1924 expedition to Mount Everest.

Many thanks to the following persons who kindly gave permission to reproduce quotations or images:

- Conrad Anker
- Phil Ershler
- Dr George Havenith
- Jochen Hemmleb
- Stuart Holmes
- Iain Johnston
- Chris Klinke
- Sondre Kvambekk @500fjell
- Veli-Pekka Mölsä
- Jake Norton
- Andrew Parkinson
- Thom Dharma Pollard
- Eric Simonson
- Julie Summers
- Mark Synnott
- Michael Tracy
- Steve Wyn-Harris.

Special thanks to Balázs Petheő, for his generous permission to use his brilliant painting as our cover; to Katinka Kun-kuty, for her diligent and meticulous transcription of key passages from Mallory's letters and Irvine's letters and diaries; and to Edó Gergely for her help and encouragement.

Finally, my thanks to you the reader, for accompanying me on this journey. You are the other half of the "we" that has appeared throughout this story.

All errors and omissions are my own. As Harry Truman used to say, the buck stops here.

Sources

1. Books

Anker, Conrad; David Roberts. *The Lost Explorer: Finding Mallory on Mount Everest*. New York : Simon & Schuster, 1999.
Carr, Herbert R. C. (ed.). *The Irvine Diaries*. Gastons-West Col, 1979.
de Schlagintweit, Hermann; Adolphe de Schlagintweit; Robert de Schlagintweit. *Results of a scientific mission to India and high Asia, Vol. 2.* Leipzig: F. A. Brockhaus, 1862; London: Trübner and Company, 1862.
Dodd, Christopher. *The Oxford & Cambridge Boat Race*. London: Stanley Paul, 1983.
Gillman, Peter; Leni Gillman. *The Wildest Dream.* Seattle: Mountaineers Books, 2000.
Hall, Lincoln. *White Limbo*. McMahons Point: K. Weldon, 1985.
Hemmleb, Jochen. *Detectives on Everest: the 2001 Mallory & Irvine research expedition.* Seattle: Mountaineers Books, 2002.
Hemmleb, Jochen. *Ghosts of Everest: the search for Mallory & Irvine: from the expedition that discovered Mallory's body.* Seattle: Mountaineers Books, 1999.
Hemmleb, Jochen. *Tatort Mount Everest: der Fall Mallory.* Munich: F.A. Herbig/Terra Magic, 2009.
Messner, Reinhold. *The Crystal Horizon*. Marlborough: The Crowood Press, 1989.
Norges Svalbard-Og Ishavs-Undersokelser. *Skrifter Om Svalbard Og Ishavet Nr. 80, The Place-Names Of Svalbard* (Oslo: Kommisjon Hos Jacob Dybwad, 1942).
Royal Geographical Society. *Mount Everest Expedition 1924, T.S. Diaries*. Unpublished, 1924.
Shu Ren, "Ascent [of] the Summit of Earth - first conquest of Qomolungma by the Chinese'. Liu Dong-ping (ed.) 刘东平 (ed.) *Records of exploration by the Chinese* 中国人探险纪实" . Beijing: International Culture Publishing Company, 1993.
Summers, Julie. *Fearless On Everest.* London: Weidenfeld & Nicolson, 2000.
Synnott, Mark. *The Third Pole: Mystery, Obsession, And Death On Mount Everest*. Boston: Dutton, 2021.
Tennyson, Alfred Baron. *Maud and Other Poems*. London: Edward Moxon, 1856.
Wolfe, Tom. *The Right Stuff.* New York: Farrar, Strauss and Giroux, 1979.
Wyn Harris, Percy. *The Memoirs of Sir Percy Wyn Harris*. Unpublished, 1978.

2.1 Digital files: e-books and e-book chapters

Beetham, Bentley. 'Section IV Photography'. *The Fight For Everest 1924.* London: Edward Arnold, 1925. https://archive.org/details/in.ernet.dli.2015.170876
Bruce, General Charles G. 'The Assault on the Mountain'. Bruce, Charles G. et al, *The Assault on Everest 1922*. London: Edward Arnold, 1923. https://archive.org/details/assaultonmountev00bruc
Bruce, General Charles G. 'The Start'. *The Fight For Everest, 1924*. London: Edward Arnold, 1925. https://archive.org/details/in.ernet.dli.2015.170876
Bruce, General Charles G. 'The Narrative of the Expedition'. *The Assault on Mount Everest 1922.* London: Edward Arnold, 1923. https://archive.org/details/assaultonmountev00bruc

Finch, George I. 'The Attempt With Oxygen - Notes on Equipment'. *The Assault on Mount Everest, 1922*. London: Edward Arnold, 1923. https://archive.org/details/assaultonmountev00bruc
Finch, George I. *The Making of a Mountaineer*. London: Arrowsmith, 1924. https://archive.org/details/makingofmountain00finc
Hinks, A. R. 'The Scientific Equipment'. *Mount Everest the Reconnaissance, 1921*. London: Edward Arnold, 1922. https://archive.org/details/mounteverestrec00howa
Howard-Bury, Lieutenant Colonel Charles K. "The Narrative of the Expedition", *Mount Everest The Reconnaissance*, 1921. London: Edward Arnold, 1922. https://www.gutenberg.org/ebooks/39421
Howard-Bury, Lieutenant Colonel Charles K. et al. *Mount Everest, The Reconnaissance*, 1921. London: Edward Arnold, 1922. Project Gutenberg edition, pdf. https://www.gutenberg.org/ebooks/39421
Mallory, George. 'The First Attempt'. Charles G. Bruce et al, *The Assault on Mount Everest, 1922*. London: Edward Arnold, 1923. https://archive.org/details/assaultonmountev00bruc
Mallory, George. 'The Highest Climb'. Charles G. Bruce et al, *The Assault on Everest 1922*. London: Edward Arnold, 1923. https://archive.org/details/assaultonmountev00bruc
Mallory, George. 'The Problem'. Charles G. Bruce et al, *The Assault on Everest 1922*. London: Edward Arnold, 1923. https://archive.org/details/assaultonmountev00bruc
Mallory, George. 'The Reconnaissance of the Mountain'. *Mount Everest, The Reconnaissance, 1921*. London: Edward Arnold, 1922. https://archive.org/details/mounteverestrec00howa
Noel, John. *Through Tibet To Everest*. London: Edward Arnold, 1927. https://archive.org/details/dli.pahar.2337
Norton, Colonel Edward F. 'The North Col'. *The Fight For Everest 1924*. London: Edward Arnold, 1925. https://archive.org/details/in.ernet.dli.2015.170876
Norton, Lieutenant Colonel Edward F. 'The March Across Tibet'. *The Fight For Everest 1924*. London: Edward Arnold, 1925. https://archive.org/details/in.ernet.dli.2015.170876
Odell, Noel. 'Mallory and Irvine's Attempt'. Norton, Lieutenant Colonel Edward F. et al, *The Fight For Everest 1924*. London: Edward Arnold, 1925. https://archive.org/details/in.ernet.dli.2015.170876
Ruttledge, Hugh. *Everest 1933*. London: Hodder and Stoughton Ltd, 1934. https://archive.org/details/in.ernet.dli.2015.210461
Somervell, T. Howard. *After Everest - The Experiences of a Mountaineer and Medical Missionary*. London: Hodder & Stoughton, 1936. https://archive.org/details/in.ernet.dli.2015.208466
Unsworth, Walt. *Everest – A Mountaineering History*. Seattle: Mountaineers Books, 1991. https://archive.org/details/everest0000unsw/
Younghusband, Sir Francis. 'Introduction'. Bruce, Charles G. et al, *The Assault on Everest 1922*. London: Edward Arnold, 1923. https://archive.org/details/assaultonmountev00bruc

2.2 Digital files: journal articles

'E.F.N.' [Norton, Lt. Col. Edward F.] 'In Memoriam - Lobsang'. *The Alpine Journal*, Vol.44 No.246 (May 1932). https://www.alpinejournal.org.uk/Contents/Contents_1932_files/AJ44%201932%20110-120%20In%20Memoriam.pdf
Blakeney, T. S. 'A. R. Hinks and the First Everest Expedition, 1921'. *The Geographical Journal*, Vol. 136, Part 3, (September 1970), https://www.himalayanclub.org/hj/31/2/a-r-hinks-and-the-first-everest-expedition-1921/
Bullock, Guy H. 'The Everest Expedition, 1921, Diary of G. H. Bullock, Part I'. *The Alpine Journal*, Vol.304 (1962). https://www.alpinejournal.org.uk/Contents/Contents_1962_files/AJ%201962%20130-149%20Bullock%20Everest%201921.pdf
Bullock, Guy H. 'The Everest Expedition, 1921, Diary of G. H. Bullock, Part II'. *The Alpine Journal*, Vol.304 (1962). https://www.alpinejournal.org.uk/Contents/Contents_1962_files/AJ%201962%20291-309%20Bullock%20Everest%201921%20Pt%202.pdf

Eckenstein, Oscar. 'Ueber Steigeisentechnik'. *Osterreichische Alpenzeitung*, Vol. 30, nr. 764. Vienna, (20 June 1908). http://www.alpinist.com/doc/web12f/wfeature-eckenstein

Havenith, George. 'Benchmarking functionality of historical cold weather clothing: Robert F. Scott, Roald Amundsen, George Mallory'. https://repository.lboro.ac.uk/articles/journal_contribution/Benchmarking_functionality_of_historical_cold_weather_clothing_Robert_F_Scott_Roald_Amundsen_George_Mallory/9346988

Hoyland, Graham. 'Testing Mallory's Clothes on Everest'. *The Alpine Journal*, (2007). https://www.alpinejournal.org.uk/Contents/Contents_2007_files/AJ%202007%20243-246%20Hoyland%20Clothing.pdf

König, Marc. 'Hadow's Sole: Mountaineering boots between the first ascents of the Matterhorn and Everest'. *The Alpine Journal*, (2016). https://www.alpinejournal.org.uk/Contents/Contents_2016_files/AJ%202016%20243-253%20Konig%20Boots.pdf

Norton, Lieutenant Colonel Edward F. 'The Problem of Mount Everest'. *The Alpine Journal*, Vol.37 No. 230 (May 1925). https://www.alpinejournal.org.uk/Contents/Contents_1925_files/AJ%201925%20Vol%2037%201-22%20Everest%20Norton.pdf

Ruttledge, Hugh. 'The Mount Everest Expedition, 1933'. *The Alpine Journal*, Vol.45 No.247 (November 1933). https://www.alpinejournal.org.uk/Contents/Contents_1933_files/AJ45%201933%20216-231%20Ruttledge%20Everest%201933.pdf

Shih Chan-Chun. 'The Conquest of Mount Everest by the Chinese Mountaineering Team'. *Himalayan Journal*, Vol. 23 (1961). https://www.himalayanclub.org/hj/23/16/the-conquest-of-mount-everest-by-the-chinese-mountaineering-team/

Suzuki, Hiroyuki. 'Asia, China—Tibet, Bodies On Mount Everest'. *American Alpine Journal*, Vol.22 (1980), http://publications.americanalpineclub.org/articles/12198065801

2.3 Digital files: news articles

author unspecified. 'Deodhunga, the Highest Mountain in the World', *The Illustrated London News*, Vol. 31, Issue 873 (15 August 1857), p.168-70. https://archive.org/details/sim_illustrated-london-news_1857-08-15_31_873

Dean, Paul. 'The Reluctant Celebrity'. *The Los Angeles Times*, (13 October 1985). https://www.latimes.com/archives/la-xpm-1985-10-13-tm-15543-story.html

Holzel, Tom. 'Look Back at Life on the Mountain: Chronicling Ups and Downs of 10 Weeks on Mt. Everest'. *Los Angeles Times,* (30 November 1986). https://www.latimes.com/archives/la-xpm-1986-11-30-vw-31-story.html

Synnott, Mark. 'The Mount Everest mystery deepens: Was there an international cover-up of a dead climber's ascent?' *Salon* (8 April 2022). https://www.salon.com/2022/04/08/the-third-pole-mount-everest-mark-synnott-mystery-china/

Verma, Somesh. "The faceless hero - Nepal's only Olympic Gold medalist in focus". *Kathmandu Post*, (22 August 2012). https://somesh.com.np/index.php/2012/08/18/the-faceless-hero-nepals-only-olympic-gold-medalist/

Zhao Zonglu, 'Mountaineering Heroine: 10 Years Later'. *Beijing Review*, Vol.29, No.32 (11 August 1986), 27. http://www.massline.org/PekingReview/PR1986/PR1986-32.pdf

2.4 Digital files: website content

Alpine Club. "Everest: by 'Those Who Were There' Exhibition Opens". http://www.alpine-club.org.uk/news/everest-centenary/825-everest-by-those-who-were-there

Bonhams. Lot 114, Mallory (George Leigh). London, 11 November 2015. https://www.bonhams.com/auction/22715/lot/114/mallory-george-leigh-series-of-ten-autograph-letters-signed-to-marjorie-holmes-a-nineteen-year-old-teacher-written-in-1923-24-during-the-year-between-his-last-lecture-tour-of-the-united-states-and-his-final-assault-on-everest-with-the-last-letter-written-from-the-boat-taking-him-out-to-tibet-new-york-england-and-en-route-to-india-2-march-1923-to-8-march-1924/

Cheng Li-lan, Dr. 'Mt. Everest Climb from North Side 2016', (YouTube, 9 July 2016). https://www.youtube.com/watch?v=ZeSqJK2Rais

Choudhury, Anjana; R. R. Kelkar, A. K. Sen Sarma. "Radhanath Sikdar: Through the Haze of Time and Neglect" (2009). https://rrkelkar.files.wordpress.com/2009/03/radhanath-sikdar-through-the-haze-of-time-and-neglect.pdf

Christie's. '1936 Everest Expedition: auction notes' (1999), https://www.christies.com/en/lot/lot-1657171

Elvers, Greg. Visual Angle Calculator, https://elvers.us/perception/visualAngle/

Getty Images. Title unknown. https://www.pinterest.com/pin/561120434817974496/

Hemmleb, Jochen. "June 8, 1924, Mallory & Irvine's ascent to 8500 m/28,000 ft". (2007). https://www.jochenhemmleb.com/english/mundi/mundi_inhalt.php#4

Hofstetter, Christoph. Contour Map Creator. https://contourmapcreator.urgr8.ch/

Ikeda, Kaneshige. 'The Northeast Ridge Of Mt. Everest (Qomolangma)'. http://www.everest.co.jp/everest95/nu-ev95-e.html

Keisan Online Calculator, https://keisan.casio.com/exec/system/1224689365

Lahiri, Ashish K. 'Radhanath Sikdar: The Atypical Derozian Scientist' (2009). https://www.academia.edu/4290137/Radhanath_Sikdar_An_Atypical_Derozian

Mallory, George. Letters to Ruth Mallory, 1921-1924. https://magdalene.maxarchiveservices.co.uk/index.php

Norton, Jake. 'Mystery' Camp Discovery on Mount Everest'. (29 August 2017). https://www.youtube.com/watch?v=S3auMLZZ2KU

Norton, Jake. 'Windproof Suits and 68 Year Old Crackers' (April 2007) https://jakenorton.com/windproof-suits-and-68-year-old-crackers/

Norton, Jake. 'One Old Sock' (February 2021). https://jakenorton.com/one-old-sock/

Norton, Jake. 'Everest Searches, 1999-2019'. https://jakenorton.com/wp-content/uploads/2022/05/Searches/output/index.html

Norwegian Polar Institute, TopoSvalbard. https://toposvalbard.npolar.no/?lat=79.11916&long=16.96731&zoom=8&layer=map

Norwegian Polar Institute, Svalbardkartet. https://geokart.npolar.no/Html5Viewer/index.html?viewer=Svalbardkartet

Outlook India. 'Joy Is The End Of Life'. (3 February 2022). https://www.outlookindia.com/website/story/joy-is-the-end-of-life/220272

Oxford University, *Spitsbergen Retraced Expedition Report*, (January 2017). https://www.spitsbergenretraced.com/static/media/spitsbergen-retraced-expedition-report.278fe75b.pdf

Pollard, Thom Dharma. 'Everest's Life-Changing Moment: Discovering Mallory with Andy Politz'. (YouTube, 18 August 2022). https://www.youtube.com/watch?v=WCraijhm7z8

Pollard, Thom Dharma. 'Sandy Irvine & the Camera Were Discovered? Mark Synnott's Revealing Intel' (YouTube, April 19, 2022). https://www.youtube.com/watch?v=glMT08zmAP0

Pollard, Thom Dharma. 'Pan Duo's TOP SECRET Discovery on Everest' (YouTube, 4 June 2022). https://www.youtube.com/watch?v=qv_sKAEeQyA

Rockfax. Grade Conversions. https://rockfax.com/climbing-guides/grades/

Simonson, Eric; Jochen Hemmleb; Larry Johnson. "Ghosts of Everest". *Outside Online*, (1 October 1999). https://www.outsideonline.com/outdoor-adventure/climbing/ghosts-everest/

The Engineering Toolbox, Clo - Clothing and Thermal Insulation. https://www.engineeringtoolbox.com/clo-clothing-thermal-insulation-d_732.html

The Himalayan Database: The Expedition Archives of Elizabeth Hawley, https://www.himalayandatabase.com

TimeAndDate. https://www.timeanddate.com/sun/india/darjeeling?month=6&year=1924

Tracy, Michael Tracy. 'Mallory and Irvine: It is known' (YouTube, 6 January 1922). https://www.youtube.com/watch?v=Qrehwt3B9nQ.

Tracy, Michael. 'Oxygen Bottle #9' (YouTube, 26 April 2017). https://malloryandirvine.com/2017/04/26/a-possible-clue/

Tracy, Michael. 'Frostbite' (YouTube, 3 December 2022). https://www.youtube.com/watch?v=bFmU1pQCvys
Tracy, Michael. 'Mallory vs. modern' (YouTube, 14 July 2021). https://www.youtube.com/watch?v=K-4lJqnim6Y
Tracy, Michael. 'Mallory & Irvine: The Plan' (YouTube, 1 May 2022). https://www.youtube.com/watch?v=yPgaRuqThog
Tracy, Michael. 'Great Climbs: Messner 1980' (YouTube, 27 May 2022). https://www.youtube.com/watch?v=aAhAycFdONg
Tracy, Michael. 'Odell's view of Mallory & Irvine at 12:50' (YouTube, 25 August 2017). https://www.youtube.com/watch?v=2SGRCaGjZf0
Tracy, Michael. 'Two and a half ice axes' (YouTube, 8 April 1922). https://www.youtube.com/watch?v=IuvUjozPkbU
Waugh, Lieutenant Colonel Andrew Scott. 'Report on the Progress and Expense of the Great Trigonometrical Survey of India, and a Sketch Map of India,* showing the Extent of the Great Trigonometrical Survey up to the Year 1849-50'. *Accounts and Papers, Thirty Volumes, -(11)- East India, Session 4 February – 8 August 1851, Vol. 11,* p.18. London: House of Commons, 1851. https://pahar.in/pahar/1851-trigonometrical-survey-india-printed-parliamentary-paper-no-219-pdf/
Yordanishvili, Dr E. K. '1960. Впервые на Эверест – с севера!' ['1960. For the first time on Everest - from the north!']. Saint-Petersburg Alpine Club, 2002. http://www.alpklubspb.ru/everest/everest52.htm

3. Film

Noel, Captain John. *The Epic of Everest: A Film by Captain John Noel* (1924). 87min. Digitised by the British Film Institute
Wyn Harris, Percy. *The Fourth Everest Expedition* (1933). 76 minutes (silent). Digitised by the British Film Institute. https://player.bfi.org.uk/free/film/watch-fourth-everest-expedition-1933-online
Wyn Harris, Percy. *Climbing Mount Everest (1933*). 32 minutes (silent). Digitised by the British Film Institute. https://player.bfi.org.uk/free/film/watch-climbing-mount-everest-1933-online

4. Journal articles

Burrard, S. G. 'Mount Everest: The story of a Long Controversy'. *Nature*, Vol.71, (10 November 1904).
Frazer, Robert A. 'Central Spitsbergen and North-East Land. I. The Sledge Journey'. *The Geographical Journal*, Vol. 64, No. 3, (September 1924)
Mallory, George. 'The First High Climb'. *The Geographical Journal*, Vol. 60, No. 6 (December 1922)
Norton, Lt. Col. Edward F. 'The Personnel of the Expedition'. *The Geographical Journal*, Vol. 64, No. 6 (December 1924), pp. 436-43
Odell, Noel E. 'Explorations in the Mountains of Eastern Spitsbergen'. *The Alpine Journal*, Vol. 35 (1923), 232-8
Odell, Noel. 'Mount Everest Dispatches, No.9, June 14, 1924'. *The Geographical Journal*, Vol. 64, No. 2 (August 1924)
Odell, Noel. 'The Last Climb of Mallory and Irvine', *The Geographical Journal*, Vol. 64, No. 6 (December 1924)
Rodway, George W. 'Mountain Clothing and Thermoregulation: A Look Back'. *Wilderness & Environmental Medicine*, Vol.23 (2012).

Royal Geographical Society, 'Dr Kellas' Expedition to Kamet'. *The Geographical Journal*, Vol. 57, No. 2 (February 1921), 124-130

Royal Geographical Society, "The Mount Everest Expedition". *The Geographical Journal*, Vol. 57 No. 2, (February 1921), 73-75

Ruttledge, Hugh. 'The Mount Everest Expedition, 1933'. *The Geographical Journal*, Vol. 83, No. 1 (January1934), pp. 1-9

Sarkar, Oyindrila: 'Science, Surveying and Scientific Authority: The Brothers Schlagintweit in 'India and High Asia', 1854–57'. *South Asia: Journal of South Asian Studies*, Vol.40, No.3 (2017). doi: 10.1080/00856401.2017.1340110

Spender, Michael. 'Photographic Surveys in the Mount Everest Region'. *The Geographical Journal*, Vol. 88, No. 4 (October 1936)

Tilman, H. W.; E. E. Shipton; C. E. C. Fischer. 'The Mount Everest Expedition of 1938'. *The Geographical Journal*, Vol. 92, No. 6 (December 1938)

Waugh, Andrew Scott. 'On Mounts Everest and Deodanga'. *Proceedings of the Royal Geographical Society of London*, 1857-1858, Vol. 2, No. 2 (1858)

West, John. 'George I. Finch and his pioneering use of oxygen for climbing at extreme altitudes'. *Journal of Applied Physiology*, Vol. 94 (2003)

Wyss-Dunant, Ed. 'The First Swiss Expedition to Mount Everest, 1952'. *The Geographical Journal*, Vol. 119, No. 3 (September 1953)

5. News articles

Guo Chao-zhen. 'Битва за Джомолунгму' ['Battle for Chomolungma']. *Sovietski Sport*, nr. 142, (15 June 1960).

Mallory, George. 'Everest Unvanquished'. *Asia Magazine*, No. 9 (1923).

Schlagintweit, Robert. 'On the Routes pursued by Herren Robert, Hermann and Adolphe Schlagintweit, in India, The Himalayas, Thibet, and Turkistan'. *The Athenaeum*, No. 1558 (5 September 1857), p.1127.

6. Personal correspondence

Odell, Noel E. Letter to Norges Svalbard-og Ishays-undersokelser, (20 September 1935).

Endnotes

Prologue

1. The modern calibration is 29,032 feet (8,849m).
2. For North American readers: ax.
3. Also known as Chu Yin-hua.
4. Also known as Gonbu, Gonpu, Konbu and other variations.
5. Now Saint Petersburg.
6. Now the Russian Geographical Society.
7. 8,600m in the published account.
8. For North American readers: suspenders.
9. No relation (as far as is known) to Wang Fu-zhou of the 1960 expedition.
10. Anker was the first to see Mallory's body.

Chapter 1: Sikdar

1. Choudhury, Anjana; R. R. Kelkar; A. K. Sen Sarma. 'Radhanath Sikdar: Through the Haze of Time and Neglect' (2009).
2. Ibid.
3. Ibid.
4. Waugh, Lieutenant Colonel Andrew Scott. 'Report on the Progress and Expense of the Great Trigonometrical Survey of India, and a Sketch Map of India,* showing the Extent of the Great Trigonometrical Survey up to the Year 1849-50' in *Accounts and Papers, Thirty Volumes, -(11)- East India, Session 4 February – 8 August 1851* (London: House of Commons), Vol. 11, p.18.
5. Then known as Calcutta.
6. Lahiri, Ashish K. 'Radhanath Sikdar: The Atypical Derozian Scientist' (2009), p.7
7. Ibid, p.8
8. Quoted in Waugh, Andrew Scott. 'On Mounts Everest and Deodanga'. *Proceedings of the Royal Geographical Society of London*, 1857-1858, Vol. 2, No. 2, p.104-5.
9. Quoted in Waugh (1857-1858), ibid., footnote to p.105.
10. *The Illustrated London News*, 15 August 1857, p.170.
11. Ibid.
12. Burrard, S. G. 'Mount Everest: The story of a Long Controversy'. *Nature*, 10 November 1904, Vol. 71, p.43
13. Waugh (1857-1858), ibid, p.104
14. Sarkar, Oyindrila: 'Science, Surveying and Scientific Authority: The Brothers Schlagintweit in 'India and High Asia', 1854–57'. *South Asia: Journal of South Asian Studies*, 2017.
15. Schlagintweit, Robert. 'On the Routes pursued by Herren Robert, Hermann and Adolphe Schlagintweit, in India, The Himalayas, Thibet, and Turkistan'. *The Athenaeum,* No. 1558 (5 September 1857), p.1127
16. Now that Sikkim is part of India, Phalut is on the Nepal/India border; the main peak is in the province of West Bengal, India. Hermann gave the location of his vantage point as

27°13'07'N, 87°59'8'E which is on the western (Nepali) side of the border. He described it as 'a mountain southeast of Falut at a height of 11,055 English feet'.

17. This name is not found on modern maps. Hermann de Schlagintweit described it as north-north-west of Kathmandu; however, he gave the co-ordinates 27°47'N, 85°09'E, which would place his vantage point about twelve miles northwest of Kathmandu. It was possibly the British resident's cottage at Koulia, near the village of Ranipauwa.
18. de Schlagintweit, Hermann; Adolphe de Schlagintweit, Robert de Schlagintweit. *Results of a scientific mission to India and high Asia*, Vol. 2, p.297.
19. Adolphe Schlagintweit's name appeared posthumously. He had been murdered in Kashgar: by some accounts, on the orders of the local chieftain.

Chapter 2: The Third Pole

1. Also known as Howard Bury (without the hyphen) and also simply as Bury.
2. Royal Geographical Society, 'The Mount Everest Expedition'. *The Geographical Journal*, Vol. 62 No. 2, February 1921, p.73
3. Blakeney, T. S. 'A. R. Hinks and the First Everest Expedition', 1921'. *The Geographical Journal*, Vol. 136, Part 3, September 1970.
4. Royal Geographical Society, 'The Mount Everest Expedition'. *The Geographical Journal*, Vol. 62 No. 2, February 1921, p.73,74
5. In keeping with his social class, Mallory had a double-barreled surname, which sometimes was written Leigh-Mallory.
6. Howard-Bury, Lieutenant Colonel Charles K. *Mount Everest, The Reconnaissance, 1921*. Project Gutenberg edition, pdf p.75
7. Mallory, George. 'The Reconnaissance of the Mountain'. *Mount Everest, The Reconnaissance, 1921*. Project Gutenberg edition, pdf p.201,202
8. Ibid, p.202
9. Bullock, Guy H. 'The Everest Expedition, 1921, Diary of G. H. Bullock'. *The Alpine Journal*, 1962, Vol.304, p.134.
10. Mallory, George. 'The Reconnaissance of the Mountain'. *Mount Everest, The Reconnaissance, 1921*, pdf, p.203
11. Ibid, p.204
12. Ibid, p.204
13. Ibid, p.205
14. Ibid, p.206
15. Bullock, Guy H. 'The Everest Expedition, 1921, Diary of G. H. Bullock'. *The Alpine Journal*, 1962, Vol.304, p.136-7
16. George Mallory, 'The Reconnaissance of the Mountain'. *Mount Everest, The Reconnaissance, 1921*. Project Gutenberg edition, pdf, p.207
17. Ibid, p.207,208
18. Dean, Paul. 'The Reluctant Celebrity'. *The Los Angeles Times*, October 13, 1985. Yeager, referring to his supersonic flight of 14 October 1947, was slightly rewriting the story; on the previous flight on 10 October 1947, he had already reached Mach 0.997.
19. Mallory, George. 'The Reconnaissance of the Mountain'. *Mount Everest, The Reconnaissance, 1921*. Project Gutenberg edition, pdf, p.210-1
20. Bullock, Guy H. 'The Everest Expedition, 1921, Diary of G. H. Bullock'. *The Alpine Journal*, 1962, Vol.304, p.139-40
21. Mallory, George. 'The Reconnaissance of the Mountain'. *Mount Everest, The Reconnaissance, 1921*. Project Gutenberg edition, pdf, p.219
22. Author's calculation based on Elvers, Greg: Visual Angle Calculator (website).
23. Mallory, George. 'The Reconnaissance of the Mountain'. *Mount Everest, The Reconnaissance, 1921*. Project Gutenberg edition, pdf, p.235
24. Ibid, p.236-7

25. Ibid, p.237
26. Ibid, p.238
27. Ibid, p.255
28. Ibid, p.258-9
29. Ibid, p.264
30. Ibid, p.277
31. Howard-Bury, Lt. Col. Charles K. *Mount Everest, The Reconnaissance, 1921*, Project Gutenberg edition, pdf p.14
32. Mallory, George. 'The Reconnaissance of the Mountain'. *Mount Everest, The Reconnaissance, 1921*, Project Gutenberg edition, pdf, p.285
33. Bullock, Guy H. 'The Everest Expedition, 1921, Diary of G. H. Bullock'. *The Alpine Journal*, 1962, Vol.305, p.305
34. Mallory, George. 'The Reconnaissance of the Mountain' in *Mount Everest, The Reconnaissance, 1921*, Project Gutenberg edition, pdf, p.286
35. Ibid, p.302
36. By this author's estimate, the crest of the First Step is 2,453 feet (0.46 miles) horizontally from the summit.
37. Spender, Michael. 'Photographic Surveys in the Mount Everest Region'. *The Geographical Journal*, Vol. 88, No. 4 (October 1936), map following p.300
38. Ibid.

Chapter 3: 1922

1. Younghusband, Sir Francis. 'Introduction'. Bruce et al, *The Assault on Everest 1922*, p15
2. Ibid, p17
3. Bruce, General Charles G. 'The Assault on the Mountain'. Bruce et al, *The Assault on Everest 1922*, p54
4. Mallory, George. 'The Problem'. Bruce et al, *The Assault on Everest 1922*, p100
5. Ibid, p.101,102
6. Ibid, p.102,103
7. Dean, Paul. 'The Reluctant Celebrity', *Los Angeles Times*, 13 October 1985.
8. Mallory, George. 'The Problem'. Bruce et al, *The Assault on Everest 1922*, p.103
9. Ibid, p.115
10. Ibid, p.115
11. Ibid, p.116
12. Ibid, p.116
13. Mallory, George. Letter to Ruth Mallory, 17 May 1922, p.2.
14. Mallory, George. 'The Highest Climb'. Bruce et al, *The Assault on Everest 1922*, p.150
15. Ibid, p.163
16. Ibid, p.163,164
17. Mallory, George. Letter to Ruth Mallory, 26 May 1922, p.1,2
18. Ibid, p.2
19. Mallory, George. Letter to Ruth Mallory, 1 June 1922, p.1 (verso)
20. Mallory, George. Letter to Ruth Mallory, 26 May 1922, p.3 (verso)
21. Mallory, George. Letter to Ruth Mallory, 26 May 1922, p.4 (recto)
22. Mallory, George. Letter to Ruth Mallory, 1 June 1922, p.1 (verso)
23. Mallory, George. 'The First High Climb'. *The Geographical Journal*, Vol. 60, No. 6 (December 1922), p.411
24. Somervell, T. Howard. 'After Everest', p.62
25. Mallory, George. 'The Third Attempt'. Bruce et al, *The Assault on Everest 1922*, p.279
26. Mallory, George. Letter to Ruth Mallory, 9 June 1922, p.2,3.
27. Ibid, p.411

Chapter 4: 'English air'

1. Noel, John. *Through Tibet To Everest*, p.163.
2. The term 'coolies' was employed universally by British expeditions in the 1920s to denote locally hired porters.
3. Kellas, Dr Alexander. Quoted by Royal Geographical Society, 'Dr. Kellas' Expedition to Kamet'. *The Geographical Journal*, Vol. 57, No. 2 (February 1921), p.126
4. Ibid, p.127
5. Ibid, p.127
6. Hill, Leonard. 'An Oxygen Generator and Inhaler: Its Use in Mountain Sickness'. *The British Medical Journal*, Vol. 2, No. 2552 (27 November 1909), pp. 1522.
7. Younghusband, Sir Francis. 'Introduction', *Mount Everest the Reconnaissance, 1921.*
8. Mallory, George. 'The Reconnaissance of the Mountain'. *Mount Everest the Reconnaissance, 1921.*
9. Hinks, A. R. 'The Scientific Equipment'. *Mount Everest the Reconnaissance, 1921.*
10. Howard-Bury, Lieutenant Colonel. Charles K. 'The Narrative of the Expedition', *Mount Everest the Reconnaissance, 1921.*
11. Somervell, T. Howard. *After Everest - The Experiences of a Mountaineer and Medical Missionary*, p.37-38.
12. West, John. 'George I. Finch and his pioneering use of oxygen for climbing at extreme altitudes'. *Journal of Applied Physiology*, Vol. 94, 2003, p.1705, 1708.
13. Younghusband, Sir Francis. 'Introduction'. In *The Assault on Mount Everest 1922*, p.10.
14. Bruce, General Charles G. 'The Narrative of the Expedition'. *The Assault on Mount Everest 1922*, p.20.
15. Finch, George. *The Making of a Mountaineer*, p.284,285.
16. Ibid, p.306-308.
17. Finch, George. 'The Attempt with Oxygen'. *The Assault on Mount Everest 1922*, p.252.
18. Bruce, General Charles G. 'The Narrative of the Expedition'. *The Assault on Mount Everest 1922*, p.9,10.
19. West, John. 'George I. Finch and his pioneering use of oxygen for climbing at extreme altitudes'. *Journal of Applied Physiology*, Vol. 94, 2003, p.1705.
20. Finch, George. *The Making of a Mountaineer*, p.293,294.
21. Bruce, General Charles G. 'The Narrative of the Expedition'. *The Assault on Mount Everest 1922*, p.58,60.
22. Mallory, George. 'The First Attempt'. *The Assault on Mount Everest 1922*, p.144.
23. Finch, George. 'The Attempt With Oxygen'. *The Assault on Mount Everest 1922*, p.254
24. Mallory, George. 'The Third Attempt'. *The Assault on Mount Everest 1922*, p.278
25. Ibid, p.291
26. Ibid, p.278
27. Ibid, p.291
28. Ibid, p.294
29. Finch, George. 'The Attempt With Oxygen: Conclusions' and 'The Attempt With Oxygen: Notes on Equipment'. *The Assault on Mount Everest 1922*, p.257,263
30. Ibid, p.252
31. West, John. 'George I. Finch and his pioneering use of oxygen for climbing at extreme altitudes'. *Journal of Applied Physiology*, Vol. 94, 2003, p.1711

Chapter 5: Windproof

1. Younghusband, Sir Francis. 'The Introduction'. *Mount Everest, The Reconnaissance, 1921*, p.18
2. Mallory, George. 'The Reconnaissance of the Mountain'. *Mount Everest, The Reconnaissance, 1921*, p.260.

3. Bruce, General Charles G. 'The Narrative of the Expedition'. *The Assault on Mount Everest, 1922*, p.36
4. Finch, George. 'The Attempt With Oxygen - Notes on Equipment'. *The Assault on Mount Everest, 1922*, p.266
5. Mallory, George. 'The First Attempt'. *The Assault on Mount Everest, 1922*, p.186
6. Noel, John. *Through Tibet To Everest*, p.129. London, 1927
7. Bruce, General Charles G. 'The Narrative of the Expedition'. *The Assault on Mount Everest, 1922*, p.115,117.
8. Somervell, T. Howard. *After Everest - The Experiences of a Mountaineer and Medical Missionary*, p.38,39.
9. For North American readers: sweater
10. For North American readers: pants
11. Finch, George. 'The Attempt With Oxygen - Notes on Equipment'. *The Assault on Mount Everest, 1922*, p.267,268
12. West, John. 'George I. Finch and his pioneering use of oxygen for climbing at extreme altitudes'. *Journal of Applied Physiology*, Vol.94, 2003, p.1704.
13. Noel probably meant Fahrenheit, equivalent to -34 degrees Celsius.
14. Impregnated with a lacquer which dried to an impermeable finish; used in fabric-covered airplanes until around the 1940s.
15. Noel, John. *Through Tibet To Everest*, p.173,174.
16. Ibid, p.174
17. Mallory, George. 'Everest Unvanquished'. *Asia Magazine*, No. 9, 1923
18. Finch, George. 'The Attempt With Oxygen - Notes on Equipment'. *The Assault on Mount Everest, 1922*, p.268
19. Duroprene was the brand name of a solution of chlorinated rubber, originally marketed by the United Alkali Company.
20. Ibid, p.268
21. Noel, John. *Through Tibet To Everest*, p.173.
22. Eckenstein, Oscar. Ueber Steigeisentechnik. *Osterreichische Alpenzeitung*, Vol. 30, nr. 764, 20 June 1908. Vienna, 1908.
23. Mallory, George. 'Everest Unvanquished'. *Asia Magazine*, No. 9, 1923
24. Ibid, p.174
25. Bruce, General Charles G. 'The Narrative of the Expedition'. *The Assault on Mount Everest, 1922*, p.62.
26. Finch, George. 'The Attempt With Oxygen – The Second Attempt'. *The Assault on Mount Everest, 1922*, p.235
27. Ibid, p.235
28. Bruce, General Charles G. 'The Narrative of the Expedition'. *The Assault on Mount Everest, 1922*, p.62
29. Verma, Somesh. 'The faceless hero - Nepal's only Olympic Gold medalist in focus'. *Kathmandu Post*, 22 August 2012.
30. Norton, Colonel Edward. 'The North Col'. *The Fight For Everest 1924*, p.96. London: June 1925.
31. Trousers [pants] with baggy knees, originally from the USA and popularized in Britain until the 1920s.
32. Trousers [pants]
33. Norton, Colonel Edward F. 'The North Col'. *The Fight For Everest 1924*, p.103.
34. Trousers that extended four inches below the knee.
35. Mallory, George. Letter to Ruth Mallory, 12 April 1922, p.6.
36. Mallory, George. 'The First Attempt'. *The Assault on Mount Everest, 1922*, p.187,188
37. Rodway, George W. 'Mountain Clothing and Thermoregulation: A Look Back'. *Wilderness & Environmental Medicine*, Vol.23, 2012, p.92
38. Hoyland, Graham. 'Testing Mallory's Clothes on Everest'. *The Alpine Journal*, 2007, p.245,246

39. The Engineering Toolbox, Clo - Clothing and Thermal Insulation.
40. Derived by author from Havenith, George (2010) fig.4,6.
41. Odell, Noel. 'Mallory and Irvine's Attempt'. *The Fight For Everest 1924*, p.126
42. Ibid, p.131,132
43. Havenith, George. 'Benchmarking functionality of historical cold weather clothing: Robert F. Scott, Roald Amundsen, George Mallory', 2019.
44. König, Marc. 'Hadow's Sole: Mountaineering boots between the first ascents of the Matterhorn and Everest'. *The Alpine Journal*, 2016, p.247.

Chapter 6: Irvine

1. Bonhams. Lot 114, Mallory (George Leigh). London, 11 November 2015.
2. Ibid.
3. Ibid.
4. Mallory, George. Letter to Ruth Mallory. TSS California, 3 March 1924.
5. Ibid.
6. Ibid.
7. Irvine, Andrew. Letter to mother, 1 March 1924, p.1.
8. West, John B. 'George I. Finch and his pioneering use of oxygen for climbing at extreme altitudes'. *Journal of Applied Physiology* Vol.94, 2003, p.1706, 2003.
9. Dodd, Christopher. *The Oxford & Cambridge Boat Race*.
10. Gillman, Peter; Leni Gillman. *The Wildest Dream*, p.232.
11. Rockfax. Grade Conversions.
12. Odell, Noel. Diary, quoted in Summers, Julie. *Fearless on Everest*, p.67
13. Frazer, Robert A. 'Central Spitsbergen and North-East Land. I. The Sledge Journey'. *The Geographical Journal*, Vol. 64, No. 3, September 1924, p.201
14. Ibid, p.202
15. This was apparently a reference to Odell's article 'Explorations in the Mountains of Eastern Spitsbergen' in *The Alpine Journal*, Vol. 35 (1923). Two photographs inserted in that article (but not attributed to Odell) refer to 'Mt. Irvine'.
16. Ibid, p.202
17. Odell, Noel E. 'Explorations in the Mountains of Eastern Spitsbergen'. *The Alpine Journal*, Vol. 35 (1923), p.237
18. Odell, Noel E. Letter to Norges Svalbard-og Ishays-undersokelser, 20 September 1935. Quoted in Norges Svalbard-Og Ishavs-Undersokelser. *Skrifter Om Svalbard Og Ishavet, Nr. 80, The Place-Names Of Svalbard* (Oslo: Kommisjon Hos Jacob Dybwad, 1942), p.203
19. Norges Svalbard-Og Ishavs-Undersokelser. *Skrifter Om Svalbard Og Ishavet, Nr. 80, The Place-Names Of Svalbard* (Oslo: Kommisjon Hos Jacob Dybwad, 1942), p.203
20. Summers, Julie. *Fearless On Everest*, p.74.
21. Ibid, p.75
22. He probably meant metamorphic (rocks which have been transformed under heat or pressure from their original form).
23. Irvine, Andrew. Quoted in Oxford University, *Spitsbergen Retraced Expedition Report*, January 2017, p.28
24. Summers, Julie. *Fearless On Everest*, p.86-87
25. Oxford University. *Spitsbergen Retraced Expedition Report*, January 2017, p.28-30
26. Norton, Lieutenant Colonel Edward F. 'The Problem of Mount Everest'. *The Alpine Journal*, No. 230, p.7, May 1925.
27. Mallory, George. Letter to Ruth Mallory from TSS California, 8 March 1924.
28. Irvine, Andrew. Diary, p.18, entry for 30 March 1924.
29. Irvine, Andrew. Letter to mother, 17 April 1924, p.1
30. Irvine, Andrew. Diary, p.38, entry for 18 April 1924.

31. Bruce, General Charles G. 'The Start'. In *The Fight For Everest 1924*, p.18-19.
32. Ibid, p.19
33. Norton, Lieutenant Colonel Edward F. 'The March Across Tibet'. *The Fight For Everest 1924*, p.37.
34. Ibid, p.37
35. Ibid, p.45
36. Mallory, George. Letter to Ruth Mallory from Chiblung, Tibet, p.3. 19 April 1924.
37. Norton, Edward. 'The North Col'. In *The Fight For Everest 1924*, p.97,98,102.
38. Irvine, Andrew. Letter to mother, 24 April 1924, p.1.
39. Irvine, Andrew. Letter to Peter [Lunn?], 30 April 1924, p.1.
40. Irvine, Andrew. Diary, p.97, entry for 4 June 1924.

Chapter 7: Brainwave

1. Norton, 'Lieutenant Colonel Edward F. 'The March Across Tibet'. *The Fight for Everest 1924*, p.35
2. Ibid, p.36
3. Ibid, p.35
4. Ibid, p.35
5. Ibid, p.36
6. Ibid, p.36
7. Mallory probably meant 'khud' (खड्ड), Hindi for 'ravine' or 'cliff'.
8. Mallory, George. 'The Highest Point'. *The Assault on Everest 1922*, p.187
9. Noel, John. *Through Tibet to Everest*, p.220.
10. Somervell, T. Howard. *After Everest*, p.105-106.
11. Norton, 'Lieutenant Colonel Edward F. 'The March Across Tibet'. *The Fight for Everest 1924*, p.36
12. Mallory, George. Letter to Tom Longstaff, 19 April 1924. Quoted by Michael Tracy in 'Mallory & Irvine: The Plan' (YouTube).
13. Norton, 'Lieutenant Colonel Edward F. 'The Problem of Everest'. *The Alpine Journal*, Vol. 37, May 1925, p.5
14. Norton, 'Lieutenant Colonel Edward F. 'The March Across Tibet'. *The Fight for Everest 1924*, p.41
15. Ibid, p.46
16. Ibid, p.46
17. Irvine, Andrew. Letter to mother, 24 April 1924, p.1-2.
18. Ibid, p.46-47
19. Tennyson, Alfred (Baron). 'The Charge of the Light Brigade'. *Maud and Other Poems* (1856).
20. Norton, Lieutenant Colonel Edward F. 'Norton and Somervell's Attempt'. *The Fight for Everest 1924*, p.117
21. Norton, Lieutenant Colonel Edward F. 'The March Across Tibet'. *The Fight for Everest 1924*, p.41-42
22. Mallory, George. Letter to Ruth Mallory, 27 May 1924, p.3-4.
23. Norton, Lieutenant Colonel Edward F. 'The North Col'. *The Fight for Everest 1924*, p.87
24. Noel, John. Through Tibet to Everest, p.248,249
25. Norton, Lieutenant Colonel Edward F. 'The North Col'. In *The Fight for Everest 1924*, p.92,93
26. Norton, Lieutenant Colonel Edward F. 'The Climb with Mr. Somervell to 28,000 Feet'. *The Geographical Journal*, Vol. 64 No. 6, December 1924, p.451
27. Norton, Lieutenant Colonel Edward F. 'The Problem of Everest'. *The Alpine Journal*, Vol. 37, May 1925, p.7

28. Norton, Lieutenant Colonel Edward F. 'Norton and Somervell's Attempt'. *The Fight for Everest 1924*, p.116
29. Here Mallory was referring to his and Geoffrey Bruce's unsuccessful climb of 1 June 1924.
30. Ibid, p.116, footnote
31. Ibid, p.116, footnote
32. Ibid, p.116
33. Ibid, p.116
34. Norton, Lieutenant Colonel Edward F. 'The Climb with Mr. Somervell to 28,000 Feet'. *The Geographical Journal*, Vol. 64 No. 6, December 1924, p.455
35. Noel, John. *Through Tibet to Everest*, p.258

Chapter 8: Tigers

1. Published in the USA as *The Story of Everest.*
2. Carr, Herbert R. C. (ed.) *The Irvine Diaries.*
3. Norton, Lieutenant Colonel Edward F. 'The North Col'. *The Fight For Everest 1924*, p.91,92,93,94.
4. Somervell, T. Howard. *After Everest*, p.122,123
5. Irvine, Andrew. Letter to mother, 26 May 1924, p.1
6. Somervell, T. Howard. *After Everest*, p.94
7. Norton, Lieutenant Colonel Edward F. 'Norton and Somervell's Attempt'. *The Fight For Everest 1924*, p.101
8. A quote from Roger Miller, 'King of the Road' (Smash Records, 1965)
9. Norton, Lieutenant Colonel Edward F. 'Norton and Somervell's Attempt'. *The Fight For Everest 1924*, p.101
10. Bruce, Charles G. 'The Start'. *The Fight For Everest 1924*, p.18
11. Norton, Lieutenant Colonel Edward F. 'Norton and Somervell's Attempt'. *The Fight For Everest 1924*, p.101
12. Ruttledge, Hugh. 'The Mount Everest Expedition, 1933'. *The Alpine Journal*, Vol.45 No.247 (November 1933), p.220
13. Somervell, T. Howard. *After Everest*, p.127
14. A Hindi word with the connotation of 'leader'.
15. 'E.F.N.' [Norton, Lieutenant Colonel Edward F.] 'In Memoriam - Lobsang'. *The Alpine Journal*, Vol.44 No.246 (May 1932), p.120
16. Bruce, Geoffrey. 'The Rongbuk Glacier'. *The Fight For Everest 1924*, p.70
17. For North American readers, roughly: a bum, a moocher, a loser.
18. Younghusband, Sir Francis. 'Introduction'. *The Fight For Everest 1924*, p.5
19. Norton, Lieutenant Colonel Edward F. 'The March Across Tibet'. *The Fight For Everest 1924*, p.39
20. Mallory, George. Letter to Ruth Mallory, 11 May 1924.
21. Norton, Lieutenant Colonel Edward F. 'Future Possibilities'. *The Fight For Everest 1924*, p.201
22. Norton, Lieutenant Colonel Edward F. 'The Return to Base Camp'. *The Fight For Everest 1924*, p.153
23. The proverbial Englishman.
24. Norton, Lieutenant Colonel Edward F. 'The Return to Base Camp'. *The Fight For Everest 1924*, p.152-153. The reference to Dr Johnson meant Samuel Johnson, the 18th century writer, with whom Norton assumed his readers would be familiar.
25. Irvine, Andrew. Letter to mother, April 1924, p.2.
26. Bruce, Geoffrey. 'The Organization of the Expedition'. *The Fight For Everest 1924*, p.338,348
27. Mallory, George. Letter to Ruth Mallory, 29 March 1924.
28. By Robert Seymour Bridges, who was the British Poet Laureate from 1913 to 1930.

29. Mallory, George. Letter to Ruth Mallory, 12 April 1924.
30. Noel, John. *Through Tibet to Everest*, p.242
31. Norton, Lieutenant Colonel Edward F. 'Norton and Somervell's Attempt'. *The Fight For Everest 1924*, p.105
32. Wolfe, Tom. *The Right Stuff*, p.228.
33. Bruce, Geoffrey. 'The Organization of the Expedition'. *The Fight For Everest 1924*, p.348
34. Somervell, T. Howard. *After Everest*, p.126
35. On 28 May 1952, Raymond Lambert and Tenzing Norgay reached 28,215 feet on the Southeast Ridge. Wyss-Dunant, Ed. 'The First Swiss Expedition to Mount Everest, 1952'. *The Geographical Journal*, September 1953, Vol. 119, No. 3, p.272
36. Norton, Lieutenant Colonel Edward F. 'Norton and Somervell's Attempt'. *The Fight For Everest 1924*, p.108
37. Ibid, p.127
38. Smythe, Frank. 'The Second Assault'. In *Everest 1933*, p.163-164

Chapter 9: Pyramid

1. For our North American readers: fired their last bullets. For surfers: wiped out.
2. Noel, John. *Through Tibet to Everest*, p.258, 259
3. Odell, Noel. 'Mallory and Irvine's Attempt'. *The Fight for Everest 1924*, p.125.
4. Odell, Noel. 'Oxygen Apparatus, etc'. *The Fight for Everest 1924*, p.421. Odell was referring to his own two climbs with little or no oxygen to Camp VI, which he estimated at 27,000 feet.
5. Norton, Lieutenant Colonel Edward F. 'The Problem of Mt. Everest'. *The Alpine Journal*, Vol. 37, No. 230 (May 1925), p.2
6. Norton, Lieutenant Colonel Edward F. *Mount Everest Expedition 1924, Diary, Camp No. IV*, no page number
7. Odell, Noel. 'Mallory and Irvine's Attempt'. *The Fight for Everest 1924*, p.125
8. Noel, John. *Through Tibet to Everest*, p.212
9. Ibid, p.259
10. Ibid, p.126
11. Norton, Lieutenant Colonel Edward F. *Mount Everest Expedition 1924, Diary, Camp No. IV*, no page number
12. Mallory, George. Letter to Noel Odell, quoted in Odell, Noel. 'Mallory and Irvine's Attempt'. *The Fight for Everest 1924*, p.126
13. The author is grateful for Michael Tracy for this observation.
14. Noel, John. *Through Tibet to Everest*, p.260-1
15. Ibid, p.260
16. Norton, Jake. 'One Old Sock', https://jakenorton.com/one-old-sock/
17. Norton, Lieutenant Colonel Edward F. 'Norton and Somervell's Attempt'. *The Fight for Everest 1924*, p.109
18. Noel, John. *Through Tibet to Everest*, image facing p.220. Transcription by author.
19. Ibid, p. 275S
20. Norton, Lieutenant Colonel Edward F. *Mount Everest Expedition 1924, Diary, Camp No. IV*, no page number
21. As documented in Norton, Lieutenant Colonel Edward F. 'The Problem of Everest'. *The Alpine Journal*, Vol. 37 No. 230 (May 1925), p.2
22. The author is grateful to the original research of Michael Tracy in drawing attention to some of these quotations.
23. Mallory, George. Postcard to Marjorie Holmes, 1923? © Bonhams.
24. Mallory, George. 'The Northern Approach'. *Mount Everest, The Reconnaissance, 1921*, p.215

25. Mallory, George. 'The Highest Point'. *The Assault on Mount Everest 1922*, p.204-205
26. Mallory, George. 'The Northern Approach'. *Mount Everest, The Reconnaissance, 1921*, p.276
27. Mallory, George. 'The Problem'. *The Assault on Mount Everest 1922*, p.125
28. Author's calculation based on Google Earth.
29. Author unidentified, *The Sphere*, 25 October 1924, p.102-3
30. Odell, Noel. 'Mallory and Irvine's Attempt'. *The Fight for Everest 1924*, p.129
31. Ibid, p.131
32. Noel, John. *Through Tibet to Everest*, p.278, 279, 280, 293.
33. Messner, Reinhold. *The Crystal Horizon.*
34. Tracy, Michael. 'Great Climbs: Messner 1980' (YouTube, 27 May 2022)
35. Hall, Lincoln. *White Limbo*, p.132
36. Ibid, p.220
37. Ibid, p.222

Chapter 10: Odell

1. Unsworth, Walt. *Everest – A Mountaineering History* (1991), p.163
2. Christie's, 1936 Everest Expedition: auction notes (1999)
3. Tilman, H. W.; E. E. Shipton; C. E. C. Fischer. 'The Mount Everest Expedition of 1938', *The Geographical Journal*, Vol. 92, No. 6 (December 1938), pp. 481-490
4. Norton, Lieutenant Colonel Edward F. In *The Fight For Everest*, p.128
5. Norton, Lieutenant Colonel Edward F. 'Mount Everest Dispatches', *The Geographical Journal*, Vol. 64, No. 2 (August 1924), p.155
6. Odell, Noel. 'Mount Everest Dispatches, No.9, June 14, 1924', *The Geographical Journal*, Vol. 64, No. 2 (August 1924), p.161
7. Odell, Noel. 'The Last Climb of Mallory and Irvine', *The Geographical Journal*, Vol. 64, No. 6 (December 1924), pp. 456
8. Odell, Noel. 'Mount Everest Dispatches, No.9, June 14, 1924', *The Geographical Journal*, Vol. 64, No. 2 (August 1924), p.161
9. Odell, Noel. 'The Last Climb of Mallory and Irvine', *The Geographical Journal*, Vol. 64, No. 6 (December 1924), pp. 458
10. Odell, Noel. 'Mallory And Irvine's Attempt'. *The Fight For Everest 1924*, p.127
11. Odell, Noel. 'Mount Everest Dispatches, No.9, June 14, 1924', *The Geographical Journal*, Vol. 64, No. 2 (August 1924), p.164
12. Ibid.
13. Odell, Noel. 'The Last Climb of Mallory and Irvine', *The Geographical Journal*, Vol. 64, No. 6 (Dec., 1924), pp. 457
14. Author unknown, 'Mount Everest Dispatches, No.9, June 14, 1924', *The Geographical Journal*, Vol. 64, No. 2 (August 1924), caption to image opposite p.160
15. Author's estimate based on 1936 map by Spender.
16. Odell, Noel. 'Mallory And Irvine's Attempt'. *The Fight For Everest 1924*, p.130
17. TimeAndDate. (website)
18. Norton, Lieutenant Colonel Edward F. 'Norton And Somervell's Attempt'. *The Fight For Everest*, p.111
19. The altitude of the base of the Second Step, as per Michael Spender's map of 1936.
20. TimeAndDate. (website)
21. Keisan Online Calculator (website)
22. Tracy, Michael. 'Odell's view of Mallory & Irvine at 12:50', (YouTube), transcription by author, with apologies to Mr Tracy for any errors
23. Odell, Noel. 'The Last Climb of Mallory and Irvine', *The Geographical Journal*, Vol. 64, No. 6 (December 1924), p. 457. Odell used an almost identical wording in Norton's *The Fight For Everest 1924.*

24. Odell, Noel. 'Mallory And Irvine's Attempt'. *The Fight For Everest 1924*, p.120
25. Ruttledge, Hugh. *Attack On Everest*, p.256, quoted by Michael Tracy
26. Ruttledge, Hugh. *Everest 1933*, p.152
27. Hofstetter, Christoph. Contour Map Creator (website)
28. Norton, Jake. One Old Sock. https://jakenorton.com/one-old-sock/
29. Odell, Noel. 'Mallory And Irvine's Attempt'. *The Fight For Everest 1924*, p.131
30. Ibid, p.138
31. Tracy, Michael. 'Odell's view of Mallory & Irvine at 12:50' (YouTube), transcription by author.
32. Noel, John. *Through Tibet To Everest*, p. 267.
33. Noel, John. *Through Tibet To Everest*, annotation to image on p.285
34. Elvers, Greg. Visual Angle Calculator.

Chapter 11: Traces

1. Ruttledge, Hugh. 'The Higher Camps'. *Everest 1933*, p.131
2. Ruttledge, Hugh. The Mount Everest Expedition, 1933. *The Geographical Journal*, Vol. 83, No. 1 (January 1934), p.7
3. Ruttledge, Hugh. 'The First Assault'. *Everest 1933*, p.137
4. Odell, Noel. Letter to Alpine Club, 8 August 1934.
5. Wyn Harris, Sir Percy. *The Memoirs of Sir Percy Wyn Harris*, p.130. By permission of Steve Wyn-Harris.
6. Smythe, Frank. *Camp Six*, p.230
7. Ruttledge, Hugh. 'The First Assault'. *Everest 1933*, p.138
8. Norton, Lieutenant Colonel Edward F. 'Norton and Somervell's Attempt'. *The Fight For Everest 1924*, p.114
9. Ruttledge, Hugh. 'The First Assault'. *Everest 1933*, p.144
10. No-one has ever rediscovered Wyn Harris's personal ice-axe.
11. Wyn Harris, Sir Percy. *The Memoirs of Sir Percy Wyn Harris*, p.130-1. By permission of Steve Wyn-Harris.
12. The Alpine Club. 'Everest: by 'Those Who Were There' Exhibition Opens'. (website content)
13. Inscription by courtesy of Anja Schauer.
14. Tracy, Michael. 'Two and a half ice axes'. (YouTube)
15. Wyn Harris, Percy. Letter to Noel Odell, 16 June 1934. By permission of Steve Wyn-Harris.
16. Wyn Harris, Sir Percy. *The Memoirs of Sir Percy Wyn Harris*, p.130.
17. Brooke-Smith, Robin. Personal correspondence, 19 April and 1 May 2023.
18. Ibid, p.144-5
19. Smythe, Frank. *Camp Six*, p.304
20. Wyn Harris, Sir Percy. *The Memoirs of Sir Percy Wyn Harris*, p.130. By permission of Steve Wyn-Harris.
21. See Dawkins, Richard. *River Out of Eden: A Darwinian View of Life*
22. Smythe, Frank. *Camp Six*, p.230-1
23. Hemmleb, Jochen. *Ghosts of Everest*, p.140
24. Ibid, p.154
25. Hemmleb, Jochen; Eric Simonsen; Larry Johnson. 'Ghosts of Everest'. *Outside Online*, 1 October 1999
26. Hemmleb, Jochen. 'June 8, 1924, Mallory & Irvine's ascent to 8500 m/28,000 ft.' (website content, 2007)
27. Ibid.
28. Hemmleb, Jochen. Personal correspondence, 7 March 2023.
29. Hemmleb, Jochen. *Tatort Mount Everest: Der Fall Mallory*, p. 109
30. Personal correspondence, 2023.

31. Norton, Jake. 'Mystery' Camp Discovery on Mount Everest. (website content, 29 August 2017)
32. Norton, Jake. 'Windproof Suits and 68 Year Old Crackers' (website content, April 2007)
33. Hemmleb, Jochen. *Detectives on Everest*, p.180
34. Ruttledge, Hugh. 'The Higher Camps'. In *Everest 1933*, p.133
35. Smythe, Frank. *Camp VI*, p.212
36. Smythe, Frank. 'The Second Assault'. In *Everest 1933*, p.152
37. Norton, Lieutenant Colonel Edward F. 'The Personnel of the Expedition'. *The Geographical Journal*, Vol. 64, No. 6 (December 1924)
38. Beetham, Bentley. Section IV Photography. In *The Fight For Everest 1924*, p.324-5
39. Irvine, Andrew. Diaries (untitled, unpublished), p.97, entry for 4 June 1924.
40. Hazard, John de Vars. Camp IV Diary, 10 June 1924. *Mount Everest Expedition, T.S. Diaries* (unpublished, 1924), no page number.
41. Mallory, George. 'The First Assault'. *The Assault on Mount Everest 1922*, p.162,
42. Ibid, p.203
43. Ibid, p.204
44. Irvine, Andrew. Diaries (untitled, unpublished), p.38, entry for 12 April 1924.
45. Mallory, George. Note to John Noel, June 7, 1924. Noel, John, *Through Tibet to Everest*, facing p.220
46. Hoyland, Graham. *Last Hours on Everest*, p.3
47. Norton, Lieutenant Colonel Edward F. 'The Climb with Mr. Somervell to 28,000 Feet'. *The Geographical Journal*, Vol. 64, No. 6 (December 1924), pp. 455
48. Mallory, George (presumed). Camp IV diary, June 4, 1924. *Mount Everest Expedition 1924, T.S. Diaries*, (unpublished, 1924) no page number.
49. Somervell, Howard. *After Everest*, p.125
50. Ibid, p.133
51. A pamphlet printed in Lynchburg, Virginia, in 1885, purporting to contain enciphered directions to the location of a (surely fictional) buried treasure.

Chapter 12: 'Old English dead'

1. 'The Himalayan Database: The Expedition Archives of Elizabeth Hawley', accessed 1 January 2022.
2. Ibid.
3. Yordanishvili, Dr E. K. *1960. Впервые на Эверест – с севера!' [1960. For the first time on Everest - from the north!]*, Saint-Petersburg Alpine Club, 2002. Translation by author. For North American readers: braces are suspenders.
4. Cheng Li-lan, Dr. 'Mt. Everest Climb from North Side 2016', (YouTube).
5. Ibid.
6. Warren, Charles. *Scraps of an Everest Diary*, quoted in Unsworth, Walt. *Everest - A Mountaineering History*, (2000) p.244-5
7. Shipton, Eric. Letter to Political Officer in Sikkim, 22 August 1935. National Archives of India.
8. Kempson, Edwin. Attachment dated 20 July 1935 to Shipton, Eric. Letter to Political Officer in Sikkim, 22 August 1935. National Archives of India.
9. Guo Chao-zhen. 'Битва за Джомолунгму' ['Battle for Chomolungma']. In *Sovietski Sport*, nr. 142, (15 June 1960), p.6 [in Russian; translation by author]
10. Shu Ren, "Ascent [of] the Summit of Land - first conquest of Qomolungma by the Chinese" in Liu Dongping 刘东平 (ed.) *Records of exploration by the Chinese* 中国人探险纪实" (1993), extracts translated by 'MH' (full name unknown)
11. *EverestNews*. (website content, 2022)
12. Yordanishvili, Dr E. K. (2002)

13. Suzuki, Hiroyuki. 'Asia, China—Tibet, Bodies On Mount Everest'. *American Alpine Journal*, Vol.22 (1980), p.658
14. Holzel, Tom. 'Look Back at Life on the Mountain: Chronicling Ups and Downs of 10 Weeks on Mt. Everest', *Los Angeles Times* (30 November 1986)
15. Poston, Pete. Personal correspondence (2022)
16. Ikeda, Kaneshige. 'The Northeast Ridge Of Mt. Everest (Qomolangma)'. World Expeditions Consultants (website content, 1995?)
17. Chhiring Dorje now lives in Steamboat Springs, Colorado, USA; This author wrote to him via Facebook and e-mail, with no reply received at the time of writing.
18. Hemmleb, Jochen. Personal correspondence (2022)
19. Hellen, Nicholas. Xu Jing. Interview with *The Times*, extracts quoted by Hemmleb and Simonsen.
20. *EverestNews*, website content (2022)
21. Shih Chan-chun. 'The Conquest of Mount Everest by the Chinese Mountaineering Team'. *The Alpine Journal*, Vol. 66 (1961), p.28-41
22. Wang Fu-zhou [spelt as Wang Fu-chou], 'On to the summit'. In *China Reconstructs*, August 1960, p.6,7.
23. Yordanishvili, Dr E. K. (2002)
24. Pollard, Thom Dharma. 'Pan Duo's TOP SECRET Discovery on Everest'. (YouTube, 4 June 2022)
25. Synnott, Mark. 'The Mount Everest mystery deepens: Was there an international cover-up of a dead climber's ascent?' *Salon* (8 April 2022)
26. Mallory, George. 'Mallory's Letters'. *The Fight For Everest 1924*, p.215.
27. Smythe, Frank. 'The Second Assault'. In *Everest 1933*, p.153
28. Hemmleb, Jochen. *Ghosts of Everest*, p.112
29. Zhao Zonglu, 'Mountaineering Heroine: 10 Years Later'. *Beijing Review*, Vol.29, No.32 (11 August 1986), p.27

Chapter 13: Finding Mallory

1. Anker, Conrad; David Roberts. *The Lost Explorer: Finding Mallory on Mount Everest.*
2. Hemmleb, Jochen. *Ghosts of Everest.*
3. Norton, Jake. Personal communication, 2022.
4. 220/430 = 0.51; arctan 0.51 = 27 degrees.
5. A landmark which is known to climbers, but is not shown on any map in the public domain; it is probably the same as the 'two rock towers', above the 1933 Camp VI.
6. Norton, Jake. Personal communication, 2022.
7. Norton, Jake. Personal communication, 31 March 2023.
8. Anker, Conrad; David Roberts. *The Lost Explorer: Finding Mallory on Mount Everest*, p.21
9. Hemmleb, Jochen. *Ghosts of Everest*, p.127
10. Anker, Conrad; David Roberts. *The Lost Explorer: Finding Mallory on Mount Everest*, p.22
11. A Nepali name for a black bird resembling a raven.
12. Pollard, Thom. Quoted in Anker, Conrad; David Roberts. *The Lost Explorer: Finding Mallory on Mount Everest*, p.139
13. Anker, Conrad; David Roberts. *The Lost Explorer: Finding Mallory on Mount Everest*, p.172
14. https://www.pinterest.com/pin/561120434817974496/
15. Tracy, Michael. 'Frostbite'. (YouTube)
16. Anker, Conrad; David Roberts. *The Lost Explorer: Finding Mallory on Mount Everest*, p.21
17. *EverestNews*, 10 November 2004.
18. Ibid.
19. Ibid.

20. Anker, Conrad; David Roberts. *The Lost Explorer: Finding Mallory on Mount Everest*, p.36
21. Hemmleb, Jochen. *Ghosts of Everest*, p.129
22. Ibid, p.129
23. Proposed to signify 'Mount Everest Expedition II'
24. Anker, Conrad; David Roberts. *The Lost Explorer: Finding Mallory on Mount Everest*, p.36
25. Ibid, p.139
26. Pollard, Thom Dharma. 'Everest's Life-Changing Moment: Discovering Mallory with Andy Politz'. YouTube, 18 August 2022.
27. Norton, Jake. Personal communication.
28. Himalayan Database, expedition EVER04134
29. Norton, Jake. Personal communication.
30. Norton, Jake. 'Everest Searches 1999-2019'. (website content)
31. Himalayan Database, expedition EVER95102
32. Himalayan Database.
33. Himalayan Database, expedition EVER04144
34. Himalayan Database, expedition EVER10142
35. Norton, Jake. 'Everest Searches 1999-2019'. (website content)
36. Himalayan Database, expedition EVER11144
37. Norton, Jake. 'Everest Searches 1999-2019'. (website content). Norton reports the Sherpas' names as Llakpa Gelu and Phurba Tashi.
38. Norton, Jake. 'Everest Searches 1999-2019'. (website content)
39. Himalayan Database, expedition EVER12127
40. Norton, Jake. 'Everest Searches 1999-2019'. (website content)
41. Himalayan Database, expedition EVER19161
42. Himalayan Database, expedition EVER19179
43. Norton, Jake. 'Everest Searches 1999-2019'. (website content)
44. Synnott, Mark. *The Third Pole: Mystery, Obsession, And Death On Mount Everest.*
45. Pollard, Thom Dharma. 'Sandy Irvine & the Camera Were Discovered? Mark Synnott's Revealing Intel'. (YouTube) 19 April 2022.

Epilogue

1. Saxe, John Godfrey. *The Poems of John Godfrey Saxe*. Boston: Houghton, Mifflin and Company, 1881
2. For North American readers: suspenders.

Index

Note: f denotes reference to figure; n denotes reference to end-note; numbers following n denote chapter and end-note number

Objects and materials

Places

Publications